THE GLOBAL ATLANTIC

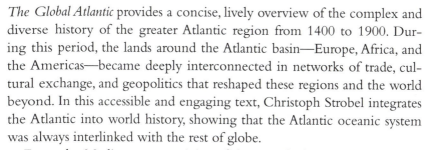

The Global Atlantic provides a concise, lively overview of the complex and diverse history of the greater Atlantic region from 1400 to 1900. During this period, the lands around the Atlantic basin—Europe, Africa, and the Americas—became deeply interconnected in networks of trade, cultural exchange, and geopolitics that reshaped these regions and the world beyond. In this accessible and engaging text, Christoph Strobel integrates the Atlantic into world history, showing that the Atlantic oceanic system was always interlinked with the rest of globe.

From the Mediterranean origins of slave-worked sugar plantations to the Chinese demand for silver from American mines, *The Global Atlantic* discusses key examples of these connections with clarity, enabling students to understand how existing ideas and incentives shaped the emerging Global Atlantic, and how these Atlantic systems in turn created the world we live in today.

Christoph Strobel is Associate Professor in the History Department at the University of Massachusetts Lowell. He is the author of *The Testing Grounds of Modern Empire*, and co-author, with Alice Nash, of *Daily Life of Native Americans from Post-Columbian through Nineteenth-Century America.*

THE GLOBAL ATLANTIC

1400 to 1900

Christoph Strobel

Routledge
Taylor & Francis Group
NEW YORK AND LONDON

First published 2015
by Routledge
711 Third Avenue, New York, NY 10017

and by Routledge
2 Park Square, Milton Park, Abingdon, Oxon OX14 4RN

Routledge is an imprint of the Taylor & Francis Group, an informa business

Library of Congress Cataloging-in-Publication Data

Strobel, Christoph.
The global Atlantic : 1400 to 1900 / Christoph Strobel.
pages cm
Includes bibliographical references and index.
1. Atlantic Ocean Region—History. 2. Europe—Relations—Africa. 3. Africa—Relations—Europe. 4. Europe—Relations—America. 5. America—Relations—Europe. 6. Africa—Relations—America. 7. America—Relations—Africa. 8. Geopolitics—Atlantic Ocean Region—History. 9. Atlantic Ocean Region—Commerce—History. I. Title.
D210.S825 2015
909'.09821—dc23 2014036343

ISBN: 978-0-7656-3951-6 (hbk)
ISBN: 978-0-7656-3952-3 (pbk)
ISBN: 978-1-315-72262-7 (ebk)

Typeset in Bembo
by Apex CoVantage, LLC

Printed and bound in the United States of America by Publishers Graphics, LLC on sustainably sourced paper.

For Kristin, Lora, and Anne

CONTENTS

ACKNOWLEDGMENTS

This book draws from the work of a large community of scholars who are cited in the endnotes of each chapter and the bibliography. Their contributions have illuminated my understanding of the histories of many global regions, as well as that of Atlantic and World history. Years of teaching students in various World, African, and Native American history courses, has also influenced my thinking on this subject. Several mentors and colleagues, too numerous to be all included here, have provided role-models, suggestions, support, and encouragement over the years. In alphabetical order I want to especially thank Al Andrea, Leonard Blusse, Kevin Boyle, Joye Bowman, Lisa Edwards, Trevor Getz, John Higginson, Jonathan Lipman, Patrick Manning, Eric Martin, Chad Montrie, Alice Nash, Carl Nightingale, Brian Ogilvie, Michael Pierson, Jonathan Reynolds, Neal Salisbury, Chris Saunders, Timothy Dale Walker, and Frederick Weaver. I want to thank the editorial team that has been involved in making this book: Steven Drummond, Jeannie Labno, Kimberly Guinta, Genevieve Aoki, Sioned Jones, and Irene Bunnell. My partner Kristin's contribution to this book has been invaluable. She has been a perceptive listener, and as an experienced teacher of World history, she has been a constructive critic on questions of organization and conceptualization. She commented on drafts of the manuscript and her editorial insights helped to greatly improve the final outcome. She did all this while being a great mother to our two daughters Lora and Anne. I also owe deep gratitude to

David Kalivas, editor of H-World and Professor at Middlesex Community College, for reviewing the manuscript. I benefitted greatly from the valuable feedback, criticisms, suggestions, but also the positive encouragement of such an experienced World historian. Of course, all this monograph's shortcomings remain my own.

INTRODUCTION

Currents of the Global Atlantic

This book provides a concise overview of the complex and diverse history of *The Global Atlantic.* By integrating the Atlantic Ocean region into a world historical perspective, this short book presents a new way to understand and conceptualize this growing field of study and hopes to encourage and foster debate and discussion. The volume explores how global exchange and interconnectedness had an impact on Europe and Europeans, Africa and Africans, as well as on the Americas and Native Americans and how these societies and places, in turn, helped to influence and reshape the world and its peoples beyond the Atlantic Ocean.

Historians and the Field of Atlantic World History

In recent years, the concept of Atlantic World history has been a popular scholarly organizing principle among historians. There has been a growing wave of books and journal articles that claim this mantle. Many of the works that successfully take on a broader Atlantic World perspective focus on certain aspects of this ocean system such as the slave trade, colonization, empire, the role of Africa and Africans, or topics such as the development of literature or natural science in the Atlantic World.

Historians have come to define the Atlantic World as a geographic region that surrounds this ocean, a body of water that has a surface area of around 31,666,000 square miles, which is a system that includes Africa, the

Americas (North America and South America), and Europe. The growth of the field of Atlantic World history has been part of a general move by some scholars toward internationalizing their research away from more traditionally focused narratives, which conventionally examine the past of nation-states and national communities. This type of approach almost exclusively dominated the writings of European and North American historians for a century prior to World War II. Since then, as part of more recent academic developments, which favor more globalized and transnational approaches, some researchers have given special relevance to the history of ocean systems such as the Mediterranean, the Indian, as well as the Atlantic oceans.[1]

The field of Atlantic World history focuses on the study of how societies in Africa, the Americas, and Europe converged, and how they were changed by the forces that were unleashed as a result of the initial travels of Christopher Columbus. This voyage resulted in significant transformations that occurred post-1492, which reached far into the African, American, and European interior—often hundreds of miles away from the coast. The cultural interchanges among the peoples of the Atlantic World were significantly influenced by the interactions and transactions among Africans, Europeans, and Native Americans.

There are some vivid debates among historians about the nature and the dynamics in the field of Atlantic World history that are also relevant for this book. Is Europe the driving engine in this ocean system, and can this perspective provide us any insights into what some scholars have called "the rise of the West" (Europe and North America) to global dominance? Does an excessive focus on Europe lead to or reinforce Euro-centric perspectives and explanations of the past? What were the roles played by Africans and Native Americans in the history of the Atlantic World? What were the power dynamics that existed between African, European, and Native American societies, and did they change through time and space? Furthermore, can we gain some deeper understanding about "multicultural" or "multiracial" issues in history by studying the Atlantic World?

Another issue that brings about scholarly disagreement in the field of Atlantic World history is periodization. Was there a beginning and an end to the history of this ocean system, and if so, what are the best dates to capture these points in time? In 1492, Columbus made his pivotal trans-Atlantic voyage establishing permanent contact between the worlds of Afro-Eurasia and the Western Hemisphere. Seems obvious enough, but with more informed contextualization perhaps 1492 is not the optimum starting point for the Atlantic era. As many Atlantic World historians point out, several of the trends and tendencies that are of special interest in this field, had clearly been in place for decades or even centuries before this date. Finding an appropriate endpoint to Atlantic World history is arguably even more controversial. Several historians argue that the Atlantic World remains valid as a distinct organizing principle into the nineteenth century, and even beyond, given the contours, currents, and legacies that shape this ocean system.[2] On the other hand, some historians, especially those whose work focuses on the British Atlantic, favor the end date of around 1800.[3] For instance, one of the deans in this field, Nicholas Canny, argues that by the nineteenth century the Atlantic World becomes integrated into world history, and ceases to be "clearly distinguished from global history."[4]

The Global Atlantic: An Exploration

Was the Atlantic World as separated from the rest of the globe prior to the nineteenth century as Canny seems to suggest? By situating the early modern Atlantic in a world historical perspective, this book argues that this ocean system emerged as a globally integrated structure. *The Global Atlantic* does not question the usefulness of the Atlantic World as a scholarly organizing principle. There are many dynamics that drove and shaped the history of this region, and historians will benefit greatly from closely studying these phenomena and developments in a trans-Atlantic perspective. However, the Atlantic World did not exist in a vacuum, and scholars and students can gain a greater understanding by placing the history of this ocean system in a trans-regional and global context.

There have been some forays by historians in this direction. Two exploratory articles by Peter Coclanis encourage Atlantic World historians to pursue a "greater scholarly cosmopolitanism" by connecting the field of Atlantic with World history. Coclanis suggests that the history of the "Atlantic basin" could be "much enriched by taking into account the East." He warns us that "[b]y fixing our gaze so firmly toward the West, the approach may, anachronistically, give too much weight to the Atlantic Rim, separate Northwest Europe too sharply both from other parts of Europe and from Eurasia as a whole, accord too much primacy to America in explaining Europe's transoceanic trade patterns, and economically speaking, misrepresent through overstatement the place of Europe

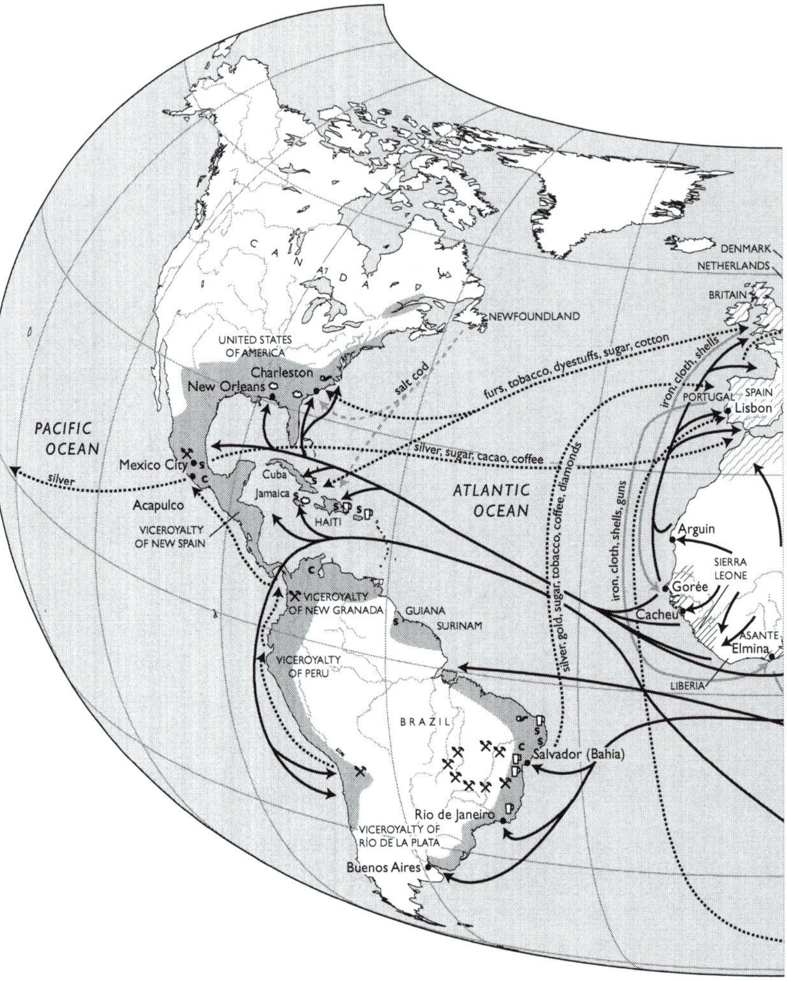

This map, while focusing on the slave trade from the fifteenth to the nineteenth centuries, shows the worldwide commodities' trade and involvement of the Global Atlantic.

Source: Pomeranz, Kenneth, and Steven Topik. *The World That Trade Created: Society, Culture, and the World Economy, 1400 to the Present*, 3rd edition. Armonk, NY: M.E. Sharpe, 2013.

in the order of things."[5] Coclanis provides a good starting point. His two pieces raise important questions and concerns, but the issues they bring up require further elaboration, research, and discussion. In addition, the edited volume *The Atlantic in Global History, 1500–2000* explores some of the global dimensions of the Atlantic World. Several of the chapters in the

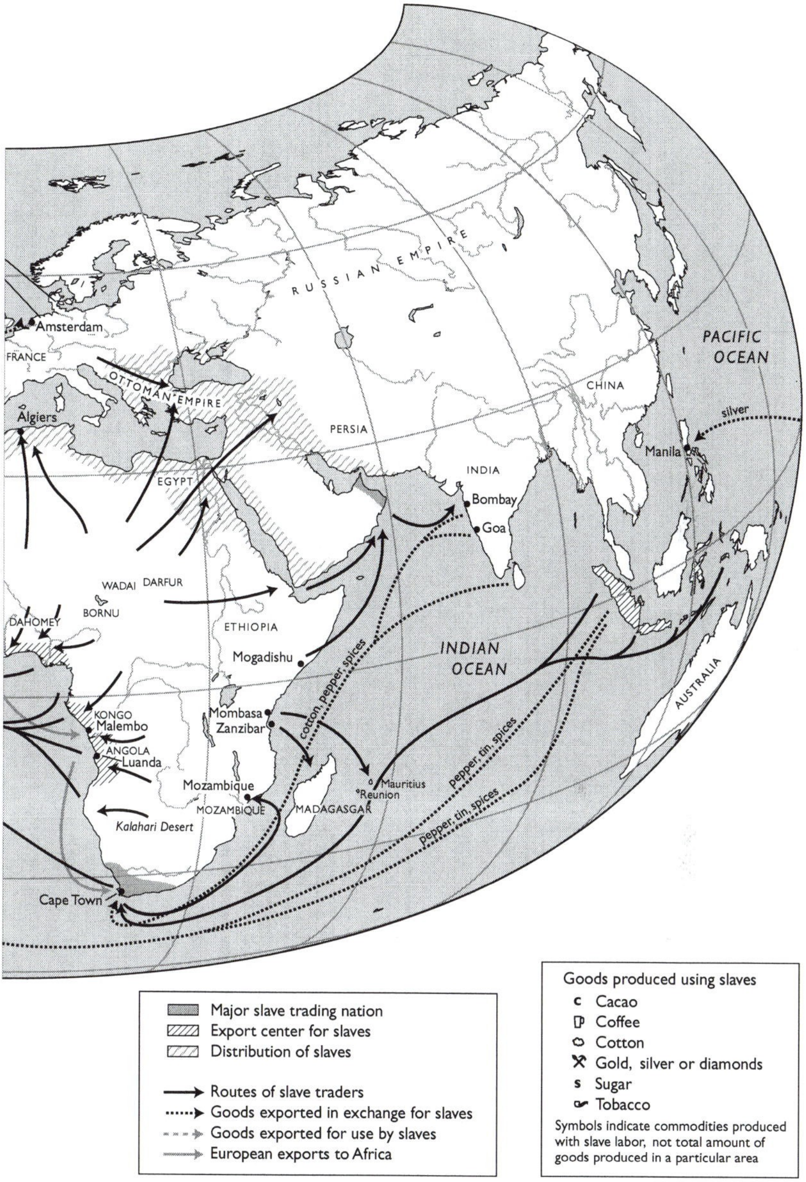

book pursue a world historical perspective of the Atlantic, but they are too focused on themes shaped by questions relevant to scholars in various area studies, and, as a result, the book does not provide a globally connected narrative.[6]

While providing a good short survey of the history of the Atlantic World, Karen Ordahl Kupperman's *The Atlantic in World History* explores very few of the global connections of this ocean system despite its promising title.[7] Alongside Kupperman's book, there are several other titles and edited collections of essays that give commendable comprehensive narrative introductions to the history of the Atlantic World.[8] While there is much to compliment about all of these books, much of the literature fails to set the Atlantic World into a world historical context.

The Global Atlantic aims to provide an accessible and tightly focused exploration of this subject. Given the sheer complexity and scope of the topic, however, this book cannot provide a complete account of the world historic connections of this ocean system. Still, by discussing several episodes, themes, trends, and tendencies of how the Atlantic World was interlinked with the rest of the globe, I hope readers will gain an appreciation of the interconnected nature of this system. Dynamics that historians often describe as "culture contact" and the "encounter" of peoples and the exchanges that occurred between them are central to this book. They led to the spread and exchange of goods, ideas, people, religion, cultural influences, plants, animals, disease, insects, and technology throughout the world. These patterns and processes were often multi-directional, complicated, contested, and diverse. They took place at various stages through time and place and rarely provide a linear story.

This book is organized into two sections. Part I, which consists of Chapter 1, examines the hemispheric connections of societies in Africa, the Americas, and Europe before 1492 and argues that Africans, Native Americans, and Europeans participated and had been integrated into trans-regional "old world" systems of exchange long before permanent contact between the Western and the Eastern Hemisphere was established. The second part of the book explores the global currents of the Atlantic World from the late fifteenth to the mid- to late eighteenth century, which was brought about by European overseas expansion. As we will learn, these efforts at empire building were often limited, a process shaped, in part, by the capacities of the many diverse local populations that Europeans encountered to keep those aspirations at bay. Specifically, Chapter 2 examines the role that Europe and Africa played in the making of a Global Atlantic. Chapter 3 analyzes how the Spanish Empire in the Americas extended into the Pacific Ocean. This led to trade with China through the Philippines, which in turn had an impact on developments in the Atlantic World. Chapter 4 investigates the connections of the Global Atlantic with the worlds of the Indian Ocean. The conclusion discusses how during the mid-eighteenth and into the nineteenth century, a shift in power dynamics in world history would take place. These changes spurred economic, political, and cultural developments that led to a period when the "West" (Europe and its former colonies in North America) became ascendant in Atlantic and global networks. They brought about an increasing break down in accommodation that occurred throughout the worlds of the Global Atlantic. Still, the Atlantic and its peoples continued to be tied in with the world at large—impacting and in turn being impacted by developments from outside this ocean system.

A Note on Terminology and Periodization

Terminology in a book of this nature poses several challenges. In fact many terms used here, such as "European," "African," "Native American," or "Asian," are problematic, as they are in part the product of a history of European overseas expansion, when they became signifiers that grouped extremely diverse peoples and distinct nations together into invented categories. These Euro-centric classifications still shape our understandings of the world today.[9]

Terms such as "Europe," "Asia," "Africa," "Indian," or "Native American" pose even more specific analytical issues still. For instance, a quick look at a world map makes clear that there is no obvious geographic division between the continents we today call "Europe" and "Asia." Designating the Ural Mountain chain as the dividing line between two notionally different continents is an arbitrary invention. As another example, there is a theory that the name "Africa" had its origins during the days of the Roman Empire, when the continent was dubbed after a Roman officer (Scipio Africanus who served in what is today North Africa). The term "Indian" was reportedly given to the inhabitants of the Western Hemisphere by Columbus because he believed he had arrived somewhere in Asia. The now more fashionable term "Native American" also raises several issues. The "American" component comes from the name of an Italian navigator and cartographer, Amerigo Vespucci. "Native" generally describes anyone's place of origin, but it has a negative connotation in the history of British imperialism when the term was widely used to describe colonized people, with the implication of "ignorance" and "backwardness." This list merely provides some highlights that emerge from our use of established geographic or ethnic concepts.[10] This book offers no solution to these problems, but the reader ought to be aware of the history and the often arbitrary and illogical roots of the "proper" names we give to places and people today.

How we categorize time also raises issues about Euro-centric legacies. For one, we use a Western Christian calendar to determine dates. Moreover, Western assumptions about "modernity" also play a significant role in the way we organize world history into a "modern" or "early modern" period. Again, no solution is provided in this work. Still, readers should be aware of the intellectual roots of the periodization used here, and of the history of Western expansion and colonization that they emerge out of. This book refers to the "pre-modern" period as the time before the fifteenth century. The "early modern" describes the period from roughly the 1400s to about 1750–1800, which is when political and industrial revolutions brought about dramatic changes in Western society. "Modern" here describes the second part of the eighteenth century all the way to the present.

Notes

1 For a general introduction to this subject see Jerry Bentley, "Sea and Ocean Basins as Frameworks of Historical Analysis" *The Geographical Review* 89 (April 1999), 215–224. See also Rainer Bushman, *Oceans in World History* (New York: McGraw-Hill, 2007). For two excellent studies that internationalize the study of history see Donald Wright, *The World and a Very Small Place in Africa: A History of Globalization in Niumi, The Gambia*, 3rd edn (Armonk, NY: M.E. Sharpe, 2010); and Thomas Bender, *A Nation among Nations: America's Place in World History* (New York: Hill & Wang, 2006).

2 See, for example, Alan L. Karras and J.R. McNeill, eds, *Atlantic American Societies: From Columbus through Abolition, 1492–1888* (New York: Routledge, 1992); and Toyin Falola and Kevin Roberts, eds, *The Atlantic World: 1450–2000* (Bloomington: Indiana University Press, 2008).

3 See, for example, David Armitage and David Braddick, eds, *The British Atlantic World, 1500–1800* (New York: Palgrave Macmillan, 2002); Nicholas Canny and Anthony Pagden, eds, *Colonial Identity in the Atlantic World, 1500–1800* (Princeton, N.J.: Princeton University Press, 1987).

4 Nicholas Canny, "Atlantic History and Global History" in *Atlantic History: A Critical Appraisal*, eds, Jack P. Greene and Philip D. Morgan (New York: Oxford University Press, 2009), 317–336.

5 Peter A. Coclanis, "Drang Nach Osten: Bernard Bailyn, the World Island, and the Idea of Atlantic History," *Journal of World History* 13 (2002), 169–182; Peter A. Coclanis, "Beyond Atlantic History" in *Atlantic History*, 342 (2009), 337–356. This chapter is an extended version of his article, "Atlantic World or Atlantic/World?" *William and Mary Quarterly* 63 (October 2006): 725–742.

6 Jorge Canizares-Esquerra and Erik Seeman, eds, *The Atlantic in Global History, 1500–2000* (Upper Saddle River, N.J.: Prentice Hall, 2006).

7 Karen Ordahl Kupperman, *The Atlantic in World History* (New York: Oxford University Press, 2012).

8 See Douglas Egerton, Alison Games, Jane Landers, Kris Lane, and Donald Wright, *The Atlantic World: A History, 1400–1888* (Wheeling, Ill.: Harland Davidson, 2007); Thomas Benjamin, *The Atlantic World: Europeans, Africans, Indians and Their Shared History, 1400–1900* (New York: Cambridge University Press, 2009); John Thornton, *A Cultural History of the Atlantic World, 1250–1820* (New York: Cambridge University Press, 2012). For a book that focuses on European exploration and trade see Paul Butel, *The Atlantic* (New York: Routledge, 1999). For edited collections see Falola and Roberts, eds, *The Atlantic World*; N.P. Canny and Philip Morgan, eds, *The Oxford Handbook of the Atlantic World, 1450–1850* (New York: Oxford University Press, 2011); Jack Greene and Philip Morgan, eds, *Atlantic History: A Critical Appraisal* (New York: Oxford University Press, 2009); Thomas Benjamin, Timothy Hall, and David Rutherford, eds, *The Atlantic World in the Age of Empire* (Belmont, CA: Wadsworth, 2001); Reinhardt, Steven and Dennis Reinhartz, eds, *Transatlantic History* (College Station: Texas A&M University, 2006).

9 See Eric Wolf, *Europe and the People without History*, new edn (Berkeley: University of California Press, 1997), IX–XIV; Martin Lewis and Karen Wigen, *The Myth of Continents: A Critique of Metageography* (Berkeley: University of California Press, 1997).

10 This section draws from Christoph Strobel, *The Testing Grounds of Modern Empire: The Making of Colonial Racial Order in the American Ohio Country and the South African Eastern Cape, 1770s–1850s* (New York: Peter Lang Publishing, 2008), IX–X.

PART I

Trans-Regional Interactions before 1492 and the Roots of the Global Atlantic

The trans-regional interactions of Europe, Africa, and the Americas before 1492 would, at least in part, influence the patterns and processes that would shape the history of the Global Atlantic. Even before Christopher Columbus' now famous voyage marked the beginning of sustained contact between Afro-Eurasia and the Americas, these regions were part of far-reaching, long-distance exchange networks. The pre-modern histories of these areas provide a partial glimpse into the motivations and the mechanisms of how European, African, and Native American interactions created cross-cultural and economic exchanges that transcended regional borders to form active global networks.

1

"OLD WORLD" LONG-DISTANCE EXCHANGE IN EUROPE, AFRICA, AND THE AMERICAS

Until 1492, the Atlantic Ocean largely divided the Western Hemisphere from Afro-Eurasia. Although some Europeans, Africans, and Native Americans had learned to navigate certain segments of this vast ocean system, Atlantic wind patterns and currents provided challenging barriers that proved difficult to overcome. Thus, prior to the 1400s, Europe's and West Africa's long-distance commerce was not focused on the Atlantic coast, but rather on the Mediterranean World and Asia. Much of pre-modern Afro-Eurasia was tied into a sophisticated system of interaction, which created connections that influenced, at least in part, European and West African consumption habits, cultures, and practices. It was part of the larger dispersion of commodities, ideas, technologies, and beliefs that shaped the cross-cultural encounters throughout the Afro-Eurasian landmass, or what some historian have called the "Old World."[1]

Meanwhile, in the Western Hemisphere, despite their geographic isolation from a global perspective, the indigenous peoples of the Americas did not live in isolation. Like the peoples of Afro-Eurasia, Native Americans were tied into far-reaching and sophisticated trans-regional exchange networks, which influenced Native American material culture, consumption, and daily lives. Native Americans, in a sense, like the peoples of Afro-Eurasia, lived in their own, vast, "Old World," which was shaped by cross-cultural encounters.[2]

Europe and Old World Exchange

When considering Atlantic exploration, historians have long emphasized the role of the people of the Iberian Peninsula, a region of Europe that contains the modern nation-states of Spain and Portugal today. Portugal, as well as the kingdoms of Castile and Aragon, the founding states of Spain in the sixteenth century, sponsored several journeys, which would eventually aid in the gradual creation of an Atlantic World starting in the latter half of the fifteenth century. Yet, the Iberians were not the only Europeans who ventured into the western ocean. From the eighth to the eleventh centuries, the Vikings, or Norse as they are also called, made significant headway in their exploration and colonization of the northern Atlantic region. As with the later Iberians, the Vikings' motivations to go out in the Atlantic were spurred, at least in part, by the lure of trade with worlds to the east and south.

The Northern Global Atlantic World of the Vikings

Scant historic records suggest that the Vikings may have been the first among the Europeans to make significant headway into the Atlantic. Their journeys of exploration brought them all the way to Iceland, Greenland, and eventually Newfoundland. Norse efforts were aided in this endeavor by the easterly flow of the Greenland current off the western coast of Norway. Easier access to this natural phenomenon, and the presence of several islands along the way, might have provided the Vikings with much more favorable conditions for ocean exploration, especially compared to other Europeans, Africans, and Native Americans.

Despite their importance to this narrative, these Atlantic voyages were only a part of a much larger process of Viking exploration and colonization that began some time before AD 800. Using their Scandinavian homeland as a base, various and vast expeditions led the Norse into today's Russia, the Eurasian interior toward the Arab World and the Byzantine Empire, as well as to the modern British Isles, Ireland, northern France, and the Mediterranean. Aided by their relatively small, open ships with square sails, the Norse frequently sailed in extremely dangerous conditions, through bad weather, storms, rough sea, and drift-ice. River systems were often used as maritime extensions to get into the European and Asian interior. At times, the Vikings portaged boats and cargo from one river system to the next or carried their belongings and vessels across shallow or hard-to-travel parts of rivers.

It is important to underscore, however, that the Vikings' efforts were not homogenous or centrally organized. Rather, Vikings came from communities all over Scandinavia and set out independently on their missions, usually led by high-ranking local men, for various reasons. Because of their northerly geographic location and the varied Scandinavian topography, there was only limited access to farm and pastoral land. As a result, food scarcity made overpopulation a continuous issue in many Norse communities and encouraged expansion. The Vikings also went out in search of adventure and booty, which they obtained through raiding. Whatever their motivations, the Norse were more than just raiders, and through their voyages they established sophisticated and far-flung trading networks.

During the so-called "Age of the Vikings," at its peak from the late ninth to the twelfth centuries, the Norse began to establish a far-flung, informal system of settlements and states, a network that had a North Global Atlantic reach. Viking colonization stretched all the way to the Western Hemisphere, where a short-lived settlement in L'Anse aux Meadows, Newfoundland was established in the early 1000s, almost 500 years before Christopher Columbus' voyage to the Caribbean.[3] Already much earlier, by the eighth century, the Vikings began to extend their sphere of influence and settlements into the forest frontiers of modern-day Russia. The participants of this eastern branch of Norse expansion, which likely originated from modern-day Sweden, are often referred to in the historic record as the "Rus." This term might have given us the modern name of the nation-state of Russia. Rus merchants created a sustained trading system that lasted several centuries that reached as far as Baghdad and Byzantium. Thus, between the 900s to the 1100s, the Vikings were able to create a tenuous, fluid, and heavily decentralized trade network that connected Eurasia with the Western Hemisphere.

Much of what we know about the Rus comes from archeological evidence and various Arab, Byzantine, and Frankish sources. But even from the scant record it is clear that the eastern frontier of the Norse's Global Atlantic was extremely active. Beginning in the mid-750s, Vikings began to move into the Russian forest zone. This expansion was accompanied by violent raiding, trading, tribute seeking, and colonization.

The Rus' advance into Eurasia was a complicated and fluid process that made use of an extensive network of river routes. The Vikings initially gained a foothold in the region by way of the Baltic Sea through the Gulf of Finland. They traveled across lakes and rivers by water and portage, and eventually connected via the Volga River all the way to the Caspian Sea. This route provided them with access to the Arab world and the Muslim metropolis of Baghdad. In later years, the Vikings also used the Dnieper River to access the Black Sea, a way that connected them to the Byzantine Empire and Constantinople. While they did trade directly with the Arabs or Byzantines at times, the Rus were often forced to exchange goods through border-states such as the Khazar and Bulgar states, who, at times, blocked the Vikings' access to southerly trade, but who also became producers of several commodities that the Norse desired. The Rus traded slaves (usually people of Slavic, Baltic, and Finno-Ugrain backgrounds), fur, honey, artic animal skin and teeth, walrus ivory, amber, as well as Frankish swords. In return they obtained silver coins, ceramics, jewelry, furniture, aromatics, silk, and tapestries, the remains of which are found today in unearthed Viking graves.

The encounter with the worlds to the east and the south significantly and relatively rapidly transformed the Viking societies of the Rus. The most significant point of cultural contact was with the Byzantine Empire. While Norse raids were reported in the Caspian as well the Black Sea, the Byzantine navy, with their effective tactical skills and their infamous, and somewhat mysterious, liquid fire bombs known as "Greek Fire," was the first sophisticated sea power that the Vikings confronted. Conflict between the two cultures was, however, only one component of Byzantine–Rus relations. Byzantium and several of the Rus states had an active commercial exchange, they created and signed treaties, and, eventually, some Norse served as mercenaries in the military forces of the Byzantine Empire. These more peaceful encounters between the Rus and the Byzantine capital of Constantinople helped to establish a lasting cultural link between the two regions. In only a few generations, the Rus elite blended with the local Slavic majority population over which they had ruled, and by the mid-1000s, they had transformed into Slavic Christian Orthodox rulers. These old trade links laid the groundwork for the later nation of Russia's eventual widespread adoption of Orthodox Christianity, the Cyrillic alphabet, art, and government structure. The evidence of this relationship, some scholars argue, can be seen by the way Scandinavian names became Slavic. For instance, Helge turned to Oleg, Helga to Olga, Yngvar to Igor, and Valdemar to Vladimir.[4]

The Vikings' western most significant efforts at colonization in Greenland and North America are linked to the figure of Erik the Red and his family. In the late 900s, Erik became an outlaw for murder in Norway and was banished from that part of Scandinavia. He and his followers resettled in northwestern Iceland, where he again ran in trouble with the law for manslaughter. Banishment from several communities spurred Erik to sail north to explore the coast of Greenland. There, Erik eventually came across several fjords in the western part of the largely arctic island, which he deemed suitable for settlement. Some Norse sagas suggest that he named the island "Greenland" because he believed this name would more likely attract settlers to follow him there from "Iceland." In 985, it is told, Erik made the difficult voyage from Iceland to Greenland with twenty-five ships to begin his new colony. After a brutal voyage, however, some ships sank and others turned back; only fourteen landed safely.[5] Despite the tremendous distance to Iceland, and especially the Scandinavian homeland of the Vikings, over time, several sizeable settlements would emerge in Greenland. Still, the overall Norse population never rose to more than 4,000.

Due to a shortage of land for pasture and for farming, as well as due to a lack of timber and iron, the Norse colonies on Greenland had to be tied to the Vikings' commercial exchange networks in order to survive. Hunters from the settlements went on excursions to obtain walrus ivory and skin, seal skin, high thick quality furs, blubber and downs. These Arctic products would fetch a high price in the trade system of the Vikings' North Global Atlantic and were widely distributed and traded.[6]

The need for timber and other resources was likely the cause for more southwardly explorations along the North American Atlantic coast. In around 1000, according to the Nordic sagas, Leif Erikson, Erik the Red's son, was the first leader to set up a more permanent camp in Newfoundland. It had a promising beginning as the Norse would call this place "Vinland" and described the location as rich in timber, game, salmon, and berries. Furthermore, and unlike later Viking settlers, Leif and his crew did not seem to encounter any Native Americans during their relatively short stay. Leif had intended to return to Vinland, yet, his father's death necessitated him to run affairs in Greenland. It would come to Leif Erikson's brother, Thorvald Erikson, to continue the Vinland project in 1004. Thorvald and his crew arrived in Newfoundland in the fall and spent the winter in the settlement established by Leif. When Thorvald and his men encountered a party of nine Native Americans, presumably Beothuk or Micmac, during an exploratory expedition, the Vikings killed eight of them. The lone survivor, however, came back with reinforcements, and during the retaliatory attack, Thorvald was mortally wounded. Without a leader, the mission was quickly abandoned.[7] Five years later Thorfinn Karlsefni, who had married Thorvald's widow, became the leader of another Vinland expedition. After an extremely difficult winter, Native Americans appeared on the scene again. This time, however, the two groups traded peacefully. Nevertheless, during one of their later encounters, a Norse killed a Native American and the result was once more an extremely violent confrontation between the two groups. Fear of further native attacks became the likely cause for Karlsefni to abandon the colony in the spring of 1012. The last of the North American Viking colonies in Newfoundland also ended as a result of violence. This time, however, it was a blood feud between the Icelandic and Greenlandic Norse factions that caused the final effort at permanent settlement to fold in 1013.

While the idea of long-term colonization in the region was abandoned, Vikings are believed to have returned to the North American shores into the 1300s. There they continued to fish, harvest timber, search for valuable goods, and trade with Native Americans. Furthermore, by the fifteenth century evidence suggests that other Europeans, such as the intrepid Basque fishermen of the Northern Iberian Peninsula, took advantage of the rich fishing grounds off the coast of Newfoundland. They would spend their summers fishing at sea, and processing the fish on land, before returning home across the Atlantic once more.

While the colonization of Vinland was abandoned, the wealth of the North American shore and the colony in Greenland remained tied into a commercial system that traded luxury goods to Europe and Asia lasting into the fourteenth century. At that time, the Hanseatic League, a commercial and military alliance of merchant guilds from various city-states, towns, and small states in the North and Baltic Sea, began to dominate and restructure trade in the region. This led to a quick decline of the Vikings' extended North Global Atlantic World. Even more important to the limits of the Norse presence in Greenland, and as an extension, the Americas, was climate change. A cooling of global climate during the Little Ice Age made an already harsh climate harsher still. Marginal agriculture and pastoralism, already strained due to the northerly climate and soil erosion, became next to impossible. Moreover, the growing threat from the Inuit made Norse survival in Greenland impossible.[8]

In a limited way, the Viking experience from the 800s to the 1100s underscores and provides a test case for the Europeans' motivations and goals in pursuing a Global Atlantic. It was, at least in part, the exposure to eastern and southern trade that was spurred by the desire for trade goods, as well as the access to potential raw materials that could be used in trade, which aided and fueled the process of Viking expansion and colonization—not only in the Atlantic, but also in other areas of the world. The Norse's North Global Atlantic pattern would become even more apparent with several other European states in the period between 1400 and 1800.

Out of the East: Europe and the Old World Long-Distance Trade Networks

Just like the Vikings in Scandinavia to the north, other parts of Europe further to the south were part of extensive long-distance exchange systems before 1492. A variety of European states, cities, and merchants from Christian Europe actively sought trading opportunities with their Muslim neighbors in the southern and eastern portions of the Mediterranean world. The Islamic world was connected in turn to the commercial networks in Asia and sub-Saharan Africa, and in this fractured manner, Europe had a degree of contact with a large section of the Eastern Hemisphere. European population centers such as Venice and Genoa in present day Italy, as well as Ghent and Bruges in the Flanders region of modern day Belgium, were just a few cities that were actively involved in and benefited from this long-distance commerce. They served as commercial and financial centers, as distribution points of goods for other parts of Europe, but also, at times, as hubs of production. The cities of Flanders, for example, were manufacturers of a variety of highly desired textiles. These early trade connections between Europe, Asia, and Africa also had a significant impact beyond commercial interactions. Cross-Mediterranean trade introduced significant cultural influences that helped to shape European society.

While Europe might have played a comparatively minor role in the pre-modern global spice trade, which was, as we will discuss in a later chapter, dominated by the commercial interests of sections of Asia and

East Africa, Europeans did purchase significant amounts of these expensive commodities for a variety of reasons from roughly AD 1000 onward. In recent years scholars have begun to criticize the conventional explanation that Europeans merely used spices to preserve food or to cover up the rancid flavor of old meat. The historian Paul Freedman argues, for example, that medieval accounts suggest that fresh meat was widely available in households of means and that the "the monthly cost of spices was almost exactly the same as expenditures for beef and pork combined." Simply put, for Europe's wealthy there was plenty of fresh meat to be had, and spices were deemed too valuable to be wasted on old meat. Medieval cuisine, at least for those who could afford it, was much spicier than what we perceive as the typical European cuisine of today. Europe's elite imported vast amounts of saffron, sugar, cloves, cinnamon, ginger, several varieties of pepper, cypress root, almonds, and nutmeg. "The medieval palate preferred overlapping fragrant taste sensations, much as is the case in India, Persia, or the Arab world." Thus, at least for much of the pre-modern and early modern period, Europe's elite, and, at least for special occasions, commoners as well, shared the food preferences of their Asian neighbors. It was only "by the eighteenth century," Freedman writes, that flavors in European cuisine "had dramatically changed in favor of a richer but blander taste."[9]

Europeans also associated spices with medicinal and religious powers. They used spices to treat sickness, believed that spices had protective qualities against certain types of disease, and burned them for aromatherapy. Furthermore, fragrances and spices were linked to the sacred and served religious functions during various ceremonies. "Once the notion of spices as not merely useful but somehow wonderful took hold," writes Freedman, "their importance was enhanced by the need to show off. As with all prestigious consumer items, spices were effective in claiming, conveying and confirming social status, but they therefore had to be consumed in a public and ostentatious manner." Europeans were willing to pay high prices for spices, and the desire to purchase these commodities aided, as we will see, at least in part, to push for overseas exploration by the 1400s.[10]

The long-distance trade in spices and other commodities with Asia and Africa left a significant mark on European culture in the years between the fourteenth and seventeenth centuries, an era that has frequently been referred to as the "Renaissance." The term, "Renaissance," which means "rebirth," was introduced as an academic organizing principle in the nineteenth century by Western intellectuals. This era, they argued, marked a significant change in

European history, a break with what they believed to be the stagnant Middle Ages of Europe and the beginning of Europe's rise to become the global power it would briefly be as a result of the Industrial Revolution in the mid-1800s. These historians saw "the Renaissance" as a time of flowering in humanist thought, science, and cultural production in art and literature, and an era of European exceptionality, ingenuity, creativity, and uniqueness.

In the last few decades, however, several scholars have begun to revise this interpretation, arguing that Europe's intellectual, artistic, and cultural life in this period was shaped, at least in part, by the long-distance trade with Afro-Eurasia. They argue that it was the exchange of goods and the ideas that accompanied them with Europe's predominantly Muslim neighbors in the Mediterranean World that helped to spur culture and creativity in the late pre-modern and the early modern era. For instance, many scientific achievements during this period were based on Hindu numerals conveyed by and identified as Arab. Indeed the overall system of math used by Europeans was significantly influenced by the Muslim world. Moreover, the rediscovery and reading of classical texts, so central to the pursuits of fifteenth and sixteenth century European intellectuals, frequently relied on the Latin translations of Greek writings that had been translated into Arabic with additional contributions by Muslim scholars. The influence of eastern elements can also be seen in European architecture during this period. In Venice, for example, the arches, decorative facades, and windows of the Doge's Palace, to name just one of the structures in one of Europe's most powerful and international cities of the fifteenth century, were influenced by the bazaars, mosques, and palaces of the Muslim World, and Islamic architecture, in turn, had been inspired by Greco-Roman architectural styles as evidenced, for instance, by the use of domes and columns. Venetian merchants had long traded with eastern cities such as Cairo, Alexandria, Acre, or Tabriz, and this extended contact influenced their esthetics and cultural tastes at home. European cartography, literature, philosophy, and art were also influenced by these encounters with the Afro-Eurasian world, just as they would later be shaped by the cultural contact with the Western Hemisphere after 1492.[11]

The Roots of the Global Atlantic: The Portuguese in North Africa

It is the Iberians who are generally given credit for being at the forefront of Europe's colonial overseas expansions, but their first forays into the Atlantic in the fifteenth century were modest and driven by long-established concerns, aspirations, and the strategic interests of their respective states. As we will discuss in the section below, several phenomena encouraged the Portuguese and later the states of Castile and Aragon, the two nations that eventually merged to become Spain in the sixteenth century, to leave the relative familiarity of the Mediterranean for the rougher waters of the Atlantic. First, the Ottoman Empire and other Muslim states at times blocked the Iberians' access to the Mediterranean trade routes, which connected them to the lucrative trade routes of the Indian Ocean world, often as a repercussion for Iberian aggression. Second, the Portuguese and the proto-Spanish states had a comparative commercial and military disadvantage with the Venetians and Genovese, arguably the most powerful European states in the fifteenth century, who, often in collaboration with Muslim states, dominated the European position in the Mediterranean trade. And third, the crusader spirit encouraged by the *Reconquista*, which was, in the fifteenth century, in its final phases, the Iberians desired to expand Christendom throughout their own lands and beyond.

Portuguese rulers initially began this expansion process by extending their control into northern Africa. Military campaigns in that region began in force after Portugal's 1415 conquest of the Muslim city of Ceuta located on the North African Mediterranean coast (modern-day Morocco). Through its access to the Saharan salt and gold trade, which will be discussed at a later point, and through its connections with the greater Muslim world, Ceuta was a city of great wealth. The Portuguese were amazed at its riches and their conquest of the city motivated them to push for greater expansion. Driven by competition with North African Muslim neighbors as well as with the proto-Spanish states, Portugal soon moved to take control of the strategically important Strait of Gibraltar, the narrowest point of the Mediterranean, which separates Europe and Africa by only nine miles. Controlling the straight meant controlling much of the trade between the Mediterranean and the Atlantic.

This new strategic position enabled the Portuguese to access new avenues of wealth in North Africa. Portugal had long experienced a shortage of bullion (silver and gold currency), but this deficiency began to subside when, through their holdings in Ceuta, they began to have access to the trans-Saharan salt and gold trade. The camel caravans that arrived in their newly conquered city enabled the Portuguese royal mint to produce gold coins in quantity. Although the centrality of the trans-Saharan trade to

Portugal's economy would gradually erode after 1450 as they continued to push out into the Atlantic and have access to West African trade routes, it was this initial financial boost that helped fund their early voyages. Finally, conquest in North Africa provided Portugal with much needed farmland. The Portuguese took advantage of Muslim infighting in what is now Morocco in the second part of the fifteenth century. They conquered several coastal towns such as Al-Ksa as-Saghi in 1458, and Asilah and Tangier in 1471, as well as, and just as importantly, the fertile regions of Atlantic Morocco. The Mediterranean climate of the area allowed the Portuguese to grow grain, a vital commodity of strategic importance that was in short supply in Portugal. This new land did not satisfy all of Portugal's need for grain, but it certainly aided in ameliorating their situation.[12]

As noted above, the third major motivating factor for expansion had political and ideological underpinnings rooted in the history of the Iberian Peninsula. Beginning in the eighth century, several Muslim states controlled most of the Iberian Peninsula for 300 years and they controlled the southern sections for much longer; Granada, for example, was in Muslim hands for 800 years. Despite their long tenure of control and the often times peaceful interaction between Muslims, Christians, and Jews in several of these Islamic states, some European Christians felt that the peninsula should be under their control and called the slow and centuries long process of pushing the Muslims from the area, the "*Reconquista*" and linked it conceptually to the Crusades against the Islamic states in the "Holy Land" of the Middle East. Given their long-established roots in Iberia, Muslims had a different view of the Christians' rationalizations for expelling them from what they naturally perceived as their homeland. To the Portuguese and the proto-Spanish states, however, theirs was a struggle for the "glory of God." It was a war against non-believers who were cast in the role of "infidels" and "savages"—literally meaning people without faith. "*Reconquista*" also became an important rationalization for expansion into North Africa. The historian of Portuguese Empire A.R. Disney writes, for example: "The kings of Portugal, Castile and Aragon all claimed to be the rightful heirs to an ancient Visigothic North Africa wrongfully taken from their forefathers by Muslim conquerors."[13] Hence, there existed a strong religious fervor among many Iberians, which motivated their advance, and often targeted Muslims and Jews in acts of violence, repression, and forced conversion. This religious zeal would also have an impact on Iberian expansion in the Atlantic World and around the globe, and terms such as "savages" and 'infidels" would be used by Europeans as part of their vocabulary of ethnic differentiation and superiority.

Yet, by the first half of the sixteenth century, Portuguese efforts in North Africa were losing momentum. The Portuguese were forced to turn to a more defensive strategy and over time they lost control over big portions of Morocco. Several factors played a role in this decline. Muslim states in North Africa took a more united position against the Iberians than they had in the previous century. Corsairs, or pirates, as the Portuguese would have called them, sponsored by the Ottoman Empire put pressure on the Portuguese and Spanish in the region. And, finally, the Muslim states caught up with military technology, eradicating the Europeans' comparative advantage in this area. By the time the Spanish Habsburg Empire took over Portugal in 1580, the Iberians had lost almost all of their holdings in North Africa with the exception of a few footholds like Ceuta, the city that had started it all. While the Portuguese and Spanish effort at empire building in North Africa was short-lived, it played a foundational role in the development of the Global Atlantic.[14]

West African Empires—Global Connections

Like the Atlantic regions examined above, West Africa was deeply involved with trans-regional trade. The extensive West African empires of Ghana, Mali, and Songhay who dominated West Africa from the ninth to the sixteenth centuries, and smaller communities as well, were economically linked with the outside world through a vast trans-Saharan trade network. With these commercial interactions came enduring cultural contact that ultimately had a significant impact on societies in the region. Historians have tended to refer to this trans-regional commercial network as "the salt and gold" trade after its predominant and most lucrative commodities, but goods such as kola nuts, ivory, books, textiles, dyes, grains, porcelain, carpets, precious woods, furniture, silk, hides, figs, and slaves were also widely purchased and sold.

The Trans-Saharan Trade

The trans-Saharan trade that the Portuguese encountered in Ceuta reached back to the third and fourth centuries, which was sometime after the camel arrived in the Sahara region from Asia. The introduction of this beast of burden gradually tied the regional economy of the larger Niger River Valley—based on farming, fishing, and hunting—to the Afro-Eurasian world. The camel, sometimes called the "ship of the desert," became the main vehicle that enabled the peoples of the region to cross the Sahara. Perfectly adapted to the harsh environment, the camel can travel long distances, survive for days without needing to consume water, eat a variety of foods, walk with relative ease through the sandy dunes, withstand sandstorms, and haul around 300–350 pounds, enabling the transport of large quantities through the desert. By employing the strengths of the camel and developing a sophisticated system of oases where they could replenish supplies of food and water, the peoples of the region began to master and cross the desert while moving substantial amounts of goods.

As the camel expanded opportunities for contact, a trans-regional commerce developed and some of the character of this trade is belayed in the regional names, which are still employed today. The region south of the Sahara desert, for instance, reaching from the Atlantic coast of modern Senegal to Ethiopia in eastern Africa, is often referred to as the Sudanic belt. The root of this term comes from the Arabic *Dar-al-Sudan* ("abode or country of the blacks"). The northern reaches of this region, adjacent to the Sahara, are often referred to as the "Sahel," which is derived from the Arabic word for shore or coast. This terminology indicates that the local populations in the region did not perceive the desert as an obstacle to trade, but rather, like the sea, saw it as a space through which one could navigate and make connections with the outside world. There were certainly dangers in the desert, but just as with the Mediterranean or the Indian Ocean, it could be traveled, and, at least to some degree, mastered.

The trans-Saharan trade grew to become a major force in the Afro-Eurasian world as a result of two main commodities: salt and gold. Although perhaps odd from a contemporary perspective, given its wide availability today, salt played an integral and valued role in the history of West African empires and the trans-Saharan trade. The mineral's historical centrality stemmed from the fact that salt was a locally scarce commodity and essential for human life. Because plant tissue does not hold as much salt as animal tissue, societies who depended on grain as the basis of their diets, such as those of West Africa, require supplemental salt to maintain their health. Salt was valued for its ability to preserve food, an important attribute in a hot climate, and, as one of the few basic tastes on the human tongue, it was prized for gastronomic reasons as well. Salt was predominantly mined in the Sahara Desert, where large blocks of it would be cut and hauled by camel caravans to the West African Sahel by the Tuaregs and other Berber merchants. Salt could also be extracted from dried lake beds and, in smaller quantities, from the Atlantic Ocean. Coastal groups often rendered salt from ocean water, but they also used vegetation to produce it. In the Niger Delta, for example, mangrove trees were cut, and burned to ash. Then the ash was leached to make a highly concentrated saltwater solution, which was then boiled down to produce salt. Once the coastal peoples had produced the salt they shipped it to the urban centers of the great empires, many hundreds of miles away into the interior, generally via the Niger, the Senegal, and the Gambia rivers.[15]

The appeal of gold as a product might need less of an explanation than salt. Many societies around the world used it as a form of currency, considered it a measure of wealth and status, and saw it as a source for profit. It was a desired trade good. For the most part, gold was produced either in the West African empires themselves, or, it was obtained by them through commerce, generally with smaller states further to the south. A lot of gold in the region, like that of the California gold rush of 1848, was found in the alluvial soils near the bends of the local rivers. The location of the gold was diffuse and its extraction required minimal technology. As a result, some agriculturalists supplemented their farming by mining and panning for gold. In addition, there also existed a wealth of gold mines in the region. As a result, West Africa, between 1000 and 1500, provided, in aggregate, the world market with a substantial quantity of the precious commodity. Gold quickly developed into the source of wealth for West African empires, and became the major device that financed the trans-Saharan trade.

While the gold and salt largely originated from western and northern Africa, the larger trans-Saharan trade was linked through North Africa to the further reaches of the Muslim World and even beyond. Rare books and manuscripts, finished goods, incense, and spices came from all over the Middle East, and porcelain, silk, and spices were traded from the far corners of Asia. Thus, West Africa was tied into long-distance commerce and became an active player in the pre-modern global economy, especially as a major supplier of gold for the Mediterranean World. From the tenth to the sixteenth centuries, many of the gold coins minted by the various peoples of the Mediterranean World were made from metal mined in western Africa. West Africans also supplied unique fabrics, animal skins, and ivory, popular products in North Africa, Asia, and Europe. Slaves were also traded on both sides of the desert: African slaves fetched high prices in the Mediterranean and slaves from north of the Sahara were profitable commodities in the West African empires. Owning human property from far-away lands was considered a status symbol in many societies across the world.[16]

The spread of Islam gradually accompanied the transport of goods along the vast trade network and increasingly gained a foothold in the urban areas of western Africa between the eleventh and the fifteenth centuries. Founded by the Prophet Muhammad and his followers in the seventh century in the Mecca and Medina regions of the Arabian Peninsula, Islam grew quickly, spreading into many parts of the Afro-Eurasian world. Within several centuries of its founding, the Muslim World reached from the western parts of Africa to the easternmost portions of Asia in what is today Indonesia. While religiously motivated military campaigns played a central role in the history of the expansion of Islam in western Africa in the nineteenth century, its spread to the empires of the Sudanic Belt during the centuries we are discussing was largely brought about through trade and was relatively peaceful. Conversion tended to take two main paths. For one, Muslim traders married local women and raised their children in their own traditions. Moreover, long-term trade and social interactions led many local merchants and others in urban areas to gradually convert. The introduction of Arabic, central to the Muslim faith as the language of the holy scriptures of Islam (the Qu'ran), and an accepted language of trade, also brought an increase in learning. Qu'ranic schools increased literacy, which was useful in business and led to a cultural flourishing in West Africa as evidenced by the trade in books and rare manuscripts, which further led to the emergence of large collections and libraries held by both institutions and private individuals. Furthermore, by the fourteenth century, Western Africa, particularly the commercial hub of Timbuktu, turned into a center of higher learning and Islamic scholarship. Hence, over time, economically and culturally, the empires of western Africa became tied into a larger Muslim world system.[17]

Ghana

Ghana, the first major West African kingdom, emerged as a centralized state in the tenth and eleventh centuries at least partially as a result of its involvement in the trans-Saharan trade. Although it shares the name of the modern nation-state of Ghana, the two regions do not share any territory. The historic Empire of Ghana is located in parts of today's Mali and Mauritania about 500 miles to the northeast. The Empire of Ghana was located in the Sahel, and, more specifically, the interior Savannah region of the upper Senegal and the Gambia River valleys. Like the West African empires that succeeded it, Ghana was composed of a variety of ethnic groups and economies. The trans-Saharan trade was driven and directed by the ruling elites and merchants, many of whom accumulated substantial wealth as a result of this long-distance commerce. However, the majority of the population worked as subsistence farmers. In addition, there were a considerable number of pastoralists who lived within the country's border, and the lack of a unifying identity between these various ethnic and economic groups provided challenges to the eventual survival of the state. Groups on the periphery of the empire often tried not to pay tribute or taxes and attempted to break away. This disunity ultimately helped weaken the power of the rulers of Ghana.

Ghana made its fortunes by its strategic location between the edge of the Sahara and the African forest regions. The gold that flowed north through Ghana came from just outside of its borders, from goldfields in Bambuk and Bure, which were located to the south in the Faleme and the Niger River valleys. The salt that came south through the empire largely originated from the salt mines of the Sahara. Copper and textiles, again largely from outside of the empire, were also popular commodities. Rather than being an actual producer of goods, Ghana facilitated trade exchanges and served as an intermediary in regional and trans-regional commerce. This position still proved lucrative. Muslim writers of the period commented on the great wealth that could be found in Ghana. The tenth-century Muslim chronicler, geographer, and traveler, Ibn Hawqal relayed what he had learned about the region during his travels to Muslim Spain and North Africa, declaring the ruler of Ghana was "the richest king on the face of the earth by reason of wealth and treasure."[18]

As in other parts of the western African savannah, involvement in the trans-Saharan trade brought Muslim traders and Islam to Ghana. Yet, unlike the later empires of Mali and Songhay, Islam does not seem to have been embraced by the rulers of Ghana. Although tolerance between those who followed the indigenous and established religions of the area and the Muslim merchants seems to have prevailed, the two groups retained clear perceptions of cultural differences. In the Ghanaian capital city, Kumbi Saleh,

Muslims lived in a separate town six miles from the Emperor and his court and this pattern seems to have been imitated in other prominent cities in the region. There is some fragmentary evidence, however, that suggests that as the empire declined, Islam may have taken a stronger hold on some of the Ghanaian elite.

Ghana's dependency on long-distance trade routes is evident in the events that led to its decline. In the eleventh century, the Muslim Almoravids, a Berber dynasty that came from today's Morocco, conquered much of western North Africa and what is today southern Spain, Mauritania, and the Western Sahara, and greatly, though temporarily, disrupted the trans-Saharan trade. As the bonds of trade deteriorated, so did the economy and organization of the Empire of Ghana. In the changing political and commercial climate, the numerous ethnic and economic groups—farmers, herders, traders, etc.—that had previously made up the empire, responded in a variety of ways: for example, some broke off into smaller political units, others became mercenaries for the Almoravids, and some became the base of the next great West African empire—Mali.[19]

Mali

More than a century later, the West African empire of Mali would step into the vacuum left by Ghana and lasted, in some form, for three centuries, reaching its peak in the fourteenth century. As we will see, the Empire of Mali provides us with a variety of evidence of West Africa's links with trans-regional trade. The borders of this massive new empire extended considerably further than those of its predecessor state of Ghana. Mali at its height controlled much of the upper Niger River Valley, and at the pinnacle of its power, reached all the way to the Atlantic Coast. On the coast, Mali controlled a region that reached all the way from the north of the Senegal River to the south of the Gambia River.

Knowing the crucial role that commerce played in the empire, the rulers of Mali attempted to create a merchant-friendly environment and established safe and transparent trading conditions within their state. They succeeded to the extent that the experienced fourteenth-century traveler Ibn Battuta, who is believed to have traveled more than 70,000 miles throughout the Afro-Eurasian world including India, Central Asia, China, and Byzantium, visited the empire and was clearly impressed by their rule of law. He observed in his writing that "the safety, too, was very great, so that a traveler may proceed alone among them, without the least fear of a thief or robber. Another of their good properties is that when a merchant happens to die among them, they will make no effort to get possession of his property: but will allow the lawful successors to take it."[20]

Mali's most famous leader, Mansa Kankan Musa, provides us with a tangible example of the empire's links with greater Afro-Eurasia. Unlike the leaders of Ghana, Mali's rulers and elite adopted Islam and in the mid-1320s, as one of the major tenets of Islam, Mansa Musa made a pilgrimage to Mecca. His remarkable journey also gives us an impression of the wealth of Mali. Historians Erik Gilbert and Jonathan Reynolds write that Mansa Musa was rumored to have "set out with 1,000 retainers and 100 camel loads of gold." Although there is likely to have been some dramatization in the sources, it is probable that Musa's entourage spent and gave away so much gold in the grand city of Cairo as they passed through that inflation increased, which created some economic headaches for the local authorities. European travelers in the Egyptian port city of Alexandria were also fascinated by this encounter and such cross-cultural contacts certainly helped to shape European views of the Mali Empire.[21] Evidence of Europe's impression of West Africa is also found in the famous Catalan map of 1375, which depicts a richly adorned king of Mali reigning over an empire with many large and powerful cities and wearing several regal insignias made of gold. Thus, in the European imagination, fourteenth-century Mali was a place of splendor, wealth, and sophistication.

Mali's defining literary work, *Sundiata*, provides evidence of both trans-regional influences in Mali and of West Africa's enduring indigenous traditions. The heavily mythologized and embellished epic of *Sundiata*, the early thirteenth-century founder of Mali, was orally passed down over generations by a professional caste of political advisors, oral historians, and entertainers called griots. The account served as a founding and unifying myth of a multicultural state by bringing together and celebrating the contributions of the various ethnic groups of Mali. The narrative also demonstrates Mali's sophistication and historic awareness. As Sundiata heroically defeats the evil magician and ruler, Soumaoro, and becomes the first ruler of one of the world's greatest empires in the thirteenth and fourteenth centuries, he is frequently compared with the classical Hellenistic conqueror Alexander the Great.

Moreover, *Sundiata* successfully mixes Islamic elements with those of the indigenous religions of western Africa. The epic reveals a tension that

The famous Catalan map of 1375 shows the wealth and power of western and northern African rulers.

Source: Wikimedia Commons. 1375. Mediterranean Catalan Atlas. Abraham Cresques. http://commons.wikimedia.org/wiki/File:Europe_Mediterranean_Catalan_Atlas.jpeg.

the newly converted Malian rulers would have contended with as Mali's Muslim elite were obligated to accommodate their non-Muslim subjects and needed to be seen as stewards of the more established traditions. These local "traditional" religions, which were often rural, were intermingled with Islam, which was often a more urban phenomenon in the region. In this process, Muslim with African elements blended to create a unique West African variety of Islam that fulfilled the needs of the people of Mali. *Sundiata* provides readers a glimpse into the religious syncretism that occurred in the region and is a source of western Africa's cultural creativity in its dealings with the outside world.[22]

During its height, fueled by the wealth of the trans-Saharan trade and ties to the Islamic world as well as the stability and openness of its traditional society, Mali became known as a place of learning and new ideas. The city of Timbuktu, for example, became famous as one of the great centers of learning in the Islamic world. Some scholars have speculated, based on the writings of Al Umari, a fourteenth-century North African writer, that Mansa Musa desired to put together a well-equipped expedition "of two hundred ships filled with men" to explore the Atlantic Ocean to find a westerly trade route. While we have no further documentation of this notion, it raises interesting questions, particularly in the context of the concept of the Global Atlantic. While it is likely that the ships were never built nor the expedition ever launched, it certainly disabuses us from the notion that it was only the Europeans who thought about Atlantic exploration.[23]

Mali's Atlantic African holdings and tributaries were, however, always on the periphery of the state. The empire's prosperity depended on its interactions with the outside world through the Sahara desert, and just as with Ghana before it, when events to the north disrupted the trans-regional trade in the fifteenth century, Mali's authority and political and economic power began to decline. The newly emerging West African Songhay state began to slowly attract trade to their borders to the north and all over the once powerful empire, ethnic groups either asserted their independence, or they were taken over by Songhay. Tuareg Berbers from North Africa captured Timbuktu in 1433. By 1500, Mali had declined into a small confederation of Mandinke speakers, and the Songhay had begun to dominate much of the middle Niger River Valley, which provided the center of their state. In 1468, Songhay conquered Timbuktu from the Tuareg. Utilizing a military built on a powerful cavalry and a navy of war canoes, the rulers of Songhay established a formidable empire.

Songhay

Songhay, the last of the three great West African Empires, had been a vassal state under the Malian Empire centered in Goa, a town on the bend of the Niger River, where the traditional base of the economy had been fishing. As Mali weakened in the fifteenth century, Songhay extended its grip as far west as Jenne and pushed aggressively northward against the Berbers to establish their influence all the way to the fabled salt-mining center of Taghaza in the Sahara Desert of Northern Mali. To the east, Songhay reached all the way to Agades in today's northern Niger and in the south its influence went as far as today's northern Nigeria.[24]

After the disruptions of conquest, Songhay gained control of the trans-Saharan trade once enjoyed by its predecessors. Leo Africanus, a North African traveler and intellectual, visited the Songhay capital, Goa, and the university city of Timbuktu, as part of a diplomatic mission in

1510 and 1530. In his writings, he provides a variety of examples of how long-distance trade influenced West African life. He was impressed by the wealth of the elites of Timbuktu, explaining that the governor of Timbuktu "has many articles of gold, and he keeps a magnificent and well-furnished court." He also noted that the people of the city used "certain shells brought here from Persia" as currency. Education and learning remained important in the city under the rule of the Songhay as Africanus observed that "there are many doctors, judges, priests, and other learned men," which were paid by the governor of the city. "Various manuscripts and written books are brought here out of Barbarie [North Africa] and sold for more money than any other merchandise."

Leo Africanus also saw evidence of the trans-regional trade in the markets of Goa. Textiles, horses, salt, and luxury goods were the main imports and gold, kola nuts, and slaves the main export. He observed:

> It is a wonder to see how much merchandise is brought here daily and how costly and sumptuous everything is. There is not any cloth of Europe so coarse, which will not here be sold for four ducats an ell [measurement unit that reaches from one's elbow to the top of one's fingers], and if it be anything fine they will give fifteen ducats for an ell: and an ell of scarlet of Venetian or of Turkish cloth is here worth thirty ducats . . . and spices also are sold at a high rate: but of all other commodities salt is most extremely dear.[25]

Of the active and ancient slave market he wrote:

> Here there is a certain place where slaves are sold, especially on those days when the merchants are assembled. And a young slave of fifteen years of age is sold for six ducats, and children are also sold. The king of this region has a certain private palace where he maintains a great number of concubines and slaves.

Just as the empires before it, Songhay both exported and imported slaves to play a variety of roles in their economic structure. Slave labor in the agricultural sector and the domestic sphere supported the more privileged clans of craftsmen and political elites.[26] Wealth in the region was often determined by the labor an individual controlled and, as a result, captives of war and exotic foreigners were seen as both an important element of economic productivity and as a marker of status. As in many Mediterranean slave-owning societies, the slaves in Songhay could also hold high positions as generals, skilled laborers, and advisors. In these positions, slaves were often seen as being more trustworthy because they did not have their own extended families to privilege. Old world slavery was notably more varied than the predominately chattel slavery that would develop later in the Americas. Nevertheless, it was the roots of this ancient trade that would be exploited on a much larger scale by the Atlantic slave traders in the centuries to come.

Songhay continued to exist into the late sixteenth century but political infighting and environmental damage weakened the region and in 1591 it was invaded by a Moroccan army with more advanced weapons. Several states emerged in the region as a result of the power vacuum. By this time the world historical importance of the trans-Saharan trade was fading. With the vast availability of gold and especially silver from the Americas starting in the sixteenth century, and the decreasing supplies of gold in the region, the global importance that West Africa once held as a major supplier of gold to the Afro-Eurasian world economy was quickly waning. In addition, the main trade routes in West Africa turned to the Atlantic coast and states in the region earned an ever increasing portion of their wealth from selling captives of their wars of expansion to the emerging trans-Atlantic slave trade.[27]

Trans-Regional Connections in the Pre-Colombian Americas

Thanks to the diligent work of archeologists, anthropologists, and historians, our understanding of the Americas prior to European colonization has dramatically changed in recent decades. Native American societies, especially those of North America, were thought to have been exclusively hunter-gatherers and, while some certainly were, the largest portion of the indigenous population across the Americas subsisted predominantly as farming societies. In addition, some of these societies created influential agrarian states and empires. Researchers have also shed light on the sophisticated nature of the trans-regional involvement of many of the native peoples of the Americas prior to European colonization. Indigenous American efforts to later shape and respond to European empire-building and their involvement in the Global Atlantic were rooted in this earlier history. Of the many agriculturally based, interconnected, societies of the pre-Columbian Americas, this section focuses on only three: the Mound Builders of North America, the Aztec of Central America, and the Inca of South America.

Mound Builders of North America

For roughly two thousand years before Columbus, the Mississippi and Ohio River valleys were the heartland of a variety of diverse Native American societies. Three of these societies, the Adena (*c.* 500–100 BC), Hopewell (*c.* 200 BC–AD 400), and Mississippians (*c.* 700–1500), despite distinct differences in culture and different time periods, shared a common practice of creating sophisticated earthworks and for that reason are known collectively as Mound Builders. Over the course of centuries, these peoples created thousands of mounds across the Eastern Woodlands, an area that encompasses what is today the eastern half of the United States and southeastern Canada. The impressive variety and quantity of mounds they constructed demonstrate such impressive organization and cultural sophistication that some European settlers even sought to prove that the mounds could not have been built by the ancestors of Native Americans. The archeological evidence of highly developed artifacts from mound burial sites suggests complex ceremonial and religious structures and the existence of ruling elites. Mound building required time, sophisticated architectural planning, and the communal efforts of a society to transport thousands of tons of earth in baskets.[28]

The Adena, Hopewell, and Mississippian cultures all built distinctive mounds for a variety of purposes and, taken as a whole, the diversity of earthworks is striking. They could be conical or flat topped, standing alone or as part of a larger mound complex that could be as large as several hundred acres across with surroundings on an earthen embankment. The mounds also had a variety of uses: burial sites, astrological calendars, meeting places, and sacred spaces for ritual. Mound structures had a variety of shapes including hexagons, squares, circles, and octagons, and, in the case of effigy mounds, the form of animals. Few of these effigy mounds remain intact today; like most of the mounds once built, they were flattened for farmland, roads, and houses. A striking exception to this destruction is the Serpent Mound in southern Ohio, where visitors can climb atop a tower and see a winding snake of mounded earth as large as a football field stretch out below them.

Before 1492, the Native Americans of the Eastern Woodlands, like societies of pre-modern Europe and West Africa, focused on their "old world" interregional interactions. As a result, they did not focus their attention on the Atlantic Coast but, as historian Lynda Shaffer writes, were oriented toward the Mississippi River leaving most of the eastern seaboard as their hinterland.[29] From their base in the interior, they developed extensive trade networks and trading centers. The largest of these centers was the city of Cahokia, the remains of which are located on the Mississippi River in southern Illinois. At its height, between CE 1050 and CE 1200, it had a population of between at least 10,000 to 20,000 people, making it larger than London at the time. It remained the largest city in the history of North America until it was replaced in this role by Philadelphia in the mid-1700s.

The intricate artifacts found in Cahokia and in other trading centers of the Eastern Woodlands demonstrate the vast trans-regional trade cultivated by the mound-building cultures. Ceramic figures, effigy pipes, engraved stone tables, copper plates, and human-shaped statues were made of materials from areas that spread across much of North America. Mica from the Appalachian mountains of North Carolina, obsidian from the Yellowstone region of western Wyoming, copper from the Great Lakes, silver from eastern Canada, and conch shells along with shark and alligator teeth from the Gulf Coast region were all found in the remains of the various river valley communities of today's American Midwest and South. The waterways of the Eastern Woodlands, major rivers such as the Mississippi, the Ohio, the Missouri, as well as their many tributaries, were used as major avenues of transportation for the trans-regional exchange networks of the Mound Builders.

The Europeans did not see mound-building culture at its height. By the time they began to colonize the Western Hemisphere in the late fifteenth and early sixteenth centuries, the Mississippian mound-building centers of the Eastern Woodlands were in rapid decline. Although the exact causes are unknown, there is convincing evidence that the mound-building cultures of the upper and middle Mississippi River Valley were already in decline before 1500, as this region underwent broader patterns of population redistribution and decline before the arrival of the Europeans. After 1492, however, historians and archeologists believe that the impact of Afro-Eurasian pathogens had a devastating impact on Native American societies. They estimate that the mortality rates in Native American communities ranged from 50 percent, to, with sustained contact over several decades, as high as 90 percent. Originating from the Spanish and other European conquistadores, shipwreck survivors, slave raiders, fishermen, and traders on the coast throughout the sixteenth century, diseases spread to the interior following the interregional river trade system of the Eastern Woodland peoples. Before Europeans and Africans actually set foot in the heartland of the mound-building region, waves of epidemics caused dramatic depopulation, especially in what is today the southeastern United States.[30]

The years following 1492 were disastrous for not only the mound-building societies but for Native people across the Americas. As disease spread, they faced a demographic collapse. While exact numbers are impossible to obtain, across the hemisphere, epidemics upended the lives of several tens of millions of people, a significant portion of the world's population, estimated at about 500 million in 1500. The impact of Afro-Eurasian disease on the Americas is unmatched in the history of the modern world and it cleared the way for European colonization and conquest of the Americas. Because of the long history of trans-regional trade between these areas, this phenomenon did not occur on a large scale in either Africa or Asia, making European efforts at colonizing these regions much more difficult. Yet, even in the Americas, it would take the Europeans and their descendants into the nineteenth century until they were able to militarily subjugate the vast majority of the indigenous people of the Western Hemisphere.[31]

The Aztec Empire of Mesoamerica

The name Aztec was never used by the Mesoamericans who built the great empire but instead evolved from the political alliance that the Mexica ethnic group created with neighboring city-states at the beginning of their rise to power. When historians refer to the rise of the Aztecs, therefore, they are generally referring to the Mexica, the ethnic group from which the modern nation-state of Mexico takes its name. When the Mexica, according to their legends, migrated from today's southwestern United States into the heart of Mesoamerica, they entered a region that had a long and rich past. It was expansive and complex. Impressive Native American civilizations such as the Olmecs, from around 1500 BC, and the

Maya, whose classical age spanned the seventh to the ninth centuries AD, created urban cultures with impressive stone architecture, complex social hierarchies, and sophisticated writing systems. While at times these societies, along with a variety of other Mesoamerican cultures, such as the peoples who built the city of Teotihuacan, one of the largest cities in the world when it was built around 100 BC, are likely to have created larger states or empires, it was the influential and powerful city-states that shaped much of the region's human political organization.

As the Mexica migrated into the Valley of Mexico, they absorbed the existing culture of the city-states of the area, and intermarried and assimilated into the older urban cultures, and eventually built their own city-state of Tenochtitlan on an undesirable location in the middle of a shallow, brackish, lake; it would become one of the world's most impressive capitals. The Mexica took advantage of the political overreach and infighting between the region's more dominant city-states to form a Triple Alliance between their Technochtitlan and the neighboring city-states of Tetzcoco and Tlacopan. In 1427, the cities of the Triple Alliance agreed that all tribute extracted by their wars of expansion would be divided between them, marking the beginning of what would later become known as the Aztec Empire. The most powerful of the three city-states, Tenochtitlan of the Mexica, would, within the course of a generation, control the vast majority of the Valley of Mexico and directly or indirectly rule millions of people from a complex array of nations and cultures.

The Mexica capital, formed on an island in the now dry Lake Texcoco in the mid-fourteenth century, at its height had an estimated population of at least 100,000, making it not only a powerful seat of government but one of the world's largest cities. Tenochtitlan was able to support such a large population through its extensive agricultural and tribute systems. The Mexica created raised fields called *chinampas* out of their lake. They dredged mud and rocks, and added reeds from the lake to raise them above the water level. They reinforced the bed's edges by interweaving sticks and planting bushes and trees to help against erosion and expanded their arable land. This effective system of agriculture was productive enough to permit the enormous population. The vast size and quantity of *chinampas* are also evidence of, and perhaps one cause of, the remarkable degree of social organization among the Mexica. Because there were no draft animals in pre-Columbian Mesoamerica, the *chinampas* were a tremendous feat of human labor. Furthermore, the deep canals between the terraced farm fields functioned as excellent waterways for transportation of crops and trade goods, which the Mexica obtained through a sophisticated long-distance exchange network.

As the understandings of the Triple Alliance make clear, tribute and trade were essential elements of the Aztec Empire from its conception. As the empire expanded, newly conquered regions would often be allowed to maintain a significant degree of local autonomy, even, at times, their own ruling family, if they would submit to the tribute requests of the Triple Alliance. Although there was some overlap between the two systems, in the region where military force could be threatened, the Aztecs tended to rely on tribute, and, in regions beyond their military control, they depended on trade. This extensive transfer of goods significantly enriched and, for a time at least, expanded the power of the Aztecs.

Because long-distance trade and tribute systems had long been present in Mesoamerica, the Aztecs were able to revive, expand, and create new links based on the economic history of the area. Although tribute goods would often include bulkier agricultural items and humans for ritual sacrifice, both tribute and trade items could be rare and valued items. Gold and other precious metals, jewels and semi-precious stones such as turquoise, desirable feathers such as the tail feathers of the quetzal bird, highly valued animal skins and furs, shells pulled from the depths of the ocean, as well as cocoa beans, which served as both a product and currency in commercial interactions, were all in demand and, in the case of the tribute, demanded.

Highly desired products could come from thousands of miles away and were widely used as evidenced in art and material culture. At the height of their empire, the Aztec exchange network reached far beyond their borders in the Valley of Mexico to both the Atlantic and Pacific Coasts. Their trade networks went at least as far north as the present states of Texas and New Mexico and as far south as Guatemala. Lacking both the beasts of burden that were so much a part of the Afro-Eurasian world and the extensive river systems employed by the Mound Builders of the Eastern Woodlands, the Aztec trade was conducted by humans who traveled commercial roads on foot carrying their goods on their backs. These goods would eventually make their way to the capital.[32]

As the Aztec Empire expanded, tribute became one of the most effective tools to not only enrich the capital but to dominate the conquered city-states. The Spanish Dominican friar Diego Duran described one of these tributary ceremonies and underscores their purpose:

> People attended with their tribute of gold, jewels, finery, feathers and precious stones, all of the highest value and in great quantities . . . so many riches that they could not be counted or valued. All of this was done to show off magnificence and lordship in front of their enemies, guests and strangers, and to instil fear and dread.[33]

By allowing the local elites to also collect tribute from their people, the Aztecs established a degree of assent from the indigenous leadership to gather quantities of agricultural goods, textiles both for common use and for displays of wealth and power, as well as the rare and valuable items noted above. They would also demand human beings to be used for labor, such as road and temple building, military expansion, and human sacrifice.

The number of people sacrificed by the Aztecs is a subject of intense debate among historians and archeologists. Mesoamerican societies had long practiced human sacrifice as part of important religious ceremonies, and the Aztecs might have increased the rate of such sacrificial killings. One root of the human sacrifice is found in the Aztec cosmology: they believed that the sun, the source of all life, depended on human blood in order to rise each day. The intensity of these rituals also tended to vary in accordance to their religious leadership and the empire's political needs over time. The manner in which human tributes were treated seems to have also fluctuated: at times, a high-ranking tribute might be treated with honor, at other times, in an effort to humiliate them, human tributes were forced to gather up refuse or inedible bugs. Demanding such a number of captives and tributes did not set the empire on strong foundations. The Spanish easily found willing Native American allies from city-states who were angry with and humiliated by the tribute system. Subjugated and disadvantaged groups were willing to work with the strange new arrivals and significantly assisted in the conquest of the Aztec overlords.

Besides providing them with allies, another element of the demand for human tribute would impact the Aztec's encounter with the Spanish. Instead of simply killing fighters on the battlefield in the manner most familiar to the Europeans, many of the Aztec war tactics were designed to take prisoners alive for sacrifice. Warriors captured in battle were thought to be favored by Aztec deities. But captives could also be used as labor and could even be adopted into Aztec military structure. The Flower Wars, as these battles for warrior tribute came to be called, were often planned in advance with the consent of the leadership of the conquered city-state. Again, this tradition of capturing fighters alive may have weakened the Aztec's actual military defense against the Europeans and their allies.[34]

When the Spanish arrived in 1519, they were amazed by the high level of urban development that existed in the region. They were fascinated by the density and size of cities as well as the sophistication of architecture as revealed by temples, causeways, aqueducts, and roads. The conquistador Bernal Diaz del Castillo observed:

> During the morning, we arrived at a broad causeway and continued our march . . . and when we saw so many cities and villages built in the water and other great towns on dry land, we were amazed . . . it was like the enchantments [that] they tell of in the legends of Amadis, on account of the great towers and buildings rising from the water and all built of masonry. And some of our soldiers even asked whether the things that we saw were not a dream.[35]

The amazement of Europeans with urban life in Mesoamerica in the early sixteenth century was matched by their appreciation of the commercial sophistication of the Aztec Empire. "Some of the soldiers among us who had been in many parts of the world, in Constantinople, and all over Italy, and in Rome," wrote Diaz, "said that so large a market and so full of people and well regulated and arranged, they had never beheld before."[36]

It was the climate of ethnic division, spurred by warfare, tribute, and sacrifice that enabled, in part, the toppling of the volatile Aztec Empire by the Spanish in the early 1520s. The Spanish aptly used the divisions among the Mesoamerican people and allied themselves with recently conquered Native nations who saw the Spanish as useful collaborators in their efforts to overthrow the Aztec yoke. As with the Native Americans of North America, the Spanish conquest was most aided by the introduction of Afro-Eurasian diseases. In this location too, disease is believed to have wiped out 90 percent of the original Mesoamerican population. The conquest of the Aztec Empire tellingly coincided with a massive and deadly smallpox epidemic, which played into Spanish military interests by significantly weakening their opponents.

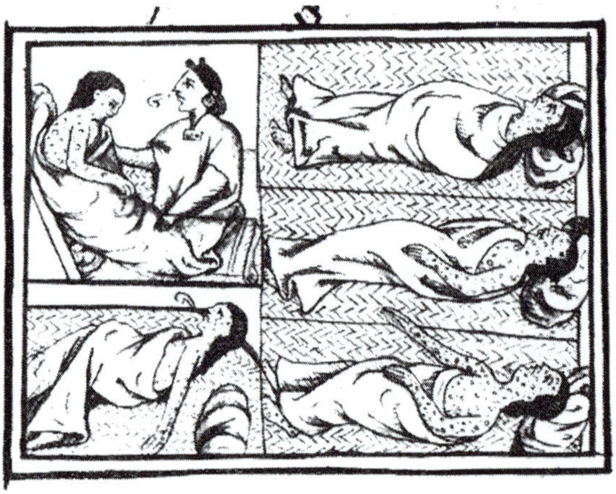

A deadly smallpox outbreak coincided with the Spanish conquest of the Aztec Empire and ravaged the indigenous population of the region. This was only one of many epidemics to hit the Americas. Since 1492, Afro-Eurasian diseases are believed to have killed tens of millions of Native Americans.

Source: Wikimedia Commons. 1540–85. Florentine Codex. http://commons.wikimedia.org/wiki/File:FlorentineCodex_BK12_F54_smallpox.jpg.

The Inca of South America

Archeological evidence teaches us that the Inca were only one society in a long line of Native American states that existed all over South America. Urban civilizations in what is today the coast of Peru date thousands of years back in history. These early societies subsisted through extensive farming supported by sophisticated irrigation systems, and by fishing in the Pacific Ocean.

For the last few thousand years or so, traders in South America's indigenous communities participated in impressive long-distance exchange networks. This was in part a maritime trade. Native Americans in the region used sailing ships along the Pacific Coast and are believed to have traveled as far north as Central America, but interregional exchange also connected coastal communities with those far inland. Trade reached across the Andean mountain chain into the Amazonian rain forest. Communities further inland in the harsher highlands of the Andes, would raise large herds of llama and alpacas; these beasts of burden, the only large domestic animals that existed in the Western Hemisphere, were used to carry goods between the Andean highlands and lowlands. Animals and human traders would travel tremendous vertical drops and distances. The colder highland regions would offer maize and potatoes, whereas the hotter lowlands provided coca, which was used as a stimulant, as well as peanuts, chilies, and cotton. In the more extensive long-distance trade network that reached beyond the Andes highlands and lowlands, and in which more valuable goods were exchanged, Native Americans dealt with gold, exotic feathers, animal pelts and skins, salt, copper, seashells, and beads. Thus, a complex and diverse history existed in these parts of the Americas, shaped by sophisticated and extensive interregional exchange systems, and the Inca actively participated in and usurped these networks when they began to build their empire.

As is the case with many Native American societies, we know much about the Inca in South America through the prism of European writers and observers. Unfortunately, scholars still have not figured out a way to decipher the *quipus*, the knotted string records that the Incas used as a form of written communication. Thus, it was Spanish authors of the early 1500s who provided much of the written documentation on the Inca. But the Spaniards, just as they did in Mesoamerica, also collected interviews and narratives from Native Americans, which provide us a glimpse into the workings of Inca society and indigenous views of the conquest. While there remain many unanswered questions about Inca and other South American societies, these sources, alongside archeological and anthropological evidence, help us to uncover the history of an imposing empire.

Like the Mexica, the Inca Empire emerged only in the 1400s as a powerful state. Most scholars assume that sometime between 1000 and 1400, the people we today call the Inca, arose from a conglomeration of several smaller allied native nations in south central Peru. These groups subsisted largely as potato and maize farmers and settled in the mountain valleys close to alpine lakes. There, despite such challenges as drought and frost, farming is possible at a height of 8,500 to 13,000 feet (roughly 2,600 to 4,000 meters).

The fifteenth- and sixteenth-century expansion of the Inca, made possible through a series of dramatic military campaigns, began an impressive effort at empire building that began from their homelands in the Peruvian highlands around Cuzco. Like the Aztec, the Inca demanded tribute in goods and labor, which was often obtained by force. Subjugated peoples would often work under dismal conditions. Furthermore, Native societies that had come under Inca control had to swear allegiance to the Inca's religion, they were often directly ruled by Inca officials, and they were pressured to adopt the Quecha language, which is still the most widely used indigenous language in the Americas today. Thus, by enforcing political as well as religious control, the Inca ruled over an extremely diverse empire. It included client states as well as occupied territories. As was the case in the Aztec empire, there existed resentment toward the Inca by the people they occupied. While their state looked outwardly strong—a large territorial domain created by an efficient military society—this was a structure built on what proved to be a fragile foundation; aiding in the eventual unraveling of the empire in the first half of the sixteenth century. Despite these issues, at the peak of their empire, the Inca dominated a vast land mass that stretched about 3,000 miles along the Andes Mountains from north of the equator in today's Equator, all the way south to central Chile in the Maule River region. The Inca's empire covered much of the Pacific coast to the West and reached into the Amazonian region to the east. The Inca state thus included a tremendous ecological diversity, ranging from equatorial rain forest regions, to alpine mountains and highlands, to lowland environments, and coastal deserts. This ecological diversity provided challenges and opportunities to the Inca, who had to integrate this difficult environment into a complicated and sophisticated interregional long-distance exchange network.

The success of the Inca was based, at least in part, on their ability to control the long-distance exchange networks of their empire. In fact, the Inca's elite strictly controlled the exchange and distribution of goods. The infrastructure and sophisticated engineering accomplishments of the empire, which are reflected in their great architectural accomplishments such as urban development at high altitudes, colossal religious structures, and sophisticated irrigation works, could also be seen in the extensive system of roads that the Inca built in one of the world's most unforgiving landscapes. Despite the incredible vertical distances that needed to be covered, connecting a tremendous area in western South America that covered coastal, desert, highlands, and jungle regions, the Inca built stone-paved roads, often using forced labor, wherever it was humanely possible. They also cut many portions of their roads into steep mountain slopes. Furthermore, armies of weavers built strong hanging bridges, which were strong enough to be used by large caravans of llamas and traders, who utilized them to cross over many dramatic canyons, valleys, and gorges. In all, the Inca's sophisticated road system covered almost 10,000 miles of the most difficult terrain. This tremendous feat in infrastructure and public work construction enabled the wide distribution of goods over the vast territory controlled by the Inca.

Andean society also excelled at creating high quality woven textiles from cotton and alpaca fiber, pottery, and especially metalwork: artisans in the Inca Empire worked on copper, bronze, silver, and gold. Their metallurgy included impressive and unique decorative pieces generally made out of silver and gold, which the Inca associated with the divine. Gold was described as the "sweat of the sun" and was connected with the veneration of the principal ruler of the Inca Empire—the Sapa Inca. Silver was associated with the "tears of the Moon," female goddesses, and the high noble women among the Inca elite. Copper and bronze, which were given less spiritual value in Inca cosmology, were often turned into tools produced for a mass market. Woven textiles also played a special diplomatic, status, and ritualistic role in Inca society. Large amounts of ponchos and blankets were, for example, used as a form of payment by the Inca elite to reward collaborating regional leaders, and certain fabrics made of special fibers were reserved for members of the elite only.

As mentioned above, the Inca state was a fragile construct, an empire shaped by constant warfare on its frontiers and plagued by reoccurring wars of succession. The Incas had conquered many peoples, such as the Chachapoyas in northern Peru who were subdued just before the arrival of the Spanish in 1525. These groups resented Inca rule, and waited for an opportunity to overthrow them. Moreover, on the eve of Spanish conquest, the Inca were consumed by a civil war over who should rule the state, Huascar or Atahualpa. This extremely bloody conflict was dearly won by Atahualpa and his supporters, and left the empire in a much weakened state. When the Spanish invaded the Andes in 1532, they were joined by many of the supporters of the defeated Huascar and other enemies of Atahualpa.

Afro-Eurasian diseases and the policies of Spanish colonization would eventually decimate the indigenous population in the region. As in the Aztec Empire, the Spanish plundered and melted down many of the Inca's golden and silver treasures—a tremendous loss to the world's artistic heritage. Although the Spanish originally came to the empire in search of gold, in the long run, and as we will see in the later chapters of the book, it was not gold but the dramatic veins of silver in the Andes Mountains as well as in Central America, that would have a tremendous economic impact on the history of the Global Atlantic.[37]

Conclusion

Long before the gradual establishment of an Atlantic World in the sixteenth century, Africans, Europeans, and Native Americans were involved in interregional long-distance exchange systems. Even with the establishment of new Atlantic-based trade routes, these traditional trans-regional links persisted. It was, therefore, through the lens of these "old world" trade connections that Africans, Europeans, and Native Americans gradually entered into the emerging Atlantic World. Recognizing how these traditional networks had shaped and been shaped by these societies helps us to appreciate the economic and social priorities of the Europeans, Africans, and Native Americans at the time of contact, as well as how they had previously approached outside goods and cultures. With the increased integration of the ocean system of the Atlantic World these older links declined but, for a while at least, they maintained social and economic relevance in their perspective cultures. These older trans-regional networks connected with the newly emerging ones and with the rise of the Atlantic World, a Global Atlantic was born.

Notes

1 For two seminal studies on the connections of the Afro-Eurasian world see Jerry H. Bentley, *Old World Encounters: Cross-Cultural Contacts and Exchanges in Pre-Modern Times* (New York: Oxford University Press, 1993); and Janet Abu-Lughod, *Before European Hegemony: The World System A.D. 1250–1350* (New York: Oxford University Press, 1989).

2 I am drawing the concept of the Native American "old world" from Neal Salisbury, "The Indians' Old World: Native Americans and the Coming of Europeans," *William and Mary Quarterly* 53 (July 1996): 435–458.

3 See Helge Ingstad and Anne Stine Ingstad, *The Viking Discovery of America: The Excavation of a Norse Settlement in L'Anse aux Meadows, Newfoundland* (New York: Checkmark Books, 2001), 1–2.

4 Simon Franklin and Jonathan Shepard, *The Emergence of the Rus, 750–1200* (New York: Longman, 1996); Johannes Bronsted, *The Vikings* (Baltimore: Penguin Books, 1965), 63–69, 88–90, 116–118.

5 Magnus Magnusson and Hermann Palsson, *The Vinland Sagas: The Norse Discovery of America* (Baltimore: Penguin Books, 1965), 49–51.

6 Ingstad and Ingstad, 24–27.
7 *Vinland Sagas*, 54–61.
8 Ingstad and Ingstad, 43–62.
9 Paul Freedman, *Out of the East: Spices and the Medieval Imagination* (New Haven, Conn.: Yale University Press, 2008), for quotes see 3–4, 25.
10 Freedman, 5.
11 Jerry Brotton, *The Renaissance Bazaar: From the Silk Road to Michelangelo* (New York: Oxford University Press, 2002). On science in particular see especially George Saliba, *Islamic Science and the Making of the European Renaissance* (Cambridge, MA: MIT Press, 2011). On these issues more generally see also John M. Hobson, *The Eastern Origins of Western Civilisation* (Cambridge: Cambridge University Press, 2004).
12 A.R. Disney, *A History of Portugal and the Portuguese Empire, vol. 2: The Portuguese Empire* (New York: Cambridge University Press, 2009), chapter 15.
13 Disney, 2.
14 Disney, chapter 15.
15 Erik Gilbert and Jonathan Reynolds, *Trading Tastes: Commodity and Cultural Exchange to 1750* (Upper Saddle River, NJ: Prentice Hall, 2006), 65–66.
16 Gilbert and Reynolds, *Trading Tastes*, 67–68.
17 For a contextualization of Islamic and world history see Marshall G.S. Hodgson, *Rethinking World History: Essays on Europe, Islam, and World History*, edited with an introduction and conclusion by Edmund Burke III (New York: Cambridge University Press, 1993).
18 This section and quote is drawn from Erik Gilbert and Jonathan Reynolds, *Africa in World History: From Prehistory to the Present*, 2nd edn (Upper Saddle River, NJ: Pearson/Prentice Hall, 2008), 105–106.
19 Gilbert and Reynolds, *Africa in World History*, 106.
20 Ibn Battuta, *The Travels of Ibn Battuta in the Near East, Asia and Africa, 1325–1354*, transl. and ed. by Samuel Lee (Mineola, NY: Dover Publications, 2004), 240. For a biography of Ibn Battuta see Ross E. Dunn, *The Adventures of Ibn Battuta: A Muslim Traveler of the 14th Century* (Berkeley: University of California Press, 1986).
21 Gilbert and Reynolds, *Africa in World History*, 107–108.
22 D.T. Niane, ed., *Sundiata: An Epic of Old Mali*. Translated by G.D. Pickett (London: Longman, 1965).
23 Basil Davidson, *The Lost Cities of Africa* (Boston: Little & Brown, 1959), 74–75. On the issue of trans-Atlantic contacts between Africans and Native Americans before 1492 see Jack D. Forbes, *Africans and Native Americans: The Language of Race and the Evolution of Red-Black Peoples*, 2nd edn (Urbana and Chicago: University of Illinois Press, 1993), chapter 1.
24 Kevin Shillington, *History of Africa*, 3rd edn (New York: St. Martin's Press, 1989), 101–104.

25 Leo Africanus quoted in Shillington, 104–105.

26 For the second Leo Africanus quote and on these issues in general see "The Story of Africa: African Slave Owners," *BBC World Service*. http://www.bbc.co.uk/worldservice/africa/features/storyofafrica/9chapter2.shtml (accessed April 25, 2014).

27 Shillington, 104–106.

28 See Christoph Strobel, *The Testing Grounds of Modern Empire: The Making of Colonial Racial Order in the American Ohio Country and the South African Eastern Cape, 1770s-1850s* (New York: Peter Lang, 2008), 20. For the Mound Builders more generally see also Lynda N. Shaffer, *Native Americans Before 1492: The Moundbuilding Centers of the Eastern Woodlands* (Armonk, NY: M.E. Sharpe, 1992); and George R. Milner, *The Moundbuilders: Ancient Peoples of North America* (London: Thames & Hudson, 2004).

29 Shaffer, 10.

30 Salisbury, 435–458; Strobel, 20; Shaffer, 85–89.

31 See for example Suzanne Austin Alchon. *A Pest in the Land: New World Epidemics in a Global Perspective* (Albuquerque: University of New Mexico Press, 2003).

32 My synthesis of the Aztec Empire is drawn from Bonnie G. Smith, Marc van de Mieroop, Richard von Glahn, and Kris Lane, *Crossroad and Cultures: A History of the World's Peoples* (Boston: Beford/ St Martin's, 2012), 519–529. See also David Carrasco and Scott Sessions, *Daily Life of the Aztecs: Peoples of the Sun and Earth*, 2nd edn (Westport, CT: Greenwood Press, 2008).

33 Quoted in Neil MacGregor, *A History of the World in 100 Objects: From the Handaxe to the Credit Card* (New York: Viking, 2011), 507.

34 Smith et al., 523–529.

35 Quoted in MacGregor, 507.

36 Bernal Diaz del Castillo, "The True History of the Conquest of New Spain," in Thomas Sanders et al., eds, *Encounters in World History: Sources and Themes from the Global Past*, vol. 2, (Boston: McGraw Hill, 2006), 61.

37 The section on the Incas is based on Smith et al., 529–538, and MacGregor, 470–475.

PART II

Navigating the Global Atlantic, 1400–1800

Part II of this book examines the global interactions that accompanied the emergence of an Atlantic World starting in the fifteenth century. The Atlantic did not function as a self-contained ocean system, but was a setting for European global expansion that resulted in culture contact and interactions that influenced the lives of Europeans, Africans, and Native Americans. The Global Atlantic also had an impact on societies and cultures beyond the boundaries of the Atlantic Ocean.

The following chapters discuss the patterns and processes of the Global Atlantic in world historical perspective, and examine the interconnectedness of this ocean system with the rest of the world. Furthermore, this part scrutinizes how in their interactions with Africans, Native Americans, and Asians, the Europeans were often limited by political, military, and economic realities, which were shaped, in part, by the abilities of local populations in Africa, the Americas, and Asia to keep the ambitions of Westerners in check.

2

EUROPE, AFRICA, AND THE EMERGENCE OF THE GLOBAL ATLANTIC

The Portuguese exploration for trade routes along the African coast in the fifteenth century and Christopher Columbus' accidental stumbling on the Americas in 1492, were the catalysts that led several other European nations out into the Atlantic in pursuit of overseas commerce and expansion. In the previous chapter, we discussed how the Iberians gained and lost their foothold in North Africa. The efforts by the Portuguese brought them further south along the West and Central African coast, which, in 1488, led them around the continent's southern tip into the Indian Ocean. For the Portuguese their mission was not Atlantic exploration, it was securing ways to navigate the globe in search of wealth.

Portugal's involvement in Africa and later in the Indian Ocean was in many ways shaped and promoted by its "Old World" interests. Motivations included the search for gold and spices, the ideology of *Reconquista* (accompanied by a Christian missionary agenda and strong anti-Muslim sentiments), and the Mediterranean slave trade, which had been spurred by the westward spread of sugar production from the Middle East to the islands of the Mediterranean. Sugar would also be grown on the Atlantic African islands and later in the Americas when Europeans began to colonize these parts of the world starting in the fifteenth, sixteenth, and seventeenth centuries. These efforts at creating an Atlantic plantation complex were accompanied by the increased use of African slaves.

It is important to underscore though that Europeans were not the only driving force in the exchange with Africa. As we have seen in Chapter 1, the peoples of western Africa had long participated in established inter-regional exchange networks. This chapter examines how African understandings, desires, needs, and interests aided in shaping cultural encounters with Europeans in the fifteenth, sixteenth, and seventeenth centuries. Africans played an active and determining role in their commercial interactions with Europeans and by focusing on African participation in these exchanges, a more complex perspective and understanding emerges about the nature of these encounters. The cultural contacts between Africans and the Portuguese complicate our perceptions of the trans-Atlantic slave trade, a staple topic examined by many high school and college history textbooks. The slave trade is generally portrayed as an Atlantic system that involved Europe, Africa, and the Americas, but which was shaped by few or no outside influences. Yet, in its early years, the slave trade followed a logic and organization different from the one that had emerged by the eighteenth century, and which we today describe as the "triangle trade." The slave trade was part of a commercial system more complicated and with more global connections, often reinforced by African consumption habits, tastes, and demands, than it is often assumed in the conventional narratives of the trans-Atlantic slave trade.

Into the Atlantic Ho! Learning the Atlantic's Currents and Wind Patterns

Even though the currents and wind patterns of the Atlantic had proved tough to master, this did not mean that the various peoples living around this ocean system did not try. We have already discussed the successful efforts by the Vikings to figure out the very northern portion of this ocean system, an accomplishment helped by the Norse's favorable geographic location. Other Europeans, as well as Arabs, became interested in accessing West Africa via the Atlantic Ocean route. Several Arab scholars, for instance, advocated that an Atlantic maritime trade route would enable the northern African Muslim states to haul bigger loads of cargo of gold and slaves than camel caravans could carry. Although none of the early Arab or European efforts to reach West Africa and return to their port of departure seem to have been successful. In 1291, for instance, the Vivaldi brothers led a maritime mission from the northern Italian city of Genoa. They hoped to access the West African trade and potentially planned to extend their voyage all the way to the Indian Ocean to get a foot in the door with the lucrative spice trade. The crew, however, never returned.

While the particular Native American and West African states discussed in Chapter 1 focused their attention away from the Atlantic, there were various Africans and Native Americans who lived on the coast and made ample use of the ocean. For one, they used the sea for fishing. Moreover, and while the evidence is somewhat scant, Native Americans in the Caribbean seemed to have used large dugout canoes and sails to propel these vessels to participate in a maritime culture, in which boats were used to participate in long-distance trade and in sea battles. Various peoples of Atlantic West Africa used large canoes as a mode of transportation to travel on the ocean and up rivers such as the Senegal or the Gambia. West Africans also used their canoes for long-distance trade, as well as for warfare. But just like the Canary current impeded European and Arab mariners going south, it stopped Africans from going further north.[1]

For various European states the exploration of the Atlantic became an extension of their established strategic and commercial interests. It was the Genovese and other northern Italians, and later the Portuguese and Castilians, who had taken the initial initiative. These states had gained experience in the eastern trade with the Byzantine, Turkish, and Arabic regions of the Mediterranean and also at times had participated in the trade with northern Europe, having gone as far as the North Sea and the Baltic Sea. The Genovese were likely the first Europeans since antiquity to reach the Canaries in the fourteenth century. But the challenging return trip, due to wind and currents, was the likely reason why the Genovese abandoned this project. It would later fall to the Portuguese and the Castilians to colonize the Atlantic African islands of the Canaries, the Azores, and Madeira.[2]

The maritime inroads into the Atlantic were made possible by several technological adaptations that seafarers in the Mediterranean had implemented over several generations, and which had been borrowed from other parts of the Afro-Eurasian world. These efforts, especially by the fourteenth and fifteenth centuries, had gradually and significantly improved the ocean-going capabilities of Europeans. For instance, the carvel, a ship that could be used for multiple tasks ranging from trading, to fishing, and which was widely used by Europeans in their early efforts at overseas exploration, was a vessel that blended shipbuilding designs and techniques from the Mediterranean with those of the North Sea.

This combination of technology helped to produce a more sturdy ship. The carvel also made use of the lateen sail, originally developed by Arabic sailors in the Indian Ocean, which gave the vessel a higher degree of mobility. Moreover, Europeans drew from the Afro-Eurasian maritime traditions in their navigational efforts. They had adopted the astrolabe from Indian Ocean navigators, an instrument that helped sailors to figure out their latitudinal position. European mariners had also adopted the magnetic compass, which was originally an invention of the Chinese.

By the fifteenth century, carvels flying the Portuguese flag were likely the first ones to have figured out how to master the Atlantic and its wind patterns and ocean currents. They learned to use the circular winds of the Atlantic and worked their way down the African coast. When they decided that they had fulfilled their trading objectives and wanted to return home, they sailed out west into the Atlantic until they caught a wind pattern and ocean current that carried them back to the Iberian Peninsula. The Portuguese called this the *volta do mar* (the return through the sea). After 1492, the geographer D.W. Meinig observes, "Mariners quickly learned to make use of this natural circulation: southwesterly outbound directly into the American Indies, returning northeasterly, arching parallel with the trend of the North American coast." This system enabled Europeans to set out on a triangular voyage, which could link Africa, the Americas, and Europe together. In the long run, it aided Europeans in their colonization efforts in the Americas and helped to boost the trans-Atlantic slave trade. These were all factors that led to the emergence of an Atlantic World.[3] Nevertheless, there remained plenty of global tangents in this newly emerging ocean world system reaching far beyond the Atlantic.[4]

Sugar and Slavery in the Mediterranean World

Sugar played an important and multifaceted role in the history of the Global Atlantic. The roots of the New World plantation complex connect back to the sugar plantations that were run by Europeans in the late medieval period in the Mediterranean World. It was on the Mediterranean islands that Europeans gradually developed a way to produce sugar, which in turn played an influential role in how it was grown in the Americas. Thus, the story of sugar has to, at least in part, be understood as an effort by Europeans to expand the production of an increasingly desirable and lucrative "Old World" commodity into new regions. Eventually, and as we will discuss in more detail later, sugar was mixed with tea and coffee, two commodities that became popular among consumers in the Atlantic World.

While sugar comes in many forms, the variety grown in the Mediterranean and later in the Atlantic World was sugar cane. While this plant is technically part of the grass family, it grows in very thick stems, which are filled with juicy sucrose that can be processed into sugar. Since it is a grass, sugar cane does not need to be sown again once it is harvested, as it just regrows in the next season. Sugar cane is an extremely productive plant in terms of how many calories can be produced per acre of land under production. In fact, to have roughly the same output of calories from wheat as from sugar cane, one would require to farm at least nine to twelve times the amount of land.

The history of the spread of sugar cane production in Afro-Eurasia is long and complex. Most experts believe that the plant likely originated in the South Pacific, and from there made its way into southern Asia, only to be adopted in various other areas of the Afro-Eurasian world. Europeans likely became aware of sugar through the Muslim World. Arabs first grew this crop in some of the wetter zones of the Middle East. Eventually Islamic states in the Levant region of the eastern Mediterranean, northern Africa, Muslim Iberia, and on the islands of Sardinia and in Sicily also cultivated the crop. This is likely how Europeans were first exposed to, and began to develop a taste for, sugar. Europeans would learn how to grow sugar from Arab farmers (or more accurately put, at least initially, they let locals do the work for them) during the Crusades when they occupied part of the Levant in the twelfth and the thirteenth centuries. With easier access, sugar became a more widely used commodity in Europe—at least among the upper classes. Thus, in pre- and early modern European food culture, sugar had many similarities with several of the other spices that we have discussed in the previous chapter. European elites loved sugar, used it for ostentatious displays of their wealth, and believed that the sweet commodity served medicinal purposes. The commodity could also serve as a useful cash crop to earn gold and silver. When Arab Muslim forces began to gradually push out the Christian European Crusader states from the Levant, Europeans had already begun to expand sugar production to several Mediterranean islands. Gradually, from the twelfth to the fifteenth centuries, sugar production spread westward to many of the islands of the Mediterranean, and with European Atlantic exploration, which led to the colonization of several Atlantic African islands, the sweet commodity was also eventually grown in several places there.

Sugar was an extremely labor-intensive crop and commodity. In many places where it was grown, irrigation was needed to keep the crop well watered and growing. This required tremendous amounts of labor as one needed to both build and maintain the intricate watering system. Harvest time was an especially demanding season. Not only was the cutting of sugar tough work, but the cane needs to be processed as soon as possible, as the sucrose begins to diminish immediately upon being harvested. Thus, each plantation either had its own sugar processing mill or was part of a collection of sugar farms that shared one. These facilities were necessarily located in close vicinity to the fields. There, the farm laborers, using various pieces of equipment and machinery, needed to crush the cane to extract the sap, then they boiled down the juice to reduce it, and finally, they separated the molasses and sugar.[5]

By the early eighteenth century, the processing of sugar in the Caribbean was so involved with its use of machinery and equipment, and some of the mills were so large and sophisticated in their use of power sources (such as water, wind, as well as human and animal muscle) that some scholars have argued that the birth of the industrial revolution did not occur in the textile factories of late eighteenth century England, but rather had its roots in the Americas, where sugar processing was being performed on an industrial scale. What aided in the development of industrial aspects of this production, according to the eminent scholar of sugar Sidney Mintz, was that the "sugar cane plantation" also created a new "form of productive organization." Thus sugar production not only changed the production process, but it also brought about important social and cultural changes in the way Western society produced things. "What made the early plantation system agro-industrial," Mintz argues, "was the combination of agriculture and processing under one authority: discipline was probably its first essential feature."[6]

While the general size of the enterprise might have increased, the basic labor process and conditions for workers were very much the same through time and space, whether we are talking about the sugar plantations of the pre-modern Mediterranean or the ones of the Americas in the eighteenth century. Fieldwork was dangerous and taxing. Laborers could inflict severe wounds on themselves or their co-workers when they cut the cane during harvest. The sugar fields were also places where creatures such as snakes, spiders, and scorpions lived. The most dangerous place, however, was the sugar mill. Equipment to crush the cane could inflict deadly injuries on human limbs and severe life-threatening burns occurred during the sugar boiling process. The likelihood of injuries and fatalities was increased by the long hours workers were forced to work during the harvesting season.

European sugar production in the Mediterranean became very quickly linked with chattel slavery, the labor system that would also spread and dominate plantation life in the Atlantic World. Although the traditional feudal labor and land arrangements of pre-modern Europe, in which a serf would work the land of a lord, was used for some time, it proved not to be conducive to the production of sugar in the long run. Sugar growers learned that production could be dramatically increased by using gang labor that worked large fields. Landlords attempted to partially adapt feudalism to serve their needs, but serfs had established different work patterns, were used to exerting at least partial control over their work day, and were reluctant to surrender control over the labor process. Serfs also attempted to avoid this dangerous work by all means necessary. Sugar producers wanted to find a solution to deal with what was a labor issue from their perspective, and they may have found inspiration in the history of the Mediterranean World. Ancient Rome, for example, made wide use of chattel slavery in agricultural production, and several of the Christian states of southern Europe recognized the legality of this labor system. European sugar growers might have also drawn inspiration from their neighboring Islamic states, where the enslavement of non-Muslims was sanctioned by law. Thus, given the long history of slavery in the region, it is not surprising that sugar lords in the Mediterranean abandoned the feudal labor arrangements and switched to chattel slavery.[7]

From the twelfth to the fifteenth centuries, to satisfy the appetites of sugar growers for workers, various sources of unfree labor were tapped by European slavers. There was an active trade in human captives in the Mediterranean throughout this period. Initially many of the unfree workers were prisoners of war taken on the battlefield, or captured civilians raided in the territories into which European forces encroached during various war campaigns, such as the Crusades or the Iberians' campaigns in North Africa. The use of war captives as a source of slave labor continued throughout this period. By the middle of the thirteenth century, an additional strategy to obtain workers was being developed. European slave raiders entered the Black Sea and began to raid the various Slavic populations of the region for captives who were then sold as forced labor to the various sugar plantations across the islands of the Mediterranean. The Genovese took the lead in this human traffic in the Black Sea just as they had in the early sugar production. Soon, however, they were joined by several other European Mediterranean states, which competed in both of these lucrative endeavors. The connection of unfree labor and Slavic peoples was so vital at the time that the root of the word "slave" was derived from the word "Slav," not only in English, but also in several other European languages.

In 1453, after conquering Constantinople (today Istanbul) and turning the city into the capital of their empire, the Ottoman Turks, the rising power of the Eastern Mediterranean, would block the Bosporus to the Genovese and other European traders. This development denied them access to the Black Sea and cut Europeans off from a vital source of slaves.[8]

"Little Americas": The Islands of Atlantic Africa

With the Ottoman's blockade of the Bosporus, Europeans needed to come up with a new source for their plantation labor. It was at this time that new sugar plantations were being established on the Atlantic African islands, which served in many ways as a testing ground for the prototype of plantation that would emerge in the Americas. The Portuguese, who worked their way down the Atlantic coast of Africa, were increasingly not only looking to trade for gold, pepper, and several other commodities, but they also gradually saw the continent as an alternative source to purchase labor. Initially, when indigenous workers were available, they were used as forced labor. As the islands' indigenous populations declined, using people of African origin as slaves became an established pattern by the time a plantation complex in the Americas began to emerge in the sixteenth and the seventeenth centuries.

The spread of European sugar plantations out of the Mediterranean to the Atlantic African islands began in the fifteenth century. The archipelagos that were located off the northwest coast of Africa, known as the Azores, Madeira, and the Canaries, were within two weeks travel from the southern Iberian Peninsula. Mediterranean sailors had known about these islands in the ancient world, and, as previously mentioned, mariners from Genoa had reached the Canaries in the fourteenth century. Still, it was not until the fifteenth century that southern Europeans began to actively pursue colonization, and unlike the fourteenth-century exploration, in which the Genovese took the lead, it was the Iberians who spearheaded the invasion of the Atlantic archipelagos. These islands, which would serve as testing grounds for what would eventually become a plantation complex in the Americas, each had distinct cultures and economies.

In the fifteenth century, the Azores, which have a cooler climate due to their northerly location roughly on the same latitude as the Portuguese capital of Lisbon but about 900 miles further west, were considered the least lucrative among the Atlantic island colonies, at least in the views of the Portuguese state. The particularly rough sea around the archipelago, especially compared to their more southerly neighbors, further isolated the Azores and reinforced their less important status. Nevertheless, the Portuguese began to settle the Azores in 1439. Sugar growing failed, so the agricultural system that emerged was based on wheat farming for export, and on fruit and wine production for largely local consumption. Over the next centuries, the islands would serve the strategic purpose as a resting and refueling station for European ships on their overseas voyages, as well as for Atlantic fishermen.

The milder climate of Madeira and the Canary Islands proved to be more conducive to the farming of sugar cane and grapes. The Portuguese began to colonize Madeira in the 1420s and large-scale sugar production took off on the islands in the 1450s. While the Canary Islands further to the south had the same agricultural potential as Madeira, the colonization of this archipelago did not prove as easy. Unlike Madeira and the Azores, which had not been settled by humans, the Canaries had long been populated by a people known as the Guanches. Their ancestors are believed to have migrated by boat over many centuries from the African mainland at least a thousand years before European contact and conquest in the fourteenth and fifteenth centuries. As the Iberian invaders took over one island after the other, the Guanches resisted European colonization and slave raiding. It was on these newly conquered lands that the Castilians began to plant sugar using Guanche prisoners of war as slave labor. Furthermore, Guanche slaves were exported to Madeira, as well as to the sugar plantations of southern Iberia and the Mediterranean. It was not an easy take-over. Indigenous resistance to slave raiding and to conquest was fierce. It was only after Columbus had stumbled on the Americas that the Castilians finally subjugated the Guanches and captured all of the Canary Islands through a series of extremely violent campaigns.

What happened to the Guanches of the Canary Islands has some significant and eerie parallels to what would happen to the indigenous peoples of the Western Hemisphere after 1492. Like Native Americans, the Guanches faced violent military campaigns of territorial conquest and slave raids, which captured and killed tens of thousands of the archipelago's indigenous peoples. In their wars and raids, the Castilians and the Portuguese rarely discriminated between Guanche fighters and their civilian population. As in the Americas, warfare was total, which included the destruction of crops and other food sources, and domesticated animals brought by Europeans, such as pigs, cattle, horses, rabbits, goats, and chickens would move onto the Guanches' farm fields and devoured and destroyed their food supplies. This, of course, would further reinforce famine and population loss among the native population. In the same vein, and again reminiscent of developments in the Western Hemisphere, Europeans took advantage of Guanche disunity. They found allies among the local peoples, which significantly aided the Castilians in their conquest of the Canaries. As in the Americas, disease was the most significant weapon in the arsenal of the Europeans. Because the Guanches had migrated so long ago, and had lived in isolation, they lacked immunity to many of the Afro-Eurasian diseases. By 1600, as a result of Spanish colonization, the Guanches, who are believed to have numbered over 100,000 prior to contact, had been practically wiped out.[9]

Given the demographic catastrophe that slavery and conquest brought to the native peoples of the Canaries throughout the fifteenth century, the Iberians had already begun to experiment with a new and more reliable source of labor. By the mid-1400s, the Portuguese had begun to purchase slaves from the African mainland, where, as we will see below, they had created extensive commercial relations with various local populations, and where many of the local states had established indigenous systems of slavery. Africans were gradually introduced as slave labor into Europe and the European colonial Atlantic plantation complex. Starting in the sixteenth century, mariners from other European nations would compete with the Portuguese over the ever expanding African slave trade.

The Iberians established a pattern on the Atlantic African islands that became a testing ground for their later colonization of the Americas.

Europeans initially used indigenous labor until it proved insufficient, at which point they switched to African slave labor to run their plantations and created a way of life based on slavery that endured until the nineteenth century.

Portuguese and Castilian Motivations for Atlantic Expansion

The motivations to explore the western African coast and to travel into the Atlantic were similar to the earlier discussed interests that had driven the Portuguese and the Castilians into northwest Africa. For one, the Iberians, led by their "Catholic majesties" were compelled by their religious beliefs. Moreover, there were clear economic and strategic interests that propelled overseas exploration, trade, and colonization.

There were numerous religious beliefs, motivations, and assumptions, which encouraged and provided ideological rationalizations and justifications to the Iberians' efforts at overseas expansion. We have already discussed the concept of *Reconquista* in the previous chapter, and established that it created an expansionary and missionary zeal among the Portuguese and the Castilians. The expansion into new lands opened the possibility of converting non-believers to Christianity. In addition, and because the Iberians were encroaching onto the lands of populations that were not Christian, this also had implications in terms of European law. By the early sixteenth century, European legal thought regarding territorial expansion was largely based on theories of canon law. The ecclesiastical law that governed the Catholic Church had influential theories about the "natural rights" of non-Christian nations that would create legitimizing narratives for Iberian colonization. During this period, legal opinions maintained that under the "doctrine of discovery," Iberians had the right to take possession of non-Christian lands, providing them with only the most limited rights to the territories they occupied.[10]

Another reason that compelled the Portuguese down the African coast was the elusive search for the mythical figure of Prester John. The popular legend of this powerful Christian ruler, whose kingdom was said to be surrounded and besieged by Muslim and pagan nations, but whose exact location was not known, enthralled many Europeans from the twelfth through the seventeenth centuries. While Europeans had failed to tackle what they perceived as a Muslim threat during the crusades, their desire to keep an Islamic resurgence in the Mediterranean in check was a high strategic priority. As we discussed earlier, this led both the Portuguese and the Castilians to invade parts of northern Africa in the fifteenth century. Some Europeans hoped that finding Prester John would open a new frontier in the fight against Islam with a powerful ally in a war against Muslims. Europeans made several attempts to locate the mythical monarch. In 1487, for example, the king of Portugal sent two Arabic speaking agents on a secret mission traveling throughout southwestern Asia, northeastern Africa, and the eastern portions of the Indian Ocean World in search for Prester John, or for other potential allies to fight against the Muslims. This mission was one of a number of similar undertakings. For instance, when the Portuguese king Henry the Navigator learned of reports of the Senegal River from his mariners in the 1440s, he hoped that this waterway could be traveled to link up with Prester John. Even after this mission failed, the Portuguese would launch several others like it in the Senegambia region, in hopes that they would be able to establish contact with the fabled Christian king.[11]

While religious motivations and strategic concerns might have aided in the initial push for overseas exploration, it was economic interests and the search for trade that ultimately sustained expansion. Recall that the Portuguese were at least in part motivated by the gold of Mali, and that they were hoping to access this precious metal through a more direct trade route. In fact, while the Portuguese failed to find Prester John, they did, however, get to Timbuktu, and established diplomatic relations with the gold-producing western African empires of the interior, relations that would be maintained into the sixteenth century. Beyond trading for significant quantities of gold on the West African coast, the Portuguese obtained melegueta pepper that would fetch a high price in the spice-obsessed European market of the fifteenth century. They also bought ivory and beeswax. By the second half of the fifteenth century, trade became so established that over time, and with the permission of local rulers, the Portuguese established several trading posts or forts in various locations on the West African coast, places that the Portuguese called *feitorias* (factories). It was a result of the Portuguese interchanges with these coastal posts that led to the purchase of relatively small but gradually increasing number of African slaves.[12]

Patterns and Processes of Interaction and Expansion in the Atlantic

The historian John Thornton argues that there are two "directions" or "wings" of European expansion into the Atlantic. He calls the Portuguese exploration down the African coast "the African wing of expansion," and refers to the westward expansion to the Americas as the "Atlantic wing of expansion." Thornton maintains that these two "directions" established two distinct patterns. The "African wing," he reasons, "sought mainland products such as slaves" and gold through trade. The "Atlantic wing," he argues "sought exploitable but not necessarily inhabited land in which to collect valuable wild products or to begin agricultural production of cultivated products in high demand in Europe.[13]

But how distinct were the African and the Atlantic wings? The colonial enterprise in the Atlantic and the Americas was about much more than the exploitation of wild products and obtaining agricultural land. For instance, and not dissimilar to the African continent, there existed slave trading and raiding of Native Americans and Guanches, and several colonial societies from the Carolinas to the Andes made use of coerced indigenous labor. The search for gold and other precious metals in the New World, though varying in success, was a prime motivator in initiating colonial endeavors not only among the Spanish, but also among various other European states, as evidenced, for example, by the fact that the first group of English colonists who founded a colony called Jamestown in 1607 included a large number of gold and silver smiths. While the dream of finding precious metals did not materialize in the region that became known as Virginia, the Spanish certainly found vast quantities of silver in their Central and South American colonies. This silver, in turn, as we will see in more detail later, boosted and financed global trade, and was mined by both unfree indigenous and African workers. In sub-Saharan Africa as well, there are exceptions to the above described patterns. By the seventeenth century, for instance, the Dutch began to settle on the southern tip of the continent, looking to establish a refueling station in what is today the city of Cape Town. What was initially intended as a small resupply post in 1652, developed into a growing Dutch and, by the nineteenth century, a British settler colony.

Rather than to think of two distinct wings of Atlantic expansion, it would be more useful to conceptualize overseas expansion as being shaped by the dynamics between European colonial capacities and by local peoples' abilities to shape the balance of power in any given area. Between 1500 and 1800, as we have seen above, patterns of trade and the search for land occurred throughout the Atlantic World, and they were, moreover, not necessarily exclusive phenomena. After all, trade could lead, and often did, to colonization. These dynamics are further complicated by processes of intergroup interaction, accommodation, rivalries, and competition among Africans, Europeans, and Native Americans. Cross-cultural encounter led the peoples of the Atlantic World, at least to some degree, to incorporate parts of each other's knowledge, material culture, and ways of subsistence. These encounters could also spur successful resistance that would limit European efforts. Given the tremendous span of hundreds of years, as well as the vast geographic space that included Africa, Europe, and the Americas, cross-cultural encounters were extremely diverse, complex, and fluid processes that defy easy characterization.

These patterns and processes of interaction are also relevant in a world historical context. Atlantic exploration has always been a global project. Europe's exploration of the African coast opened up a sea route to the Indian Ocean, and what Thornton terms the "Atlantic wing of expansion" would also extend into the Pacific Ocean.

Early Contacts between Africans and Portuguese

The Euro-African contacts of the fifteenth and sixteenth centuries certainly led to complex patterns and processes of interaction. The Portuguese, the first among the Europeans to actively explore options in sub-Saharan western coastal Africa, did so without ever having a clear power advantage and did not dictate, but had to negotiate, their encounters with Africans. Indeed, this situation was the archetype of commercial relations between Africans and Europeans throughout much of the early modern period.

Early African–Portuguese relations were complex, fluid, and were shaped by violence and resistance, but most importantly by accommodation. In 1446, for instance, a Portuguese slave-raiding mission on the Gambia River failed miserably when Africans, using war boats, fought back the European intruders with poisonous arrows. Still, it would be wrong to assume that West Africans were disinterested in commerce with Europeans, as Atlantic Africa had long been involved in the trans-Saharan trade. African elites, however, attempted to put themselves in control of the interactions, and certainly did not want their people to be raided by Europeans. The historian Donald Wright observes that "it is likely that residents of" the coastal states "were just as eager as Europeans to find access to greater and more direct participation in the expanding market." Hence, over time, with the coming of the Portuguese and other Europeans, Africans on the western shores of the continent were gradually drawn into the emerging economic system of the Global Atlantic. By 1455 on the Gambia River, less than ten years after the above mentioned violent altercations, the local leader of a small state came to an arrangement with the Portuguese about what products could be traded in this region. As this example vividly demonstrates, despite their desire to do so, the Portuguese could not dominate trade with African states through the use of force. They could achieve much more through negotiation and peaceful trade. Shaped by African rules and understandings of reciprocity, the Portuguese had to change their medieval Mediterranean patterns of raiding for slaves and forceful trade, and had to adapt to, and comply with, local commercial circumstances.[14]

Despite what conventional narratives of the Atlantic slave trade often tell us, several historians of western Africa point out that for much of the early modern period Africans did not depend on European manufacturing imports, that they made many of the commodities and manufactured goods they needed themselves, and that they instead desired to exchange high quality prestige goods and luxury items in their trade with the outside world. In the middle of the fifteenth century, for instance, at the *feitoria de Arguim*, a trading fort that was located on an island off the coast of present day Mauritania, the Portuguese traded annually for a decent quantity of gold dust, gum Arabic (which was at that time used especially to print patterns on fabrics as part of European textile production), as well as a couple of hundred slaves per year. In return, the Portuguese traded horses, bridlery, wheat, textiles, alcohol, adornments, and other items that African traders would consider high prestige objects.[15]

The cultural exchanges and commercial interactions between Portuguese and Africans also led to sexual relations and ethnic–cultural changes, as was the case on the West African Cape Verde islands. Portugal began to colonize this archipelago in the 1460s, when mostly male Portuguese colonists held large estates that produced agricultural crops, bred horses, and manufactured woven textiles for export to West African markets. Much of this work was done by African slaves, who were brought to the archipelago from the continent. Eventually the slave population on the islands would surpass the free one by an estimated six to one ratio. In addition to the slave diaspora, there were also African migrants to Cape Verde who arrived as free persons, some of whom were members of the coastal elite of various western African states sent to the island to encourage close diplomatic ties with the Portuguese. Out of the relations of Portuguese men and African women emerged a group of people of mixed parentage who are often called the Luso-Africans. The Luso-Africans would have cultural and language skills that were useful in both worlds, and they would play an important role as intermediaries for several generations in Portuguese–West African trade and diplomatic relations.[16]

On the African mainland, the socio-cultural encounters between Africans and Portuguese in the late fifteenth and sixteenth centuries were not confined to trade, but were also shaped by the interactions of coastal Africans with Portuguese settlers. The newcomers to the continent sometimes originated from the Iberian Peninsula, but in most cases, they came from Cape Verde. This migration happened in violation of the expressed wishes of the Portuguese monarchy as indicated by the name this group of settlers was given: *lancados*, a term that implied these colonists had thrown themselves (*se lancar*) among the Africans, and, through this act, had become outcasts from mainstream Portuguese society. Still, Portugal's authorities were largely unable to curtail the illegal settlement efforts. Ironically, in the long-run, it was the *lancados* and Luso-Africans who significantly assisted the fledgling Portuguese maritime empire in maintaining their commercial interests in West Africa.

The encounter between West Africans and the *lancados* provide an interesting case study in how African elites remained in control of much of the commercial interactions during the early contact period. In order to settle on the mainland, the Portuguese and Luso-African traders would require the permission of African rulers. They had to undergo a traditional African arrangement, in which the *lancados* or Luso-African "strangers" had to attach themselves to a local "landlord." The African landlord had oversight over the newcomer's dealing with Africans. He also allocated a place of settlement, provided food, at least initially, and guaranteed the business and credit worthiness of the newcomer, and served as mediator when disputes with locals arose. Yet, this was not a one-sided relationship to merely benefit the "strangers." The old West African Mandinke proverb "strangers make the village prosper," indicates that this was a relationship based on African understandings of reciprocity. Once the newcomers were established and successful, they were expected to provide gifts and favors to their African rulers. More formally, landlords charged the strangers rent for the land they occupied, as well as fees and taxes for commercial interactions.

The Afro-Portuguese socio-cultural interactions in the Senegambia and Guinea regions also underscores the complex and ingenious processes and patterns of accommodation, cultural recreation, intermixing, and adaption that happened throughout the Global Atlantic. After some time, often with the assistance of their African landlords, the newcomers would take a wife from the local populations. The spouse was often a daughter of the landlord himself or a woman from a notable lineage in the state. Such a union would further tie the *lancados* and Luso-Africans into the structures of their state of residence, and over a few generations the newcomers became physically indistinguishable from the local populations. That said, the *lancados* maintained a unique identity, which became part of the diverse cultural mosaic of West Africa's ethnic landscape. They continued to call themselves Portuguese, used Portuguese names, wore European-style clothing and crucifixes, maintained that they were Catholic (although in many instances they had never seen a priest), and used an Iberian-inspired building style for their homes. The *lancados* spoke a creole language—Crioulo—likely developed on Cape Verde. Crioulo was based on Portuguese, with strong African influences, and served as a major trade language in West Africa.[17]

To search for gold and trade, expand sugar production, and discover new sources of labor, the Portuguese worked their way down the African coast, where they eventually took control of the islands of Sao Tome and Principe, which are located in the Gulf of Guinea about 150 miles west off the coast of modern day Gabon. In the last decades of the fifteenth century, they began to produce sugar, and by the early 1500s, Sao Tome had superseded Madeira as Europe's largest provider of the commodity. Initially, the slaves that worked the plantations of Sao Tome came from what is today the coast of Cameroon, Nigeria, Benin, Togo, Ghana, and the Ivory Coast. By the 1480s, however, as part of their southward encroachment on the western African coast, the Portuguese established close relations with the African kingdom of Kongo, which quickly became a new and very important source of African slave labor.

Portuguese relations with the Kingdom of Kongo, a populous state located in Atlantic Central Africa from the fourteenth to the eighteenth centuries, provide an interesting glimpse into Afro-European interactions. Trade with the Europeans certainly strengthened the position of the Kongolese elite, but the Portuguese also supported their African ally militarily. They helped the state to geographically expand, and aided allied members of the Kongolese elite to expand their control and to put down a civil war. The Kongolese also sent several young members of their elite to get educated in Portugal. Most significantly, the kingdom's elite traded a growing number of slaves to the Portuguese, and while their initial involvement in the slave trade might have been materially beneficial, the long-term dynamics to the Kongolese state were tragic and aided in its decline and eventual demise.

While there was tremendous regional diversity in terms of the Atlantic slave trade's impact on the continent, over time, the overall demographic effects were destructive. Europeans' demand for slaves and African desires for the goods that were offered in return eventually led to many bloody conflicts for captives among African states, which spurred a climate of constant warfare. Obtaining slaves through war was, however, only one method. To serve their short-term interests, the elite in various Central African states devised systems of punishment and taxation to push their own subjects into slavery, which, in turn, fueled the Atlantic slave trade.

Over ten million slaves are believed to have been brought to the Americas, several millions likely perishing in transit, which added an additional demographic burden on the African continent. Slave caravans would bring captured Africans from the far interior, marching them at times up to 2,500 miles to coastal slave-trading centers. Conditions were horrendous during this march. Shackled or bound, often carrying heavy loads of ivory, copper, and other items of interest to traders, African captives had to march for miles in the heat of the day and sleep in exposed conditions. At times, this ordeal could last for months. While it is hard to assess the exact demographic impact, as reliable numbers are not available, it is clear that a large number of Africans died during the trek to the coast, and the situation did not improve once captives arrived there. Once on the Atlantic seaboard, they were imprisoned in trade depots or slave forts, experiencing crammed and unsanitary conditions in dark holding cells, until they were purchased by European merchants, who then shipped them to the Americas. This trans-Atlantic voyage, often called the middle passage, was

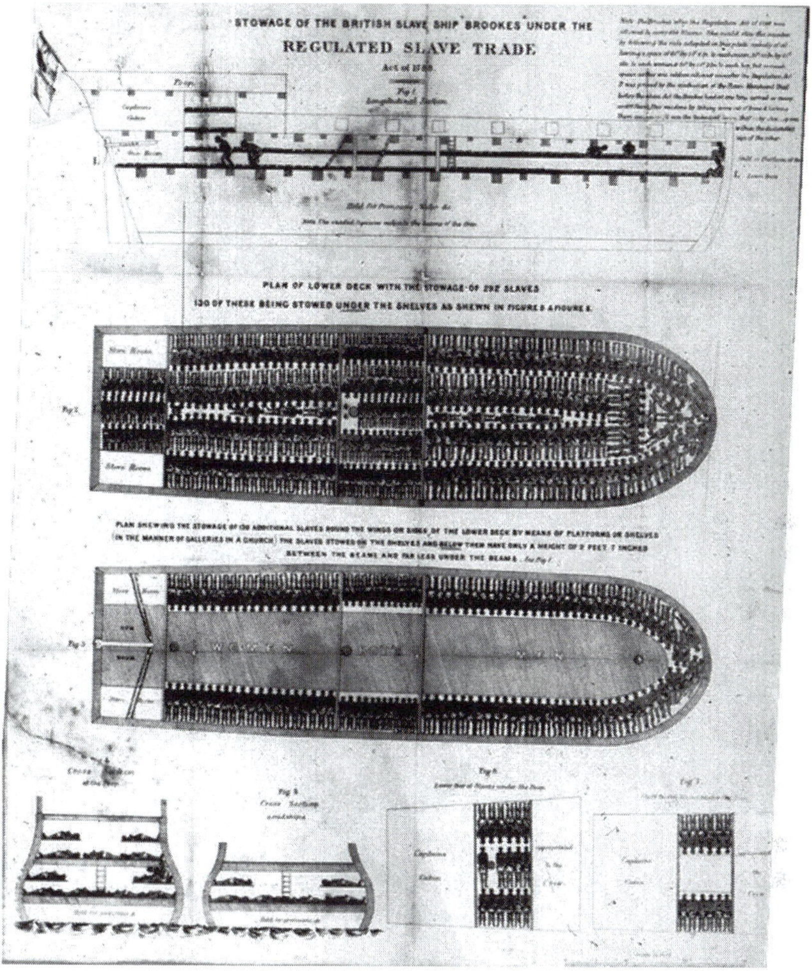

This picture shows the crowded conditions on a slave ship during the Middle Passage.
Source: Wikimedia Commons. 1789. Slavetrade. http://commons.wikimedia.org/wiki/File:Slavetrade.jpg.

the middle part of the voyage for European merchants in the triangle trade that went from Europe, to Africa, to the Americas, and back to Europe. While slave mortality rates fluctuated, depending on the duration of the trip, hygiene on the ship, on-board slave resistance, and disease outbreaks, most historians estimate that an average of about 10 to 20 percent of the Africans did not survive the journey.[18]

Africans and the Emergence of the Global Atlantic

In the early modern period, African and European interactions certainly furthered the integration of West and West-Central Africa, not only into an Atlantic "triangle trade," but also into a broader world economy. While the long-term implications of this exchange were certainly destructive to many African societies, this was a system, whose dependence on trade in human captives arose only over time. Early commerce was complex. Africans were more than just mere consumers of European manufactured goods, despite what simplistic depictions of the triangle trade so often seem to suggest. In fact, they turned raw materials imported by Europeans into sophisticated products, and also traded manufactured goods to Europeans. In the exchange of commodities, Africans were astute merchants on whose consent and participation European traders often depended. Africans were far from being exclusively the victims or pawns of slave-raiding Europeans, an image still too often maintained by popular presentations of the Atlantic slave trade. While a number of trade goods, such as horses, alcohol, cloth, tobacco, and later firearms, were popular among Africans, they often looked for additional items to trade. Along with the products listed above, which originated from Europe or their Atlantic colonies, African tastes required Portuguese and other Europeans to serve as intermediaries in an inter-African trade system, where they purchased African goods from one part of the continent and sold them in another region to make a profit. Moreover, once the Portuguese opened up the easterly trade route to Asia, desired goods also came from the Indian Ocean World. These developments tied Africa squarely into the worlds of the Global Atlantic.

The trade interactions around a Portuguese fort, founded in the last decades of the fifteenth century on the coast of what is today the modern nation-state of Ghana, give us a specific and representative perspective into how one place in West Africa was tied into this expanding world economic system. This example provides a glimpse into how a diverse Global Atlantic commerce influenced this region, and how the importance of the slave trade only grew gradually as a major feature of Euro-African exchange. The fortress in question was Sao Jorge da Mina, but among English language speakers it is usually more commonly known by the name of its neighboring African settlement—Elmina. The community of Elmina emerged and rapidly grew adjacent to the fortified Portuguese structure and became a major African commercial center, one of many that could be found all over the western coast of the continent. The fort at Elmina is usually associated with the slave trade. But in fact, as the Portuguese name for this particular coastal region, Mina (mine), or its English designation, the Gold Coast, makes clear, the precious metal played a much more important role in the initial European commercial interests. Local populations on the Atlantic seaboard obtained the gold they traded with Europeans from the interior Ashanti kingdom, as well as from other gold mining states located in the upper parts of the Volta River region. In exchange for gold and in later years increasingly slaves, the Europeans traded a wide variety of goods to the Africans at Elmina.

The commerce that flowed through Elmina was truly global. Among the particularly desirable goods were textiles. While some European textiles were certainly sold, more popular among African buyers were clothing items and cloth from Morocco, as well as from various regions of sub-Saharan Africa. Starting in the sixteenth century, Indian and Chinese materials also became admired by African consumers. The popularity of Asian textiles did not cease as the nature of the Gold Coast trade gradually shifted. Europeans continued to bring Indian calicos to the western African coast into the eighteenth century, but by then, they were increasingly exchanged for slaves. Other common items of trade in the fifteenth and sixteenth centuries were European-made hardware, such as pots and pans, as well as iron ingots, brass and copper bracelets—materials, as we will explore below, that Africans often further processed. Alcohol was another central trade item. Initially it came predominantly from Europe or the Portuguese-occupied Atlantic African islands, but, in later years, it would also be produced in the Western Hemisphere for export to Europe as well as Africa. Tobacco imported from the Western Hemisphere also became an increasingly popular commodity in Africa, especially by the eighteenth century, when it was consumed in large quantities. Glass beads from Venice and the Canaries also appealed to African merchants at Elmina, and corals were traded from the Mediterranean, parts of Africa, and later Asia. Furthermore, cowries from the Maldives, an island chain to the south of the Indian subcontinent, began to make inroads into West Africa starting in the sixteenth century. While cowrie shells were not worth much on the archipelago, they were valued across the Indian Ocean World as a currency because they were durable and light in their consistency and had a resilient texture. Once introduced to West Africa, they also became popular there.

As this brief overview of the number of products and their diverse origins in Elmina demonstrates, West Africa was truly integrated into a Global Atlantic economy.[19]

The magnificent artwork, particularly the sophisticated metal castings produced by West African artists in various states in the region, further complicates our understanding of the nature of the Atlantic slave trade. For instance, in the pre-colonial kingdom of Benin, in what is today modern southern Nigeria, artisans who created many of the magnificent plaques that this African state is famous for, worked metals imported from Europe for this purpose, which would be brought to West Africa in ever larger amounts in the fifteenth and sixteenth centuries. Historically, these plaques were the exclusive property of the rulers of Benin. Today, however, hundreds of these art treasures can be found in museums all over the Western World, because they had been looted by the British who had defeated this African kingdom in 1897. The British booty included hundreds of plaques, metal statues, many carved ivory pieces and tusks, as well as jewels made of corals. The original purpose of the plaques in Benin's society was to celebrate the ruler of the state who bore the title of the Oba, and multitudes of these metal panels were used to decorate the palace compound of the Oba, as the following description by a Dutch traveler makes clear.

> The King's court is square. . . . It is divided into many magnificent palaces, houses and apartments of the courtiers, and comprises beautiful and long square galleries, about as large as the Exchange at Amsterdam, from top to bottom covered with cast copper, on which are engraved the pictures of their war exploits and battles.

But it is important to reiterate, the exceptionally skilled bronze smiths of Benin were not the only importers of European metals, but a number of western African states increasingly relied on importing such European raw materials for their manufacturing.

European-made brass was generally shipped as big and heavy bracelets or hand rings, which the Portuguese named *manillas*. The volume of brass *manillas* exchanged with West Africa was impressive. For instance, in 1548, the Portuguese ordered 432 tons of them from one German trading company alone. *Manillas* and other metals, such as iron ingots, were not only turned into court art and statutes, but they were also manufactured

An example of a Benin plaque.

Source: Wikimedia Commons. 1500s–1600s. Benin Plaque. http://commons.wikimedia.org/wiki/File:Plaque,_possibly_1500s-1600s,_brass,_Benin_Kingdom,_Cleveland_Museum_of_Art_II.JPG.

into various goods, trade items, tools, and weapons. Like the cowrie shells of the Indian Ocean, the *manillas* could also serve as a form of currency in West Africa. They became an important part of the Euro-African trade as Africans figured out that it was easier to import metals rather than to produce these raw materials themselves.[20]

Europeans also eagerly traded African manufactured goods. For instance, throughout the fifteenth and sixteenth centuries, the Portuguese obtained many items made from ivory in West Africa. Artisans in present-day Nigeria, Sierra Leone, and Guinea Bissau, produced elaborately decorated spoons, magnificent salt cellars, and exquisite hunting horns for the European market. In many of these museum-quality creations, the artists incorporated both European and Christian symbols, especially interesting given that many of the artisans lived away from the coast, and likely had never seen a European. Many of the ivory trade items also displayed African inspired and influenced motifs.[21]

Africa's interactions with the worlds of the Global Atlantic occurred, however, not only through the exchange of goods, but it was also accompanied by the gradual introduction of new crops and foods, a development that significantly changed the patterns of daily life on the continent in the early modern period. After it was introduced to the continent from South America, manioc, also known as cassava, dramatically helped to alter subsistence farming in West Africa. Manioc was grown in a similar fashion to yams, a crop indigenous to Africa, and once Africans learned how to properly remove the toxic cyanide, the large root crop became a major food staple on the continent. The plant does not need much light, does well in poor soil, and is relatively drought resistant. Thus, it grew extremely well in the tropical forest regions of western and West Central Africa. While the plant is not particularly nutritious and not a good source of protein, it provides a rich source of carbohydrates. The incorporation of manioc helped population growth on the continent, a development that was, of course, offset by the ever growing population drain of the Atlantic slave trade. Furthermore, maize (corn), another plant introduced from the Americas, also became a major food staple. It became widely grown in various parts of the continent and, like manioc, helped to revolutionize the diet of many Africans.[22]

Black Majority: Africans and the Making of the Americas

It was in the beginning of the seventeenth century that trade in African slaves across the Atlantic started to dramatically increase, rising from a few thousand individuals per year in the sixteenth century, up to around an estimated 10,000 people during the 1600s. The Atlantic slave trade would reach its peak in the late eighteenth and early nineteenth centuries, when close to an average of 100,000 Africans per year were shipped to the Americas, making Africans by far the largest group of migrants to arrive in the Western Hemisphere in the early modern period.[23]

The slave trade and the patterns of the Global Atlantic had a significant influence in reshaping the Americas. As we have discussed, Afro-Eurasian pathogens had a devastating demographic impact on the indigenous populations of the Western Hemisphere, which gradually opened the Americas to increased colonization by European states. Yet, it is important to underscore, that colonial European populations were susceptible to tropical diseases from Africa, such as malaria and yellow fever, and suffered high mortality rates from disease outbreaks in the Americas as well. Malaria, yellow fewer, and other diseases had also kept the European presence confined to small coastal enclaves on Africa's Atlantic shoreline. Moreover, and as the above cited numbers make clear, from 1600 to 1800, African-forced migration to the Americas outnumbered that of Europeans by several million people. Vast portions of the colonies in the Western Hemisphere, from the Carolinas to Brazil, were in fact demographically black-majority areas where people of African descent contributed significantly to the economic and cultural development. By the end of the early modern period in 1750, peoples of African origin constituted about 80 percent of the total migrant population that had arrived in the Americas. In hemispheric terms, it was only starting in the 1840s that the European descended population would catch up with, and eventually overtake, the African-American population. Still, it is important to remember, that there remain many pockets all over the Americas, where people of African descent remain in the majority today.[24]

While the use of Africans never entirely replaced forced indigenous labor in the early modern period in the Americas, African slave labor significantly helped in the economic development of the European colonies in the Western Hemisphere. African workers provided the productive backbone of the Atlantic plantation complex, and, alongside indigenous forced labor, they also helped to mine and produce several commodities that would play an important role in the Global Atlantic. Whether they worked on plantations or in mines, African slaves, alongside indigenous forced labor, often endured dehumanizing conditions and violence, such as whippings and other tortures, and many were worked or beaten to death by abusive owners and overseers. In addition to chattel slavery, people of African descent would also work as domestic servants, sailors, and skilled or semi-skilled urban laborers. Thus, they played a variety of essential roles in the growing colonial economies of the Americas.

Despite the often oppressive nature of slavery, people of African descent brought with them to the Western Hemisphere their foodways, music, and religions, all of which helped to shape a variety of cultures and societies in the post-contact Americas. Africans influenced the cuisine of the Western Hemisphere through stews such as gumbo or jambalaya, as well as through dishes like several of the varieties of "greens" that are eaten all over the Americas today. Many of these recipes originated from African cooking, but blended with European and Native American cuisines. Afro-American musical styles, such as the blues and jazz in North America, or the samba in South America, also had their roots in the music of African slaves, and have become influential in shaping musical styles in the twentieth and the twenty-first centuries around the world. The banjo and a variety of percussionist instruments can also be linked to West African roots. Religion was also influenced by the cultural encounters in the Americas. Africans in the Western Hemisphere converted to Christianity and influenced it in many ways. Yet, people of African origin also developed and transplanted their religious systems and practices to the Americas, as can be seen, for example, with such religions as Santeria in Cuba or Macumba in Brazil. These beliefs survived by outwardly accommodating with and by placating the Catholicism practiced by the European elites, at least to a degree. Nevertheless, and despite some incorporation of European religious traditions, Africans still continued many of their traditional practices. Thus, religions like Santeria or Macumba were influenced by, but in turn also helped to shape, Christianity in the regions where they were practiced.

African slaves, at times, attempted to re-establish their political and economic independence all over the Americas. In their efforts to do so they created runaway slave communities, often called maroons (possibly derived from the Spanish *Cimarron*, which denoted an escaped farm animal or slave) or *quilombos* (a term that probably originated from an Angolan word meaning "encampment"). Escaped slaves developed hundreds of settlements all over the Western Hemisphere. These settlements were a serious threat to the social order imposed by the colonial elite and plantation owners and they used their military and political authority to destroy them. At times, they also engaged in diplomacy and signed treaties with colonies. Some of these communities managed to survive as independent communities for several decades and small remnant populations survive to this day. Runaway slave societies subsisted by farming, gathering, hunting, and raiding. In addition, their political and military organization was influenced by their trans-Atlantic roots as many operated councils and had militias organized on the blueprint of Atlantic African coastal states.

One of the most notorious *quilombos* was Palmares. Located in northeastern Brazil, the settlement lasted for almost a century, beginning in 1605 and surviving into the late seventeenth century. When it came to the organization of its military or to its interactions with Europeans, this large maroon settlement acted very much like a small independent Atlantic African state. At its height Palmares is believed to have been over 10,000 people strong, and, in its efforts to maintain its independence, it successfully fought both the Portuguese and the Dutch to a standstill on several occasions. Palmares was finally defeated in 1694 by a militia from Sao Paulo which consisted of a rag tag of slave raiders, fortune hunters, adventurers, as well as their Native American allies.[25]

Conclusion

The economic, political, social, and cultural interactions between people of European and African origin played a significant role in the history of the Global Atlantic. As we have seen, Europeans and Africans were motivated and influenced by their established histories in the way they approached each other. African and European understandings, priorities, and desires shaped these interactions. Biological realities as well influenced societies in Europe, Africa, and the Americas. The interactions and connections highlighted in this chapter helped to create and shape an Atlantic World that emerged as a result of the search for trade, the impact of Afro-Eurasian diseases, the Atlantic slave trade, and the colonization of the Americas. However, as we will explore in more detail in the following chapters, the Atlantic Ocean system was a complex and diverse nexus of contacts with other parts of the world.

Notes

1 Rainer F. Buschmann, *Oceans in World History* (Boston: McGraw Hill, 2007), 42–43.

2 D.W. Meinig, *The Shaping of America: A Geographical Perspective on 500 Years of History. Vol. 1: Atlantic America, 1492–1800* (New Haven: Yale University Press, 1986), 5; Buschmann, 45.

3 Meinig, 6, Buschmann, 45.

4 Buschmann, 44.
5 My discussion of sugar draws from Erik Gilbert and Jonathan Reynolds, *Trading Tastes: Commodity and Cultural Exchange to 1750* (Upper Saddle River, NJ: Pearson Prentice Hall, 2006), 84–87; Douglas R. Egerton et al., *The Atlantic World: A History, 1400–1888* (Wheeling, Illinois: Harlan Davidson, 2007), 44–49.
6 Sidney W. Mintz, *Sweetness and Power: The Place of Sugar in Modern History* (New York: Penguin Books, 1985), 50–51.
7 Gilbert and Reynolds, *Trading Tastes*, 88–90.
8 For an introduction to Mediterranean sugar production and the adaption of slave labor see Egerton et al., 44–49; and Felipe Fernandez-Armesto, *Before Columbus: Exploration and Colonization from the Mediterranean to the Atlantic, 1229–1492* (Philadelphia: University of Pennsylvania Press, 1987), 108, 117–118, 198–200, 206, 242.
9 On the Azores, Canaries, and Madeira as a testing ground for the Americas, and the concept of ecological imperialism see Alfred W. Crosby, *Ecological Imperialism: The Biological Expansion of Europe, 900–1900* (New York: Cambridge University Press 1986), see especially chapter 4; and Egerton et al, 51–54.
10 See Robert Williams, *The American Indian in Western Legal Thought: The Discourses of Conquest* (New York: Oxford University Press, 1990), chapter 2. On the issue of European conquest and early Native American dispossession in the Americas see also Patricia Seed, *Ceremonies of Possession in Europe's Conquest of the New World, 1492–1640* (New York: Cambridge University Press, 1995).
11 A.R. Disney, *A History of Portugal and the Portuguese Empire, From Beginning to 1807, vol. 2: The Portuguese Empire* (New York; Cambridge University, 2009), 35, 42–43.
12 Disney, chapter 17.
13 John Thornton, *Africa and Africans in the Making of the Atlantic World, 1400–1800*, 2nd edn (New York: Cambridge University Press, 1998), 28–36. See also John Thornton, *A Cultural History of the Atlantic World, 1250–1820* (New York: Cambridge University Press, 2012), 15–28.
14 Donald R. Wright, *The World and a Very Small Place in Africa: A History of Globalization in Niumi, The Gambia*, 3rd edn (Armonk, NY: M.E. Sharpe, 2010), quote 38, for general description see 11–13.
15 See for example George Brooks, *Landlords and Strangers: Ecology, Society, and Trade in Western Africa, 1000–1630* (Boulder, CO: Westview Press, 1993); Wright, Part II; and Thornton, *Africa and Africans in the Making of the Atlantic World*. See also Disney, chapter 17.
16 See Wright, 75. See also Brooks, 189–192.
17 On the *lancados* see Wright, 76–78.
18 My discussion of Luso-Kongolese and Central African relations draws from Erik Gilbert and Jonathan Reynolds, *Africa in World History: From Prehistory to*

the Present, 2nd edn (Upper Saddle River, N.J.: Pearson & Prentic Hall, 2008), 190–192; and Egerton, et al., 65–66.

19 On Elmina see Disney, 56–61; on West Africa in the 15th and 16th century global economy more generally see Gilbert and Reynolds, *Africa in World History*, 176–187.

20 On the plaques from Benin and the *manilla* trade see Neil MacGregor, *A History of the World in 100 Objects: From the Handaxe to the Credit Card* (New York: Viking, 2011), for quote see 499–500, in general see 497–502.

21 Paula Girshick Ben-Amos, *The Art of Benin*, revised edition (Washington, D.C.: Smithsonian, 1995).

22 Gilbert and Reynolds, *Africa in World History*, 193.

23 These numbers are drawn from Gilbert and Reynolds, *Africa in World History*, 183.

24 The concept of "black majority" is drawn from Peter Wood, *Black Majority: Negroes in Colonial South Carolina from 1670 through the Stono Rebellion* (New York: Knopf, 1974). For numbers see Gilbert and Reynolds, *Africa in World History*, 165.

25 For Africans in the Americas see for example Gilbert and Reynolds, *Africa in World History*, 165–167; and Eric Nellis, *Shaping the New World: African Slavery in the Americas, 1500–1888* (Toronto: University of Toronto Press, 2013).

3

THE GLOBAL ATLANTIC AND THE "SPANISH SEA"

The 1492 voyage of Christopher Columbus was a milestone in the history of the Atlantic World. As we have seen, there had been earlier trans-Atlantic voyages, but the expedition backed by Castile and Aragon marked the first sustained human contact between Afro-Eurasia and the Western Hemisphere. Just as with the Portuguese exploration of Africa, Columbus' mission was motivated by a European desire to gain access to Asian and African goods. In this framework, at least initially, the Atlantic was viewed by the Europeans as a means to access the wealthy, vibrant trade routes of Asia. This early mindset continued even after Columbus accidentally stumbled on the Americas and the Europeans continued to expend considerable resources in their pursuit to generate direct commercial links with Asia. Thus the Europeans developed various sectors in the Atlantic system across the globe simultaneously: Africa and the Indian Ocean, the Americas, and the pursuit of Asian trade in the Pacific. These diverse regions of the Global Atlantic created their own histories, economies, and cultures.

The encounters and interactions within the extended world of the Global Atlantic transformed the Western Hemisphere. The Columbian voyage set into motion a series of events that forever changed Native American cultures. Afro-Eurasian diseases brought by the first trans-Atlantic ships to the Americas traveled through the indigenous trade routes, resulting in massive population losses that had an impact on all aspects of Native American societies. Sustained contact with the Africans, the vast majority of the newcomers, and Europeans also dramatically altered indigenous economies and broader patterns of daily life in the Western Hemisphere. In this new era, Africans, Europeans, and Native Americans were all tangled up in processes that dramatically reshaped their lives in the Americas. In a sense, Africans, Europeans, and Native Americans all faced "new worlds" as a result of empire-building by Europeans in the Western Hemisphere.[1]

As the following two chapters will point out, these processes, encounters, and changes extended well beyond the Americas, and the global Atlantic connections reached far beyond the confines of this ocean system into various corners of the planet where they had significant global ramifications. For instance, silver, and to a lesser extent gold, obtained in the Americas, helped Europeans in their purchase of highly desired Asian goods. Europe's ability to obtain Asian exports was aided by the fact that economies, such as China, the Mughal Empire in India, and several other states in the Indian Ocean World used silver as a basis for their monetary system. As discussed below in more detail, the Spanish accessed this trade through the Pacific Ocean, bringing plenty of silver from their mines in Central and South America to Manila, and shipping many Chinese goods back to the Americas and Europe in this exchange. Furthermore, cultural contacts and trade in commodities were also accompanied by significant biological consequences that transformed agricultural systems, diets, ecosystems, and had significant demographic impacts beyond the Americas.

Christopher Columbus and the Medieval European Patterns of Expansion in the Americas

Despite the fact that Columbus' voyage led to the so-called and often touted "discovery of the New World," the man and his mission were in many ways representative of Europe's medieval cultural, trading, and strategic paradigms. Columbus was a mariner who came of age in a Mediterranean trading world and his goal of finding a trans-Atlantic trade route to Asia was spurred by his desire for spices, gold, and Christian converts.

As a review of Christopher Columbus' life illustrates, his efforts, along with those of his Iberian contemporaries, to establish colonial rule in the Americas were deeply rooted in European feudalism and the crusading spirit. Columbus grew up and lived in a Mediterranean that was an integrated part of an Afro-Eurasian world of cultural exchanges and long-distance trading networks. His native Italian city-state of Genoa, alongside Venice, was one of the important trading centers in the Mediterranean connecting Europe with Asian and African trade routes. Genovese merchants, frequently flying the flags of other states such as Portugal and Castile, had also played a key role in Atlantic exploration, as well as in the early trade on the African coast for gold, slaves, malaguetta pepper, and various other goods. In addition, the Genovese played a key role in the Mediterranean slave trade. As a member of a merchant family, Columbus was in the thick of this world; he went to sea at an early age and, like many of his compatriots, Columbus participated in both slave trading and piracy. In fact, he ended up stranded on the Portuguese coast after a shipwreck that occurred during a voyage to raid Venetian ships. Columbus was thus well versed in even the more sordid aspects of Mediterranean trade.

The fifteenth-century Portuguese state, where Columbus had been shipwrecked and which became his main residence for many years, had arguably become the most engaged and advanced maritime power among the European states. To achieve this goal, the Portuguese had built a small fleet of highly maneuverable and speedy caravel ships. They also had developed sophisticated navigational technologies and resources. By the time Columbus arrived in Portugal, as we have seen, ships flying the Portuguese flag had been trading with coastal states and communities in western and central Africa, and the Iberian states had begun to establish several colonies on the islands off the coast of the continent. In fact, while living in Portugal, Columbus married Filipa Moniz Perestrelo whose deceased father had been a minor noble and a former governor of Porto Santo, a small island in the archipelago of Madeira. This provided the Genovese with at least some, albeit limited, access and status in Portuguese society. It is also probable that it was while living in Portugal that Columbus began to seriously research his plan to sail westward to access Asian trade routes.

Despite his Portuguese residency, when he had devised his plan to explore a western maritime connection to Asia, he was willing to work with any nation that would fund his expedition. He famously struggled to secure financial backing and the reasons he was so frequently rejected by the crowns of Europe offer us a window on the events and priorities of his times. Columbus turned first to the Portuguese monarch for funding. Initially the king declined his request because he had already sponsored a failed mission to find a potential trade route to Asia via the Atlantic Ocean and, as he was perhaps reconsidering this initial rejection, another major event in extension of the Global Atlantic occurred. His second meeting with Columbus coincided with Bartholomeu Dias' return to Lisbon from his circumnavigation of the southern African Cape in 1488. Portugal had stumbled upon an eastern maritime trade route to Asia, making Columbus mission now seem especially unnecessary.

Maintaining his vision of a western route, Columbus and his associates looked abroad for support. They approached the then less affluent royalty of France and England to no avail, as well as the kingdoms that today make up much of modern Spain, where again significant events played a role in the royal response. Queen Isabella I's state of Castile and her husband's King Ferdinand V's state of Aragon were pre-occupied with the final stages of conquering the Muslim-held territories of southern Spain, so she turned him down as well. The lure of Eastern wealth must have been strong because she reconsidered her earlier position and called together a team of advisors to study Columbus' proposal. After years of examination, they turned it down again. Not, as some popular history accounts still maintain, because they believed that the mission would sail off the edge of a flat earth, but rather because the team of scholars believed that Columbus, by suggesting that the trip to Asia would require about 2,400 miles, had grossly underestimated the distance of travel there. In fact, even the most eastern points of the Americas (about which neither Columbus nor Isabella's advisors had any clue) were located several hundred miles further than that. Thus, in the opinion of the experts, it would be hard to adequately provision for a mission to Asia, and so Isabella turned Columbus's project down for a second time. Ultimately, as we all know, she funded the trip, but not until her circumstances had changed. In 1492 Isabella and Ferdinand's armies conquered Granada, the last remaining Muslim state on the Iberian Peninsula, ending over 700 years of Muslim rule in the area. In the spirit of victory and triumph, Isabella, with the support of her husband Ferdinand, and despite reservations, changed her mind and decided to financially support Columbus' Atlantic voyage.

Columbus and a crew of about ninety or so sailors sailed in search for a trade route to Asia on three ships. After a brief stopover in the Canaries, they traveled further west, but having covered the distance that Columbus predicted it would take to get to Asia, the crew was increasingly agitated. Luckily for Columbus, who his dissenters had planned to kill, they finally found land. After a trip of close to 4,000 miles, which had lasted thirty-six days, the crew had finally reached part of what is today the Bahamas.

In a letter to Isabella and Ferdinand about the first voyage, Columbus repeatedly assured the monarchs of Castile and Aragon that he had found great riches in "the Indies" and a promising area for colonization. He had seen "many spices," such as "cinnamon," "cotton," and "great mines of gold and of other metals." In order to highlight his proximity to Asia, Columbus also wrote that he found "rhubarb" a plant originating from China, and which had reached Europe via the inner Asian trade routes and the Muslim World during the late medieval period. While today the stems are usually either eaten as cake or turned into compote, in the pre-modern and early modern world the plant was cherished for its medicinal purposes. Emphasizing the importance of religion as a motivation for early modern European expansion, he also wrote that the native peoples "might become Christians." They would "be inclined to the love and service of their highnesses and of the whole Castilian nation, and strive to aid us and to give us the things which they have in abundance and which are necessary to us." To garner Isabella's and Ferdinand's support for a larger colonial mission, Columbus vastly exaggerated the availability of spices, gold, and the "incurably timid" indigenous populations' readiness to become Christian converts. During three more missions, Columbus and his crews would travel much of the circum-Caribbean, covering many of the region's islands but also reaching the mainland in modern-day Venezuela at the mouth of the Orinoco. Still, Columbus seemed to have believed until his death in 1506 that he had reached Asia.[2]

Especially insightful for the purposes of this study, are the Afro-Eurasian experiences, patterns, and interests that influenced the Iberians' early attempts at colonization in the Western Hemisphere. Like the Portuguese in Africa, early European colonizers in the Americas were interested in obtaining gold. Columbus and his crew, for example, pushed the indigenous peoples hard to bring them the valuable metal and the methods they used were so violent that in response the first garrison built by Columbus' crew on the island of Hispaniola (modern-day Dominican Republic) was attacked, destroyed, and the small force in it killed. Still, despite resistance, the Europeans relatively quickly subjugated the Native American peoples of the Caribbean, with disease being their most potent ally in this conquest. On the island of Hispaniola, for instance, the Taino might have numbered around 300,000 in 1492. By 1508 the number had shrunk to 60,000, plummeting down to 20,000 in 1512, and leaving as few as an estimated 500 Taino survivors by 1548. While the Spanish were able to obtain some gold by putting pressure on the indigenous populations through a feudal forced labor and tribute arrangement, they did not obtain the resources in bullion and spices they had hoped for.[3]

Starting with Columbus, the Iberians put in place a land and labor use arrangement that was inspired by medieval feudalism, and which would eventually be called the *encomienda* system. The precursors of this feudal structure had been put in place by Castile and Aragon on newly conquered Muslim lands on the Iberian Peninsula and the Canary Islands. It was transferred to be used in the Caribbean in 1493 by Isabella and Ferdinand, and later was used in other parts of the Americas. Technically, in this arrangement, the monarchs had title to the land, but they gave the land, alongside with the people residing on it, to a person known as an *encomendero*. In the idealized version of the *encomienda* system, and like a feudal vassal in Europe, the *encomendero* was to maintain allegiance and pay tribute to the crown. At the same time, the *encomendero* had obligations to the residents on his estate. He had the responsibility to protect and to convert Iberian Muslims, Guanches, or Native American inhabitants, and provide them with adequate land to subsist on. In reality, however, the *encomienda* system tended to deviate from the ideal model discussed here. Just as abuse of serfs occurred by landlords in Europe, and given the even longer distance of, and the lack of oversight by, representatives of the Crown, in places like the Canaries, the Caribbean, and later other parts of the Western Hemisphere, ruthless exploitation, violent abuse, and murder of laborers was widely reported.[4]

Native Americans and Spanish Colonization

Iberian efforts at empire-building in the Western Hemisphere had complex and diverse impacts on indigenous peoples and Europeans. On the one hand, colonization turned the world of Native Americans upside down and caused some significant suffering in many communities. The writings of missionaries such as Bartolome de Las Casas in his book, *A Short Account of the Destruction of the Indies*, as well as the works of other clergy, provided a glimpse and a critique of the abuses brought about by Spanish conquest in the Americas; they led to a debate in the Habsburg Spanish Empire about the treatment and the rights of indigenous Americans.[5] Yet, on the other hand, and even though there was violence and destruction during the history of Spanish colonization in the Americas, the interactions between Native Americans and Spaniards were also often more complicated and nuanced. Throughout the early modern period, Spanish power in the Americas was limited. While they might have claimed to control wide swaths of territory on maps, Spanish rule over many of the Native American peoples that supposedly lived within that massive empire, was often marginal or imaginary—territory largely used to raid for Indian slaves.

In Chapter 1 we mentioned the Spanish conquest of the massive Aztec and Inca empires. Disease was the most lethal weapon in the Iberian arsenal, and as we have seen, it had a destructive impact on the indigenous populations in the Americas. Furthermore, the Spanish used internal indigenous rivalries to their advantage. The conquest of the Aztec Empire, for example, would not have been possible without the assistance of the massive armies of Native American allies, such as the Tlaxcalans and others. Disgruntled factions of the Inca state who had resisted the ruler Atahualpa in an earlier civil war, also helped in the take-over of that empire, as they did, for example, during the capture of the capital Cusco, in which indigenous forces played a central strategic role. The quick transformation of power there was also enabled by Indian supporters and was followed by the crowning of an Inca ruler who was seen by the Spanish as a useful collaborator. Thus, indigenous allies played a key role in supporting relatively small Spanish forces that were largely made up of adventurers, a rag tag group that included some soldiers, but also minor nobles, traders, artisans, mariners, craftsmen, and notaries. Thus, it was often the freelance swashbucklers in search of plunder or *encomenderos* seeking to claim an *encomienda* who helped establish a Spanish Empire in the Americas.[6]

That said, and while the conquest of the Aztec and Inca empires might have been impressive feats, the Spanish were far less successful with "conquest" when they did not deal with Native American empires. Several of their attempts at establishing colonies failed miserably or had, at best, mixed results. For much of the sixteenth and the seventeenth centuries, Spanish control over much of what they claimed to be their empire in the Americas was tenuous at best. Colonial Spanish settlements were largely confined to the coastal regions of the Caribbean and the Pacific. Native American groups, communities, and states successfully resisted Spanish efforts at colonizing their lands, and were able to resist, defeat, and fight back several consolidated attempts in South America and in the North American Southwest and Southeast.[7]

Hernando De Soto's military expedition in the North American Southeast in the late 1530s and early 1540s provides an interesting case study of the complexity of indigenous Spanish power relations, but it also underscores the heavy toll that contact took on Native peoples. De Soto, a veteran of the campaign against the Inca, led a force of over 600 men. Like so many *conquistadores* before and after, the expedition came in search of silver and gold. De Soto's campaign depended on commandeering food from indigenous communities, using Native Americans as slaves and guides, and took local notables as hostages for blackmail. Treasures of gold and silver never materialized for De Soto's expedition, but they did meet with intense indigenous resistance. This opposition to the Spanish incursion came at a severe cost to the Native peoples of the region. During one attack on a Mississippian state, for instance, the Spanish force is believed to have killed over 3,000 people. Largely due to the comparative advantage of being on horseback and wearing protective armors, the Spanish forces and their auxiliaries reputedly suffered less than 150 fatalities. Nevertheless, over time, the consistent native resistance forced the Spanish into retreat. Thus the Mississippian states achieved what the Aztec and Inca empires failed to do. They had defeated the Spanish invaders.

While De Soto's expedition had failed to conquer the region, it likely sowed the seeds of the eventual destruction of the Mississippian Mound Building societies of the Southeast. The Spanish and African fighters, their horses, and the pigs that De Soto brought along as a portable food supply (the ancestors of today's razorback pigs in the South) introduced several epidemics that killed huge numbers of indigenous people. Disease disrupted patterns of daily life as the populations of cities, towns, and villages were decimated. Given estimated population losses from 50 to 90 percent, North American indigenous societies were weakened and disabled. These developments ensued in political, cultural, and social upheavals. Few of the Mississippian states survived these traumas, and those that did, did so in destabilized form. Many archeologists and ethnohistorians argue that, out of necessity, survivors had to reorganize into smaller towns and villages, which were often part of loosely organized confederations. This led to the creation of Native American nations, which are today known as the Cherokee, the Muskogee (Creek), or the Chickasaw. Scholars also maintain that as a result of the massive disruptions and upheavals connected to De Soto's *entrada*, mound building ceased in much of the North American Southeast.[8]

The impact of Afro-Eurasian diseases on the indigenous populations of the North American Southeast was illustrative of what happened all over the Western Hemisphere. While Native Americans were able to fight back and resist Spanish encroachment militarily, the impact of foreign pathogens carried by unsuccessful conquistadores and their entourages, slave raiders, traders, as well as survivors of shipwrecks, proved to be extremely disruptive to Native American societies all over the Americas.

Sexual relations in the Spanish colonies further complicated the history of intergroup dynamics in the Americas. Most European and African newcomers to the Western Hemisphere were male and searched for partners, often finding them among the indigenous population. Given the shortage of European women, many Spanish conquistadores and colonists also had native mistresses and wives. Most famous among these relationships was that between Cortes and Marina, an indigenous woman who served as a translator during the conquest of the Aztec Empire. Cortes, who had a wife in Cuba, never married Marina, but he is believed to have fathered several sons with her, and Marina would eventually marry a Spanish *encomendero*. Many other Spanish elite landholders married Native women who were often from indigenous notable lineages. Several of the women in the last Aztec ruler Montezuma's family, for instance, married Spaniards with significant *encomiendas*. Another prominent example of this phenomenon from Peru was the marriage of the Spanish *conquistador* Garcilasco de la Vega with Isabel, a niece of the Inca ruler Atahualpa. Their son, who shared the de la Vega name of his father but who often also referred to himself as "El Inca," wrote about Inca history and was proud of his Native American and European roots. Members of the Spanish elite who married Native American women often had family portraits drawn that showed them proudly with their mixed families. At the same time, people of mixed descent, like de la Vega, also would face discrimination by family members and by Spanish society due to their ethnic backgrounds. In the Spanish colonies in the Americas, "class" as much as "race" could serve as mechanisms to differentiate between different groups, and aided in the emergence of a complicated *casta*, or racial stratification, system in the seventeenth and eighteenth century.[9]

The European and African presence changed and dramatically disrupted Native American life, while, at the same time, requiring indigenous peoples in the Western Hemisphere to adapt to outside influences brought about by these settlements, a process that also helped to shape colonial societies. Native Americans traded with the outside world, adopted horses and other Afro-Eurasian animals such as sheep or chicken into their daily life, and they embraced Afro-Eurasian technologies, weaponries, and material culture. In turn, the indigenous peoples of the Americas also influenced the histories of the colonial encounter through their economic, social, and cultural contributions. In testimony to their impact on European society, many Native American place names survived in the Americas. Indigenous peoples contributed to the economies as laborers, suppliers, merchants, and entrepreneurs and were members of churches and other organizations. Furthermore, and as explored in more detail below, European overseas expansion did not only lead to contacts with Europe and Africa, but also to the increasing emergence of Global Atlantic patterns that would connect Native Americans—just like Africans and Europeans—to a much wider world.[10]

"The Spanish Sea": The Pacific Connection of the Global Atlantic

The importance and the extent of the Global Atlantic becomes apparent as we begin to follow the histories and patterns and processes that began to spread further afield via the Americas into the Pacific. In the early sixteenth century an ambitious political and legal Spanish elite would claim the entire Pacific Ocean as "the Spanish Sea"—a single oceanic domain to be controlled by their empire.[11] Central to this story would be the commodity of silver and its importance to the massive economy of China. Starting in the sixteenth century, the mines of Spanish America would, in part, feed, not only the Chinese demand for silver, but also that of several other Asian economies. The global exchange of silver would help to finance early modern Europe's trans-regional trade and would reinforce patterns and processes that would lead to cultural, ecological, and demographic changes. "New World" silver played such an extensive role in this newly emerging global economy that the Spanish silver coins came to be an accepted currency in many societies around the world.

Silver, China, and the Roots of the Global Atlantic Economy

The reasons why silver from the Americas would have such an appeal in China, and would play such a crucial role in helping to consolidate the patterns of a Global Atlantic, were a result of the complex and long monetary history of the pre-modern world's most powerful economy. During the period of the Tang dynasty (645–907), and again during the Song (960–1127), the Chinese authorities had been unable to issue an adequate amount of coins to satisfy their economy's needs. As the Chinese markets, commercial activity, and trade were expanding during this period, the state could not mint enough coins, which were predominantly made from copper, bronze, and some gold. During the eleventh century alone, Chinese authorities increased the amount of available coins twenty times. Yet, even such dramatic increases were not enough to satisfy the demand of a rapidly expanding economy for currency. Thus, Chinese merchants would use commodities such as tea, silk, and other luxury items as means to pay for exchanges. In addition, merchants, especially those active in long-distance trade, as well as some tax officials, had begun to issue printed notes in their transactions that could then later be redeemed for their value either in coins or in a pre-determined commodity. The government, in an effort to regulate, monopolize, and financially benefit from these new paper currencies, began to issue official notes, and theoretically, at least, their value was supposed to be backed by copper coins.

China's imperial government, by this act, created the world's first paper money. The use of paper money occurred during the Song, the Yuan (1271–1368), and during the early Ming dynasty (1368–1644). It was certainly less cumbersome to carry a piece of paper, than to have to haul a large volume of the widely used copper coins. The paper currency experiment, however, did not find wide use in the day to day financial actions of Chinese consumers. Rather its use was "ideal" as historian Kenneth Pomeranz and Stephen Topik write "for large-scale domestic trade and made considerable headway against all coins of all sorts." The use of paper as money demonstrated the power of the imperial Chinese state, which had to give and guarantee the value of a currency, which, of course, on its own did not have any real value. The paper money system was based on trust in the monetary stability of a currency backed by the imperial authorities of various dynasties. During periods of political unrest, such as the overthrow of the Mongol Yuan dynasty by the Han Chinese Ming dynasty, paper currencies became of lesser use due to instability.

In summary, what ultimately led to the suspension of the use of paper money by the Ming government in the 1420s was the overprinting of paper currency. China lacked a centralized bank that would oversee the production of money. Paper money was printed and ultimately overproduced at a local level leading to extremely high rates of inflation. Public trust in the system disappeared, and was accompanied by a rapid decline in the value of currency. To restore the monetary stability of their empire, the

Ming created a system of currency based on silver bullion. The Chinese economy's transition to silver ultimately provided the financial incentives for much of the Global Atlantic trade, and significantly boosted silver production in the Spanish mines of the Americas starting in the late sixteenth century.[12]

"The Spanish Sea" as an Alternative Maritime Trade Route to Asia

Before the silver trade could connect Spain and China in a truly global commodities' exchange, the Spanish had to first learn about the existence of the Pacific, and needed to develop a trans-Oceanic western route to Asia. By the early sixteenth century, European geographers and mariners had produced enough evidence to conclude that Columbus had not discovered a direct trade route to Asia as he had believed, but rather that the Western Hemisphere was in fact a separate continental landmass from Afro-Eurasia. A major piece of this puzzle was provided by the maritime mission led by Amerigo Vespucci. Inspired by his travels, which took Vespucci and his crew along hundreds of miles of the Atlantic South American coast, the German geographer Martin Waldseemuller created a map of the world in 1507 that depicted the Western Hemisphere as a separate continent from Eurasia. In the first edition of this map, Waldseemuller christened the continent "America" in honor of Vespucci's first name. This

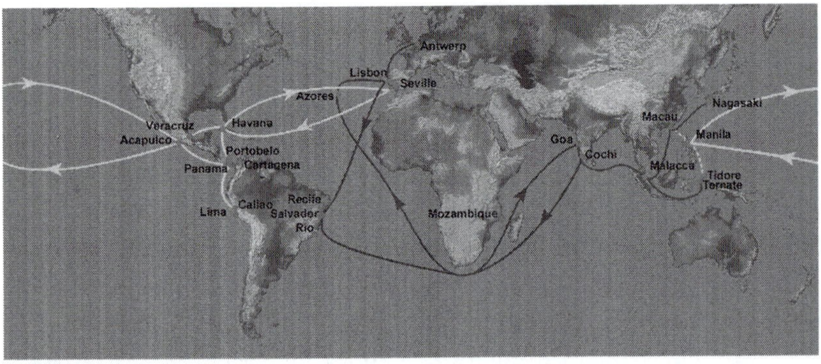

This map shows some of the Spanish and Portuguese Global Atlantic trade routes.

Source: Wikimedia Commons. Image in the public domain. Original source World_Topography.jpg licensed with PD-USGov-NASA-SRTM. http://commons.wikimedia.org/wiki/File:16th_century_Portuguese_Spanish_trade_routes.png.

was a word that gradually came into common use and slowly replaced "Indies" as the term to describe the Western Hemisphere.[13] Thus, finding an alternative and faster trade route to Asia that could compete with Portugal's Indian Ocean route, and to develop connections with the world beyond the Americas, remained a central strategic and economic interest of the Spanish kingdoms; and it also played a central role in the emergence of a Global Atlantic. There were two events that especially aided this development along. The first was Vasco Nunez de Balbao and his expeditionary force's crossing of the Isthmus of Panama in 1513, which introduced the Spanish to what we today call the Pacific Ocean. This mission established a relatively short overland route across the Western Hemisphere that eventually linked the Spanish to the lucrative Asian trade. The second development, discussed in more detail below, was a maritime mission led by Magellan, which circumnavigated the globe between 1519 and 1522 and provided the Spanish with additional information in their quest to build an empire. Eventually those two events aided in the rise of an Atlantic–Pacific trade route, which connected Spain, and by extension much of Europe, to the world's most coveted economy—China.

There were vibrant, cosmopolitan, and long-standing Asian maritime trade networks throughout the South China Sea and all along the Asian mainland when the Spanish arrived in the sixteenth century. However, the vast Pacific beyond had not been much traveled, at least not since the times when Polynesian migrants had begun to settle many of the islands in the region by sailing tremendous distances in their outrigger canoes. This Polynesian settlement process had started several thousand years ago and was likely completed before AD 1000. Although the Spanish called this ocean system "the Spanish Sea," unlike the Polynesians before them, they were not interested in large-scale settlement of the Pacific. Instead, the Spanish were predominantly interested in creating an exchange route that would link their empire with the lucrative Asian trade via the Americas. Thus, the Iberian presence in the Pacific Rim was regional, and it was not until the development of nautical instruments such as the maritime chronometer in the late 1700s that European states would begin to more fully incorporate this ocean system into their efforts of empire building and overseas expansion. For much of the 1500s and 1600s, Europeans had merely a marginal knowledge of the Pacific Ocean system.

The earliest outlines of this marginal knowledge of the Pacific were put into place by the voyage of Ferdinand Magellan who staged the first successful effort to find a maritime passage to Asia via the Pacific, an expedition accompanied by ruthless tactics toward the local peoples they encountered, which would set a precedent for future European interactions with the Pacific Islands. While Magellan was a minor Portuguese noble, and despite his participation in various Portuguese campaigns in the Indian Ocean World, he had felt that the Portuguese monarchy had never adequately compensated him for his service, or that the king had supported his aspirations. Magellan found the Habsburg Emperor Charles V more supportive, which was significant as Charles had just recently become the ruler of Castile and Aragon, while also ruling over other large sections of Europe. Charles V provided backing for Magellan's expedition and in 1519 the explorer headed out into the Atlantic with a fleet of five ships. Sailing through the dangerous southern strait of the Americas, today named after Magellan himself, he eventually sailed into a new ocean system. Due to the calm state of this ocean during the first weeks of his voyage, Magellan decided to name it the *mar pacifico*. Eventually, after traveling for some time in the Pacific, Magellan and his expedition would reach the island of Guam in March 1521. After initial peaceful interactions with the local population, the crew found itself soon in a violent conflict. The Spaniards accused the natives of "theft," as the Chamorro people apparently took some items from the mariners. This exchange would, however, have likely been understood by the norms of the Chamorro as a sharing of resources with one's hosts, who had after all welcomed the newcomers to their island and had supported them. These cultural subtleties were lost on Magellan and his crew. In an act of brutality that provided no mercy to even the youngest or meekest of the Chamorro population, they landed a war party that killed everyone that had not fled, burned some forty to fifty villages, looted the island for provisions, and kidnapped a local to serve as navigator for their mission. This was the first among a series of battles that the Spanish would lead against the Chamorro in their effort to establish a refreshment station in the Pacific. These campaigns were reminiscent of some of the genocidal campaigns against the indigenous peoples of the Americas. By March 1521, Magellan and his fleet reached an archipelago that would later be called the Philippines, in honor of King Philip who in 1556 succeeded Charles on the Spanish throne. Magellan claimed the islands for the Spanish kingdoms. Yet, as in Guam, relations with the local population soured quickly, and Magellan was killed in a military engagement with the locals.

With Magellan gone, it was left to the remaining members of his crew to circumnavigate the globe. They sailed back toward Spain but made a stopover via the Moluccas to obtain spices. Only one ship of the five returned to Seville in September of 1522, and less than 10 percent of the original crew survived the ordeal, but the tremendous profits made on the sale of spices, and the intelligence that the trip provided, made the circumnavigation a widely celebrated success. It reinforced the belief that a westward Atlantic–Pacific trade route to Asia was a feasible option.

Maritime Southeast Asia, where Magellan arrived after crossing the Pacific, was a vibrant point of convergence in the Indian Ocean world system, a well-established long-distance exchange network that reached, as we will discuss in more length in the next chapter, from China to southeastern Africa. The Portuguese were already present in the region in 1521. Emblematic of the hubris and confidence of the newly emerging European states, the Portuguese claimed Asia by the rights of the Treaty of Tordesillas of 1494. This treaty was an agreement by the Spanish kingdoms and Portugal to divide their global spheres of influence. The Iberian powers did not consider the national interests or territorial sovereignty of other states around the world. Nor did the treaty reflect the economic and political realities of the world in 1500, since, at the time, the Iberian states were rather minor players on the geopolitical stage. What attracted the Iberians, and other Europeans, to this region were spices and the close proximity to China, which, after all, was the world's largest economy; but the arrival of Europeans did not lead to European domination. Despite the frequent use of brutal military conquest and violence as a strategic tool of expansion used by the Iberians and other European states, many local Asian societies remained strong and continued to play influential roles in the interregional trade. Thus, throughout the early modern period, Europeans faced real limitations in their aspirations in the region. Through trial and error, just as they had learned in Africa and parts of the Americas, they discovered that seeking accommodation was frequently a more fruitful strategy than violence if they wanted to be successful players in Southeast Asia.

On the margins of Southeast Asia's established cosmopolitan trading system, lay an archipelago now named for a former Spanish King—the Philippines. Given its strategic location as a potential launching pad to access trade with Asia, the Spanish were keen to explore the possibility of the colonization of this archipelago. They launched several expeditions in the sixteenth century in hopes of securing a base to support their quickly expanding overseas empire. In the early 1540s, for example, the Spanish colony of New Spain sent a fleet to the archipelago, but local resistance made it impossible for this mission to establish a colonial settlement. An even larger Spanish force left Mexico in the 1560s and returned to the Philippines. This expedition defeated a local force on Cebu, put the island under their rule, and established a colonial foothold there. In 1571, the Spanish also established a settlement called Manila on the island of Luzon; this community turned into a growing city, which became the Spanish administrative seat of the archipelago. It was a capital that was blessed with a great natural harbor and was surrounded by fertile farmlands.

The colony of the Philippines was quickly integrated into the Global Atlantic World of the Spanish Empire, there were similarities between colonization efforts in both areas, and the colony had strong economic and political links with the Viceroyalty of New Spain in the Americas. Similar to what they had done in the Western Hemisphere, the Spanish soldiers and colonization efforts in the Philippines were accompanied by missionaries as the Christianization of the archipelago's diverse populations was ordered by Spain's King Philip II. The Spanish also introduced the feudal *encomienda* system to the archipelago, and began growing tobacco as a cash crop, a plant native to the Americas.[14]

Silver Mountain of the World: Western Hemisphere Bullion as Global Currency

The founding of Manila coincided with an extremely fortuitous development for the emerging Spanish Global Atlantic Empire—the discovery and exploitation of massive silver deposits in the Western Hemisphere by the Spaniards. The Americas would prove to be a massive source for global bullion in the early modern period. The scholar Ward Barrett has estimated that between the sixteenth and through much of the eighteenth centuries 85 percent of the globe's silver and 70 percent of gold originated from the Americas.[15] While these numbers, as well as the percentage of bullion that made it into the Asia trade, is a subject of fierce debates among historians, one issue is undisputable: gold, and especially silver, from the Americas fueled the Global Atlantic trade patterns discussed in this and the next chapter.

While the Spanish came in search for gold, they had more success exploiting established Native American silver mines, as well as establishing new ones. The Spanish hit the jackpot when, in the 1540s, they came across massive deposits in the Andes Mountains in modern-day Bolivia. The most productive mountain in the region came to be known as *Cerro de Potosi* or *Cerro Ricco*, and it was in the high plateau region of the Andes, an extremely dry, cold, and inaccessible part of the world. Still, in the inhospitable valley below the "silver mountain" emerged a massive city that would reach, at its peak in the early seventeenth century, a population of over 150,000. The city thus competed in size with the major European cities at the time such as Amsterdam, Seville, or London. The massive flow of silver coming from their mines in the Americas made Habsburg Spain the European superpower of the sixteenth century and aided in the financing of a massive military and naval fleet. But the empire incurred tremendous military and war expenditures to secure its treasure to fight not only various European powers, which attempted to challenge their supremacy in much of Europe and other parts of the Atlantic World, but also the Ottoman Empire, with which the Habsburg battled for control over the Mediterranean World and on its eastern European frontier. Ultimately the cost affiliated with permanent conflict to maintain its position as a global power proved damaging to the Spanish Empire and aided in its decline. Nonetheless, Spanish America continued to remain a vital source of silver for the global economy into the nineteenth century.

Although silver brought previously unimaginable wealth to Spain, the mining of this bullion came at a devastatingly high price for the laborers who procured the ore. Native Americans worked under brutal and often deadly conditions in the mines, where they endured violence, abuse, constant deprivation, and beatings. Accidents, such as mine shaft cave-ins, suffocation, a wide array of workplace injuries, including falling off long ladders into the darkness, happened frequently. Additionally, silver refiners suffered from mercury poisoning, and the often freezing conditions in the Andes led to pneumonia and other illnesses that were already rampant among native populations under more ideal conditions. In Potosi the death rates of Native American miners soared so much that Native American villages held funerals for the conscripted laborers before they went to the mines. In order to maintain a steady supply of labor, mine operators brought in additional African slave labor. African workers also suffered tremendously and perished in large numbers, and the use of Native American labor continued widely despite the introduction of the new source of slave labor.

Silver was both mined and turned directly into currency in the Americas. The first silver coins were minted in various places in the Western Hemisphere as early as the 1570s. These "pieces of eight" or "*real de ocho*," silver "pesos," "piasters," or "Spanish dollars" came to be known the world over.

Once the silver was mined and processed it would be distributed throughout the exchange networks of the Global Atlantic. Silver from Potosi and other parts of the Andes was brought down to Lima on the Pacific coast by Llama trains and from there it was shipped by boat north to the Isthmus of Panama along the Pacific coast. Once in Central America the silver was further redistributed. From Central America, it would be carried by mule train overland to the Atlantic coast, where it was again, alongside the silver mined in Mexico and other parts of the Americas, shipped by heavily protected fleets across the Atlantic to Europe. By the 1560s, silver would also begin to make its way across the Pacific to Asia via the Manila galleon trade. Furthermore, silver did not just enter Asia through the Pacific route. As we will discuss in the following chapter, a significant portion of the silver from the Western Hemisphere also ended up in Asia via Europe and its Global Atlantic Indian Ocean trade networks.[16]

Example of a Spanish silver coin, which served as currency in many parts of the world.

Source: Wikimedia Commons. 1739. Philip V Coin. http://commons.wikimedia.org/wiki/File:Philip_V_Coin.jpg.

Describing the world-wide influence of Spanish silver, the late historian of Latin America, John Jay TePaske, wrote: "In fact, American silver was so ubiquitous that merchants from Boston to Havana, Seville to Antwerp, Murmansk to Alexandria," from Istanbul to New Zealand and Australia, "to Macao to Canton, and Nagasaki to Manila all used the Spanish peso or piece of eight (real) as a standard medium of exchange; these same merchants even knew the relative fineness of the silver coins minted in Potosi, Lima, Mexico and other sites in the Indies thousands of miles away."[17] Thus, silver from the Americas, produced by coerced Native American labor and African slaves, would help drive Global Atlantic trade into the nineteenth century.

Manila Galleon Trade and Chinese Trade Diaspora

After being founded in 1571, Manila functioned as a cross-cultural transfer market city, which connected the Spanish Empire in the Americas and Europe with China and other economies in Asia. In the sixteenth century, with regularity, Spanish galleons journeyed from Acapulco (Mexico) across the Pacific to Manila (today the capital of the Philippines) and from there they headed back to Central America. The Spanish decided the return trip was less dangerous, faster, and more preferable to transport goods across the Isthmus of Panama by land, rather than to travel the hazardous Strait of Magellan around the southern tip of South America. Intercultural relations in Manila were violent at times, but they were also diverse and these complex interactions also had benefits for Asians and Europeans. For example, in a mutually beneficial arrangement, the trade in the Philippines provided the Chinese and other Asians with reliable access to silver currency, while also providing the Habsburg Spanish Empire with a wide array of desirable goods. While porcelain and silk were the most prized, Chinese and other Asian merchants also traded lacquer ware, textiles, gemstones, furniture, ivory, iron, cotton, carpets, pepper, cinnamon, cloves, and perfumes, as well as a wide variety of food items and farm animals for the day to day consumption of the colony.

Despite the access to goods it provided, the Manila galleon trade was not wholeheartedly embraced by everyone in the Spanish Empire. There were critics who saw this type of exchange as harmful to their society. For instance, many members of the Spanish elite were concerned about the amount of silver bullion that was being hemorrhaged in the trade. How much of the silver mined in the Americas actually flowed into the China trade via the Manila galleon trade is difficult to determine. Estimates range widely, but most scholars would put the number somewhere between 25 and 50 percent. In Spain itself certain sectors of the economy were disadvantaged, particularly in manufacturing, as trade with China harmed the Spanish Empire's struggling silk production, since Chinese manufacturers were able to produce high-quality silk at significantly lower prices largely due to lower labor costs. As a result, tailors and garment workers in colonial Mexico made clothes from imported Chinese silk that would be sold all over the Spanish Empire, the rest of Europe, and the Atlantic World. But even in this market there was strong competition as the Chinese tailors were quite masterful at making up-to-date fashionable European-style clothing, which was brought to Acapulco via the Manila galleons and from there redistributed to other corners of the Atlantic World.[18]

Although Manila was a Spanish colony, much of the commercial interaction within the city was conducted by Asian traders, many of them Chinese from the Fujian region of southeastern China. These Chinese were part of the growing Chinese trade diaspora in Southeast Asia, but many of them also put down roots as farmers in the Philippines.[19] Thus, and not unlike other European ruled colonial cities in the region, much of the trade in Manila was conducted by East Asians. The Chinese demographic presence in Manila was significant. One scholar estimates that from the period of 1571 to 1600 an estimated 7,000 Chinese visited the city per year—most of them mariners and merchants. This is an especially significant tally, given that residents from Spain and the Americas numbered less than a thousand. Even more dramatically, in 1600, the number of permanent Chinese residents in Manila had grown to an estimated 8,000. By the late 1630s the Chinese population around the city, many of them living in the countryside, is believed to have been as high as 45,000. The significant size and growth of the Chinese population was often a concern for the Spanish. Moreover, given the large percentage of males among the Chinese, the community intermarried with the local Filipino population and aided in the creation of a mixed ethnic community, which often functioned as cultural brokers politically and commercially. The name that the Spanish gave to the Chinese in the Philippines, *sangleye*, is also instructive of the role that this diaspora community played in the city, as it is derived from a Chinese dialect meaning trade. Chinese merchants provided the vast majority of goods that were shipped to the Americas via the galleon trade and from there on to Europe, and they provided most of the skilled crafts and services in Manila.[20]

Still, while the Spanish benefited economically from the relationship with the Chinese, this was often an ambiguous interdependence that could burst into mass violence. In 1603, for example, the Spanish and their allies massacred thousands of Chinese. Another wave of mass violence against the Chinese occurred in 1639 when Spanish colonial forces and their Filipino allies brutally suppressed a revolt by Chinese settlers who complained about ill-treatment and demanded increased autonomy. This episode resulted in the slaughter of an estimated 17,000 to 22,000 diaspora Chinese around the Manila region.[21]

The Columbian Exchange: Plants from the Americas and the Global Atlantic World

The expanding networks of the Global Atlantic led to the spread of Afro-Eurasian diseases into the Americas and the global distribution of silver, commodities, and manufactured goods, as well as numerous plants and agricultural crops, such as maize, potatoes, peanuts, tomatoes, tobacco, and chilies. The plants that produced all these crops came also to be grown in places far from their points of origin in the Western Hemisphere, and came to play an essential part in the daily life of people in the new places to which they were introduced. We have already discussed the impact that maize and manioc had on African diets, and chilies and tomatoes, for instance, would be widely adopted by societies in Afro-Eurasia. These global biological and cultural exchanges were part of a phenomenon that the historian Alfred Crosby first described as *The Columbian Exchange*. In turn, a wide variety of Afro-Eurasian plants and animal life, including European and African grasses, fungi, mosquitoes, bees, rats, horses, cockroaches, just to name a few, significantly altered the biological and cultural landscape of the Americas.[22] This exchange of goods, crops, insects, and animals significantly shaped human history post-1492 and was brought about by the patterns and processes of the Global Atlantic.

Brought to Asia by the Spanish via the Philippines, but also by the Portuguese and the Dutch via Indian Ocean routes, the Chinese, for instance, embraced several crops from the Americas. The sweet potato, in particular, began to play an especially important role in the Chinese diet. It was adopted by the Chinese alongside maize, chili peppers, tobacco, peanuts, and cassava. In fact, the introduction of crops from the Americas helped to bring about and sustain the population increases that took place in China in the eighteenth century. It is important to underscore though, that while the Chinese, according to Crosby, were the quickest to incorporate "food plants" from the Americas among the peoples of the "Old World," other societies all over Afro-Eurasia did so to an ever increasing degree.[23]

The story of potatoes after 1492 demonstrates how a relatively, at least globally speaking, marginal South American crop grown in the Andean highlands, would be introduced to various corners of the world, and underscores the Global Atlantic dynamics of this process. Increasingly, several varieties of this crop would help to feed the masses of Europe and Asia. Historians Kenneth Pomeranz and Steven Topik remind us that "Today, potatoes are the fourth largest food crop in the world." European sailors helped to introduce the plant to Asia, but potatoes also had a significant impact in the Atlantic World. For instance, in the Americas, the Spanish used the potato as a main food source to supply their Native American coerced labor force in the silver mines of the Andes. Across the Atlantic Ocean, in Europe, the potato gained an initial foothold as a luxurious dish for Europe's elite. It was only in the seventeenth, eighteenth, and the nineteenth centuries that the potential of the potato to become a staple to feed the hungry masses was gradually implemented in various European regions, most noticeably Ireland, the German states, and Tsarist Russia.[24]

Chocolate or cacao provides a Global Atlantic case study of how, over the course of about 400 years, a valuable product from the Americas generally consumed and used by elites, would turn into a mass consumer product for the people in Europe, even though it was never grown there. Before 1492, various indigenous Central American societies, such as the Olmecs, Maya, and Aztecs, had used the cacao bean as currency and valued the beans and drink as a medicine, for ceremonial purposes, as a stimulant, and as a drug. The Spanish carried on with the practice, at least for some time, and used the beans as a means of payment in several areas in Mesoamerica. In the sixteenth century, the Spanish also embraced the chocolate drink, mixing the powder with water and some flavoring derived from the vanilla orchid that originated in Mesoamerica, but also with spices foreign to the Americas, such as sugar and cinnamon, which had become accessible to the Spanish due to global trade and cash crop production. It was only in the seventeenth and the eighteenth centuries that Europeans increasingly began to mix cacao powder with milk. For much of its early modern history the drink was expensive and was consumed by the European elite, but gradually grew in popularity in Europe, which benefited suppliers in Spanish America and further drove the global economy. Due to an ever-increasing demand, cacao producers increasingly stopped to collect the beans in the wild, and began to grow the crop in ever-expanding plantations in various suitable parts of the Spanish Americas. Over time, European colonists and colonial officials also took the cacao tree to places like the Philippines, Indonesia, Brazil, and eventually Africa, where they successfully experimented cultivating the crop. By the nineteenth century, when the drink of hot chocolate had transformed from an elite product to a mass commodity consumed widely especially in continental Europe, the world's cocoa plantation fed an ever-growing consumer demand. It was also in the nineteenth century that cocoa was increasingly used to make chocolate and other sweets. Thus, to feed their ever-growing sweet tooth, Western powers increased cocoa production in their colonies. This was part of an ever-growing Western-controlled, global, imperial plantation complex, which produced a wide variety of cash crops for the Western market.[25]

Conclusion

Just like the extension of the Spanish Empire into the Pacific had dramatic ramifications, as we will discuss in detail in the next chapter, so did European colonial expansion into the Indian Ocean World. Globally speaking these developments aided the process of global integration. They illustrate a world economy integrated with the Global Atlantic.

Notes

1 I am drawing this concept from Colin Calloway, *New Worlds for All: Indians, Europeans, and the Remaking of Early America* (Baltimore, MD: John Hopkins University Press, 1997).

2 For quotes and general background see Christopher Columbus, *The Four Voyages of Columbus*, ed. Cecil Jane (New York: Dover, 1988), 1–18. My discussion of Columbus draws from Kenneth Pomeranz and Steven Topik, "Better to be Lucky than Smart," in *The World that Trade Created: Society, Culture, and the World Economy, 1400 to the Present*, eds, Kenneth Pommeranz and Steven Topik (Armonk, NY: M.E. Sharpe, 2013), 57–60;

and Glenn J. Ames, *The Globe Encompassed: The Age of European Discovery, 1500–1700* (Upper Saddle River, N.J.: Pearson & Prentice Hall, 2008), 60–64.

3 Ames, 69.

4 Ames, 68; see also David J. Weber, *The Spanish Frontier in North America* (New Haven, CT: Yale University Press, 1992), 124–125.

5 Bartolome de las Casas, *A Short Account of the Destruction of the Indies* (New York: Penguin, 1992).

6 Henry Kamen, *Empire: How Spain became a World Power, 1492–1763* (New York: Harper Collins Publishers, 2003), chapter 3.

7 See for example Kamen, chapter 3.

8 My account of De Soto's mission and its impact on Native Americans draws from Alice Nash and Christoph Strobel, *Daily Life of Native Americans from Post-Columbian through Nineteenth Century America* (Westport, CT: Greenwood Press, 2006), 106–107.

9 See for example Kamen, 240–241; and Ilona Katzew, *Casta Painting: Images of Race in Eighteenth Century Mexico* (New Haven, CT: Yale University Press, 2004).

10 For a general discussion of the impact of European colonization on Native Americans see John Kicza, *Resilient Cultures: America's Native Peoples Confront European Colonization, 1500–1800* (Upper Saddle River, NJ: Prentice Hall, 2003). For a study that situates the indigenous peoples of the Western Hemisphere in a world historical context see Jack Weatherford, *Indian Givers: How the Indians of the Americas Transformed the World* (New York: Crown, 1988).

11 For the historic use of the term "Spanish Sea" to describe the Pacific see William Lytle Schurz, *The Manila Galleon* (New York: E.P. Dutton and Company, 1939), 288.

12 This section draws from Pomeranz and Topik, "Funny Money, Real Growth," in *The World that Trade Created*, 15–17; and Neil MacGregor, "Ming Banknote: Paper Money, from China AD 1375–1425," *A History of the World in 100 Objects: From the Handaxe to the Credit Card* (New York: Viking, 2011) 465–469.

13 On this issue see for example Jerry Brotton, *A History of the World in 12 Maps* (New York: Viking, 2013), chapter 5.

14 See Ames, 69–71, 79–81; and Buschmann, 77–80.

15 Ward Barrett, "World Bullion Flows, 1450–1800," in J.D. Tracy, ed., *The Rise of Merchant Empires: Long-Distance Trade in the Early Modern World, 1350–1750* (New York: Cambridge University Press, 1990), 224.

16 See MacGregor, "Pieces of Eight: Spanish Coins, Minted in Potosi, Bolivia," *A History of the World in 100 Objects*, 517–522.

17 John J. TePaske, "New World Silver, Castile and the Philippines, 1590–1800," in J.F. Richards, ed., *Precious Metals in the Later Medieval and Early Modern Worlds* (Durham, NC: Carolina Academic Press, 1983), 425.

18 Charles Mann, *1493: Uncovering the New World Columbus Created* (New York: Knopf, 2011), 154–156.

19 On this issue see for example Pomeranz and Topik, "The Fujian Trade Diaspora," in *The World That Trade Created*, 10–12.

20 John E. Wills, Jr., "Maritime Europe and the Ming," in John E. Wills, Jr., ed., *China and Maritime Europe, 1500–1800: Trade, Settlement, Diplomacy, and Missions* (New York: Cambridge University Press, 2011), 51–61. For the use of the word *sangleye* and a general discussion see Philip Curtin, *Cross-Cultural Trade in World History* (New York: Cambridge University Press, 1984), 150, for a general discussion see chapter 7.

21 Wills, "Maritime Europe and the Ming," in *China and Maritime Europe*, 51–61.

22 Alfred Crosby, *The Columbian Exchange: Biological and Cultural Consequences of 1492* (Wesport, CT: Greenwood Press, 1972). See also Alfred Crosby, *Ecological Imperialism: The Biological Expansion of Europe, 900–1900* (New York: Cambridge University Press, 1986).

23 Crosby, *The Columbian Exchange*, 199–201; Weatherford, chapter 6.

24 Pomeranz and Topik, "One Potato, Two Potato," in *The World that Trade Created*, 143–145.

25 Pomeranz and Topik, "Chocolate: From Coin to Commodity," in *The World that Trade Created*, 86–88.

4

THE GLOBAL ATLANTIC AND THE WORLDS OF THE INDIAN OCEAN, 1500–1800

The reaches of the Global Atlantic stretched not only into the Pacific via the Americas but also into the Indian Ocean. In their efforts to explore the western African coast, the Portuguese circumnavigated the southern African Cape of Good Hope and were the first European nation to sail into this ocean system. As a result, they found themselves in a commercially vibrant and integrated region of cosmopolitan cultures. This chapter will examine the patterns and processes of intercultural exchange that came about as a result of the encounters between the Europeans and the local peoples of the Indian Ocean World. It will also explore the Indian Ocean World system's connection with the Global Atlantic.

The Indian Ocean region had long been a center of commerce and exchange. In previous chapters we have briefly explored the impact of Indian Ocean goods like shells from the Maldives or textiles from India on West African consumers. We have also read how pre-modern Europe's desire to break into the traditional spice trade helped spur European overseas trade and expansion into the Atlantic and Pacific Oceans.

With the establishment of a Global Atlantic system the importance of this trade would only grow. Earlier we read about the impact of silver on Ming China and just as it did there, silver from the Western Hemisphere played an important role in trade with the Indian subcontinent. The Mughal Empire, as well as several other smaller Indian Ocean states that emulated Mughal forms of government, also based their monetary system on silver. Europeans found that, to their consternation, in order to purchase highly desired Indian Ocean World products, they would need to pay, despite their efforts to trade goods in kind, with precious bullion.

We have explored how the Spanish accessed Chinese goods largely through the Pacific Ocean via their base in Manila. Some European states, however, such as the Portuguese and Dutch, attempted to access Chinese commodities predominantly via the Indian Ocean. The Indian Ocean connection between Europe and China was in many ways a natural extension of older trade patterns and Chinese diaspora populations had long been active participants and players in the region.

This maritime trade continued even after China underwent a major dynastic change. In 1644, a group of invaders from Manchuria, a region in what is today northeastern China, overthrew the ethnic Chinese Ming Dynasty and established a Manchu-led dynasty called the Qing Dynasty. Under the Qing, China expanded its borders and, especially during the early years of the dynasty, resumed its role as the definitive power in the region. Beginning in the seventeenth and especially by the eighteenth centuries, Europe's interest in trade with China began to shift as Europeans became increasingly interested in purchasing tea. This new and at times seemingly insatiable desire for Chinese tea gives us an example of the breadth of the Global Atlantic. The consumption of Chinese tea spurred the production of Chinese porcelain and, because so many Europeans drank it sweet, sugar grown in the Americas. The booming sugar plantations generated a demand for slave labor, which came predominantly from West Africa. Some of these slaves were paid for with Indian textiles bought with South American silver. These seemingly disparate global processes combined to produce what would become the signature drink of Great Britain. Such connections and exchanges, brought about by the extension of the Global Atlantic, helped to alter the early modern world.

Defining the Indian Ocean World

Unlike the Atlantic, the Indian Ocean trading system was an established center of trans-oceanic maritime interaction. As far back as 3,000 years, long-distance trade networks and intercultural exchanges shaped the region's politics, diplomacy, agriculture, urbanization, food and cuisine, dress, manufacturing, architecture, and construction. The historian K.N. Chauduri defines the Indian Ocean World as a spatial, temporal, and structural system and it reached far beyond the coastlines of East Africa, Arabia, and Asia, to include China, the steppes of inner Asian, and northern Africa. Like the burgeoning Atlantic system, the influence of the Indian Ocean World was vast.[1]

Long-distance intercultural exchange was made possible by the regular monsoon winds. In the western portions of the Indian Ocean, for example, the monsoon blows reliably in a northerly direction from April to September, and in a southerly direction from November to February. Thus, for several millennia, traders from such diverse places as eastern Africa, Arabia, South and Southeast Asia, as well as China, used the monsoon wind patterns to create a system of maritime interaction in the region. Portuguese explorer Vasco da Gama gives us an example about the effectiveness of the monsoons; with the help of an experienced navigator he traveled from East Africa to India in twenty-three days but when he ignored the monsoon schedule on his return trip, the same stretch took him 132 days. The secret of the monsoons helped to create a commercial network that reached from eastern Africa to China, and, during its height from the 700s to the 1400s, it was the most cosmopolitan and valuable trade zone in the world.

The luxury goods traded on the Indian Ocean have become the stuff of legends: spices, cloth, silks, porcelains, fragrances, aromatics, ivory, perfumes, textiles, medicines, precious metals (such as gold), gem stones, dyes, rare woods, and slaves. In recent years, however, scholars have also underscored that commerce in more common staples, such as rice, metals such as tin and copper, or woods also took place. These bulkier products were sometimes shipped considerable distances as trade goods, and would increase in value when they traveled the distance from a region where they were widely available, to parts where they were a rare commodity.

The pattern of the monsoons also contributed to the cosmopolitan nature of the region's trading culture. Traders would often cross the ocean with the monsoons and then spend six months there waiting for the winds to change. As a result, traders often formed relationships with local women and maintained families and children on both sides of the Indian Ocean. Trading communities throughout the region regularly had neighborhoods devoted to the various ethnic groups involved in the regional exchange where residents expected a certain amount of cultural autonomy and self-rule. Thus they maintained their own cultural identity but also accommodated that of their host region. As traders desired to educate their children in the ways of their ancestors, schools, music, food, and language, cultural elements gradually spread from one region to another. After 650, Islam spread out of the Arabian Peninsula, and while certainly not all traders converted to the new faith, the social codes and religious tenets of the religion were influential and acted, at least to some degree, as a further unifying cultural strand that helped to facilitate commerce and interaction among various ethnicities involved with the trade.

Long-term financial stability in the long-distance trade required a high degree of trust between business associates. In the pre-industrial Indian Ocean network, trustworthy trading partners were often found within one's family or ethnic or religious groups. As a result, commercial activity was often conducted within extended family networks and the diaspora communities made up of other members of one's faith or ethnicity. Arab, Swahili, Chinese, Gujarati, Jewish merchants, or trade guilds such as the Karimi, to name just a few trade communities and organizations that participated in maritime commerce, each dominated certain sectors of the trade and had diaspora communities throughout the regions of the Indian Ocean World. Merchants would focus on one leg of the trade, specializing, for example, in commerce between the eastern African Swahili city-states and Arabia or India, or from India to Southeast Asia, and be in contact with associates focused on corresponding routes.

Trading tended to be, however, not only dominated by family and commercial guilds, as well as ethnic and religious groups, but states all over the Indian Ocean region played a frequent and central role in influencing, facilitating, and sometimes attempting to monopolize trade. Some regions featured autonomous or semi-autonomous city-states who looked to interregional trade to fill their coffers. City-states, as well as larger states, could sponsor trading fleets, passed laws that gave ruling elites commercial monopolies, and competed to draw the most merchants to their shores and tax the profits of the exchanges; occasionally even going to war over trading privileges. Security was also a concern within the trade network and states would also occasionally deploy their navies to deter piracy.[2]

The most famous and extravagant example of state-sponsored maritime activity in the pre-modern Indian Ocean World also demonstrates the interconnectivity and enormity of the trading zone. Between 1405 and 1433, the Chinese Ming Dynasty sponsored their Treasure Fleet to take seven expeditions throughout a vast portion of the trade zone. The massive armada included over 300 ships, and nearly 30,000 people with different social positions and skill sets including diplomats, doctors, sailors, highly

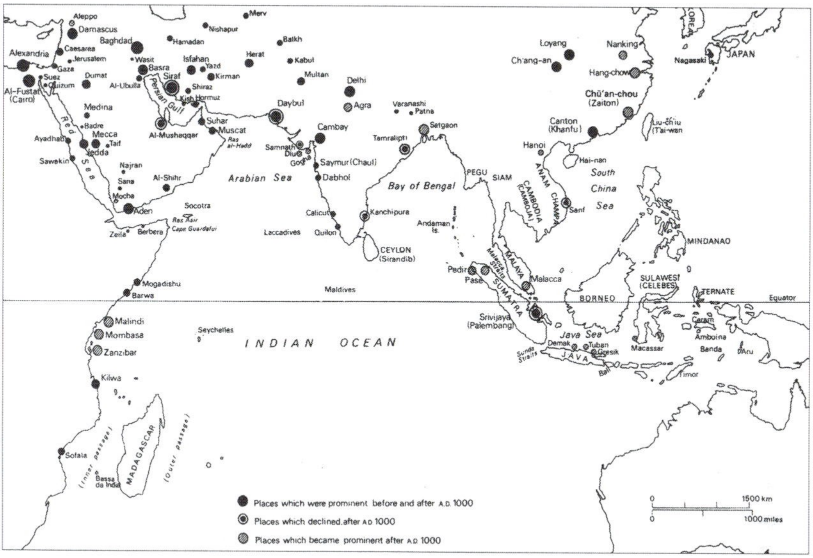

Map of trading ports and cities in the Indian Ocean, 618–1500.

Source: Adapted from K.N. Chaudhuri, *Trade and Civilisation in the Indian Ocean: An Economic History.* New York: Cambridge University Press, 1985.

educated concubines, translators, soldiers, gardeners to tend the crops on deck, and many others. The most famous aspects of the fleet were the size and structure of the Chinese Treasure ships, which were said to feature nine masts, be longer than a football field, and contain riches enough to impress those who came in contact with them of the vast wealth and power of the Chinese state of the Ming Dynasty.

These maritime missions were led by the Admiral Zheng He, a man who had been captured by the Ming Chinese forces as prisoner-of-war as a young boy, enslaved, and made a eunuch in the household of the future emperor. When the Yongle Emperor took the throne, Zheng He became one of his most trusted advisors and was eventually selected to lead the massive trans-regional voyages. During the seven voyages, Zheng He's fleets traded all over the Indian Ocean World from Southeast to South Asia, to the Arab world, to the Swahili coast of East Africa. They fought pirates, attacked states that were seen as uncooperative, demanded tribute, and put in place a commercial and diplomatic network with many Indian Ocean World states. During the rule of the Yongle Emperor, emissaries from states all over the Indian Ocean World were transported from the coast and welcomed at the Ming court in a highly organized, supervised, and ritualized diplomatic ceremony. Foreign emissaries brought goods, offerings, diplomatic messages, and prostrated in front of the emperor, and, in return, would receive gifts. Yongle officials believed that close and reciprocal political and economic ties would lead to an increase in power and wealth for China. In addition, they used the visits of emissaries and diplomats for propaganda purposes, arguing that the foreign contacts were a sign of the emperor's standing in the world.

With the death of the Yongle Emperor in 1424, the Chinese state gradually pulled out of overseas trade and failed to fund any future endeavors. By the mid-1430s, after a final effort to launch one more mission, China's once significant fleet was left to rot. This disengagement was likely in part motivated by a power struggle in the imperial Ming administration between eunuchs, who generally favored the Treasure Fleets, and Confucian scholars, who generally opposed the missions, and who seemed to have won this battle.[3] Moreover, growing threats from the Mongols on the northern steppe increasingly preoccupied the Ming Empire in the fourteenth century. Thus, southern maritime activity was in part also neglected because the imperial authorities had to engage with their northerly neighbors, a struggle exemplified by the renewed, expansive, and costly wall-building activity. Much of what Westerners call the "Great Wall" of China that survives today had been ordered built by the Ming Dynasty.[4]

Still, Zheng He's mission brought an even larger awareness about Chinese products to other parts of Asia than had already existed prior to the fifteenth century, and it introduced a larger number of Chinese consumers to more foreign products—a development that continued to aid the desire for trade in the region. Furthermore, while the Ming Chinese state might have pulled out of the maritime endeavor, Chinese merchants and diaspora communities, as we have seen in the previous chapter, continued to play an important role in the history of Asian trade, often in violation of the laws of their imperial government.

Europeans Enter the Indian Ocean World: A Short Overview

It was Portugal's exploration of the Atlantic coast of Africa that ultimately aided in the development of the easterly connections of the Global Atlantic. Bartolomeu Dias and his small fleet's accidental circumnavigation of the southern tip of the continent in 1488 provided Portuguese officials with the knowledge of an access route to Asia. Nevertheless, for several years afterwards, the small Portuguese maritime state remained focused on developing their commercial potential in sub-Saharan Africa. News about Christopher Columbus' 1492 trans-Atlantic voyage, sponsored by Portugal's major competitors, the kingdoms of Castile and Aragon, changed their more modest ambitions and spurred the Portuguese crown into action. In the summer of 1497, the Portuguese monarch ordered a small fleet of four ships under the command of Vasco da Gama to explore their commercial options in the Indian Ocean.

Da Gama's voyage marked Europe's entrance into the Indian Ocean. Although European states would not dominate the trade in the early modern era in the way they would have liked, they did alter it and fought the local population and each other fiercely in pursuit of that goal. The ferocious competition between European states, exemplified, for example, by the Hundred Years War, which ended in 1453, had resulted in great advancements in European weaponry. In contrast to Indian Ocean trade, the Mediterranean Sea trading culture that the Europeans, especially the Iberians, were more familiar with was an armed trade where heavily fortified ships jealously defended their trading monopolies. Thus, attaching the new cannon technology to ships made commercial sense. Along with these gunships, the Europeans also brought with them a sense of distrust and sometimes contempt for non-Christians, especially Muslims, that was burnished in the Crusades and, again, especially for the Iberians, the *Reconquista*. These factors combined with the fact that the Europeans had almost no domestic goods that were of interest to the Indian Ocean merchants, motivated the Europeans to take different approaches to access trade. They often pursued the objective to establish a trade monopoly and were willing to reach these ends by using considerable violence. These were dynamics that merchants in the Indian Ocean trade network were traditionally less accustomed to.

Starting with Vasco da Gama, the Portuguese were the first Europeans to develop a presence in the Indian Ocean. They dominated eastern trade among the Europeans until the 1590s when the Dutch, banned from the port in Lisbon for political reasons, began to develop their own routes to the East. While both overseas colonial powers made an effort at trading and empire-building in the Atlantic, their expansion into the Indian Ocean played a central role in the strategic and economic interests of their widely dispersed maritime empires. The Dutch, through their efficient management and ruthless tactics, managed to overtake the Portuguese trade within a few decades and dominated the trade into Europe for much of the seventeenth century. Throughout the 1600s, the British gradually began to challenge the Dutch position in the region. The French also had ambitions in the Indian Ocean, especially in India, and competed as fiercely with the British there as elsewhere in the world. Their competition came to a climax in the Seven Years War (1756–63), a conflict of Global Atlantic proportions, which some historians have called the first global war and is known in the United States as the "French and Indian War." As part of this widely dispersed conflict, the British defeated the French in South Asia and forced them to give up their small-holdings on the subcontinent. After 1783, when the British lost control of their most populous colonies in North America, they focused their energies in the Indian Ocean. Their increased attention to the area combined with a spike in the South Asian textile trade and a drop in the Southeast Asian spice trade, allowed the British to overtake the Dutch as the dominant European player in the region in the early eighteenth century.

Already in the first decades of the sixteenth century, not long after Vasco da Gama rounded Africa's Cape of Good Hope, the Indian Ocean maritime route replaced the Mediterranean trade that had once been Europe's main source for spices. Venice and Genoa, which had long dominated the earlier commerce, were quickly overtaken by Portugal. Throughout much of the early modern period trade was focused on commodities that consumers were familiar with: textiles, diamonds, other gem stones such as rubies and sapphires, pearls, porcelain, rhubarb for medicinal purposes, and lacquer ware were just some of these products. Throughout the sixteenth and early seventeenth centuries, however, it was the spice trade that dominated European commercial interests, followed in the eighteenth century by tea and textiles.

Early modern trans-oceanic travel was dangerous. As many of the trade goods originated in Southeast Asia, a successful sixteenth-century voyage to procure a cargo and ship it back to Europe could last anywhere from 2 to 4 years. Bad weather, ships from a competing trading power, and pirates could rapidly end a maritime mission. Yet, if a trip was successful, high profits could be obtained from selling spices in Europe. One boat carrying exotic spices could cover the expenses of several others lost at sea and make stalwart investors fabulously wealthy.

The Portuguese, Dutch, French, and English, were primarily interested in obtaining profits by selling Asian goods throughout Europe. But, as we will see in more detail below, despite their ambitions to dominate the trade, they had to purchase Asian products by participating, often as minor players, in an intra-Asian network of seaborne trade, or after the mid-sixteenth century, they would need to use significant amounts of gold and silver bullion from the Western Hemisphere.

The Indian Ocean World was not only influenced by the encounter with the Atlantic through the vast amounts of silver that flowed into the region. As we have seen, exchange also led, for example, to the adaption and the dramatic spread of agricultural products such as tomatoes, chili peppers, and potatoes. These plants from the Western Hemisphere made amazing inroads and would be widely adopted throughout the cuisines of the Indian Ocean, including China, India, and East Africa.

While the connections with the Indian Ocean World played an important role in the history of the Global Atlantic, for much of the early modern period, Europe's position in the region itself remained marginal. From the 1500s through the 1750s, European efforts at empire-building in the Indian Ocean were not as dramatic as they had been in the Western Hemisphere, where Afro-Eurasian disease had aided the Spanish and other Europeans to claim vast amounts of territory for their crowns. Portuguese efforts in the sixteenth century were largely confined to coastal forts and their surrounding territories. In the seventeenth century, while making some territorial inroads in Java and on other islands in Southeast Asia, the Dutch remained relatively minor players in the region. For much of the eighteenth century, French and British efforts at trade and empire-building in India also were secondary developments in the history of the subcontinent.

The European presence in the Indian Ocean World was often disruptive to traditional trading cultures. For instance, the Portuguese and later the Dutch trade systems in the region were, in part, built on looting and extracting tribute from local states. The Portuguese and the Dutch, at times, acted more like pirates than merchants when they raided Indian Ocean ships and attempted to control sea lanes and cities.

It is important, however, not to exaggerate the economic impact of the limited European presence on Asian and African societies in the Indian Ocean World during the early modern period. Local merchants and traders continued to virtually hold a monopoly on the overland trade routes

Theodorus de Bry's painting shows a fantastical depiction of "cannibals"—some hairy or with weird skin. Like much of the cultural production in art and writing in the sixteenth century, this image provides insights into Europeans' imaginations about the so called "New World," rather than a realistic depiction of the indigenous peoples of the Americas.

Source: Wikimedia Commons. 1592. Theodorus de Bry's America Tertia Pars. http://commons.wikimedia.org/wiki/File:Theodore_de_Bry_-_America_tertia_pars_3.jpg.

of Asia and Africa. European coastal trading posts also heavily depended on local merchants for many of their commercial interactions and access to trade. Furthermore, and while Europeans might have had a comparative advantage at sea, local seafarers persisted as effective players and competitors on most maritime trade routes in the Indian Ocean World. Traders from the South China Sea and the Indian Ocean, such as Chinese, Arabs, Javanese, Swahilis, Malay, Persians, and Indians, continued to play an important role and profited significantly from the integrated and extended trading networks of the Indian Ocean system. This would remain a reality until the coming of the steamship in the nineteenth century, a development that revolutionized global trade.[5]

Europe and the Global Atlantic Intellectual Encounter

The cross-cultural encounters resulting from Europe's maritime expansion in the Western Hemisphere and in the Afro-Eurasian world, brought not only highly desired trade goods to the continent, but it also significantly influenced the intellectual life there. Overseas expansion led, according to historian Olive Patricia Dickason, to a "rage to know" in Europe. Some Europeans craved knowledge about far-away places, specifically about the people, animal and plant life there. Yet a significant portion of this cultural production, in the form of essays, books, images, and other artworks were fantastical fabrications. Throughout the early modern period, European writers and artists produced pieces that showed one-footed men, humans with faces in their chest, with large ears, and with hairy, fury, scaly, or feathery skin. They also drew images of monsters and other invented animal creatures as well as plants. One particular obsession of sixteenth-century Europeans, as we can see in the depiction of the indigenous peoples of the Americas by Theodorus de Bry, was to show some of the people they encountered as cannibals. At times, Europeans, in their efforts to make sense of the cultural meeting with often perplexingly different peoples and environments, had a taste for the exotic, the bizarre, and the grotesque. These were perceived oddities that were often a testimony of the vibrant imagination of Europeans, rather than a reflection of reality of the cultures and the places that Europeans encountered.[6]

The woodcut print by the Renaissance artist Albrecht Dürer, called the "Rhinocerus," provides us a unique glimpse into the dynamics of the processes of cultural creation and imagination in Europe about the overseas encounter with the Indian Ocean World. The image was produced in 1515 and was based on a real creature, which the Portuguese colonial official and major architect of Portugal's fledgling empire in the Indian Ocean World, Alfonso d'Albuquerque, had been given as a gift by the Sultan of Gujarat, a state located on the western coast of the Indian subcontinent. D'Albuquerque decided to send the rhinoceros to Portugal as a special gift to his king. The animal survived the 120-day long trip with lay-overs in Mozambique, St. Helena, and on the Azores. The rhinoceros' arrival was celebrated by European writers, artists, and intellectuals, who considered the animal as proof of the writings of the ancient Roman writer and thinker Pliny who had written about the existence of the rhinoceros in his influential book *Natural History.* This find seemed to confirm the knowledge of the ancient Romans, whose writings were of great importance to many of the intellectuals of the period in European history often referred to as the Renaissance.

The rhinoceros, however, did not survive long in Europe. The Portuguese king decided to gift the animal to the Pope in Rome, in hope that this would lead to the pontiff's continued support of Portugal's global empire. Yet, the rhinoceros did not survive the passage. The boat that carried the animal sank and, because it was chained to the deck, it was not able to swim to shore.

Despite its short life in Europe, the rhinoceros became a popular cultural icon of the early sixteenth century. It was the subject of poems, writings, and images—the most famous among them was Dürer's "Rhinocerus." But as we can see in the illustration, the woodcut print that Dürer made

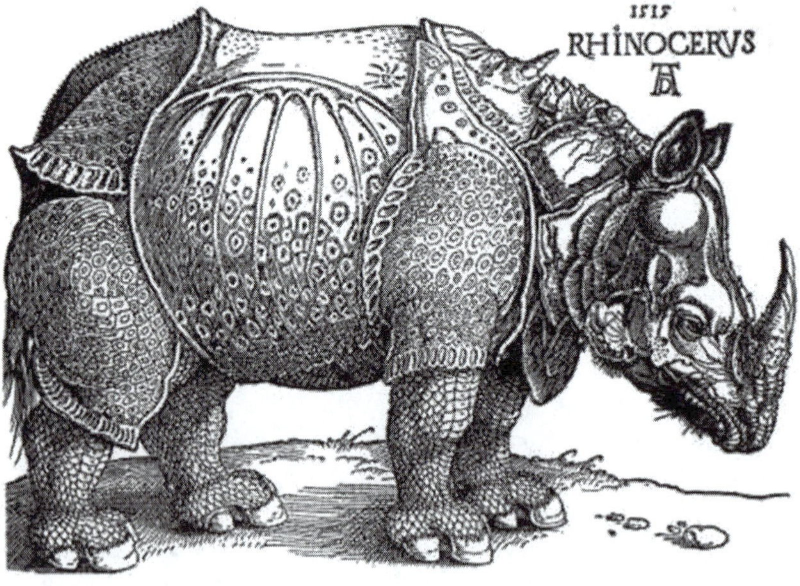

Dürer's Rhino

Source: Wikimedia Commons. 1515. Dürer's "The Rhinoceros". http://commons.wikimedia.org/wiki/File:D%C3%BCrer_-_Rhinoceros.jpg.

in the city of Nuremberg, likely from a sketch by another artist, as Dürer had never seen the actual rhinoceros, left much room for his artistic license and imagination. While the features of the body appear at first glance a lot like a rhinoceros, on further viewing there are some very unnatural things about the beast. It has an extra horn where the back meets the neck. Its skin consists of armor, scales, and swirls. The animal has also very unusual toes. Still Dürer's artistic power and Nuremberg's prominent position in sixteenth-century European commerce, printing, and publishing led to a wide dispersion of the image. Dürer sold several thousand copies of the print during his life, and the prominence of the piece continued after his death. Ironically, with the actual rhinoceros perished at the bottom of the sea, it was Dürer's image that became the realistic depiction of the animal in the minds of many Europeans. Throughout much of the early modern period, Dürer's image survived and continued to be used in biology books as the "accurate" image of this animal, even when more realistic depictions of the South Asian rhinoceros became available.[7]

Portugal's Overseas Expansion and the Roots of the Global Atlantic

The small southwestern European state of Portugal was in many ways the first example of a Global Atlantic Empire. As we have seen, Portugal's commercial activity took its fleet down the entire coast of Africa, connected with Brazil, and also interacted with Arabia, South as well as Southeast Asia, and China. Portugal was an Atlantic nation with a strong eastward focus. Lisbon, with its deep-water harbor, was Portugal's political, commercial, and cultural center. The city became a major center of exchange where expensive goods, including spices, gold, and sugar, came from all over Portugal's fledgling empire in Africa, Asia, and South America. Given its relative size and power, Portugal was nonetheless able to organize a Global Atlantic maritime commercial and colonial empire with holdings spread out all over the world.[8]

Like the European nation-states that followed, the Portuguese used violence to establish themselves in the Indian Ocean. Vasco Da Gama's initial expedition (1497–99) produced the first gun battles with some of the Swahili city-states on Africa's eastern coast. Da Gama and his men also violently captured several emissaries from the Swahili city of Malindi and used these hostages to blackmail the Malindians into providing their fleet with a navigator who could guide them to Calicut on the Malabar Coast of southwestern India. Once there, Da Gama and his men quickly realized that the trade goods they had brought were not equal to the quality of merchandise available in the markets of Calicut. Despite these circumstances, the small exploratory fleet was able to secure a small cargo of spices, which proved extremely profitable upon their return to Portugal.

Even this initial modest voyage proved how lucrative this new route to India could be for the Portuguese, and the Italian city-states of Venice and Genoa immediately saw the implications. When the Portuguese mariner Pedro Alvares Cabral arrived in Lisbon on July 31, 1501, with a haul of spices and gold, the Venetians and Genovese were filled with panic. "This," wrote an early sixteenth-century Venetian observer, "was considered very bad news for Venice. . . . Truly the Venetian merchants are in a bad way." [9] Subsequent Portuguese fleets that set out into the Indian Ocean increased dramatically in size and firepower. The Portuguese pursued a strategy of striking quickly against strategic maritime locations, occupying them when possible, and trying to keep them in their possession by reinforcing them with fortified structures. The Portuguese also attacked and plundered the unarmed merchant ships of the Indian Ocean World. Where European products failed to attract interest, these aggressive strategies became effective ways to obtain Asian products and control the maritime trade routes of the Indian Ocean. Once established in the region, they used their naval strength and sea port maritime empire to establish what was fundamentally an extortion scheme, where Asian mariners were forced to purchase "protective" passes or permits called *cartazes.* The Venetians, as it turned out, were right to be worried about Portugal's new routes to Asia as the supply of pepper in the markets of Alexandria (Egypt) dropped precipitously within just a few years. The Portuguese had cornered the market.

The Swahili city-states of East Africa and their unarmed trading vessels would be among the first to experience the impact of the new Portuguese efforts of monopoly building and attempts at conquest. For centuries the various coastal city-states competed with each other to maintain their status as centers of Indian Ocean trade. Trans-regional traders from the Arabian Peninsula, Persia, and Gujarat, among others, traded and intermarried with the local Bantu-speaking peoples of East Africa. This cultural exchange helped shape a cosmopolitan Swahili culture whose language, Ki Swahili, is grammatically a Bantu language featuring considerable Arabic and Persian loan words, and whose cuisine, to this day, features striking similarities to that of India and the Arabian peninsula. Islam came to the region through trade connections around 900 and the religion became an important element of Swahili identity. The city-states traded a wide array of goods into the Indian Ocean trade network, including ivory, animal skins, mangrove poles, slaves from the interior, and, especially in the city-state of Kilwa located in modern Mozambique, East African gold from the Great Zimbabwe region. The money made from the trade was evident in the Swahili's fine coral stone homes, the finest of which featured elaborate baths and rows of Chinese porcelain along the walls. In the 1300s, the homes of affluent Swahilis were among the most sophisticated and livable in the world. Gaspar Correa who traveled to the region with Vasco da Gama wrote of the city of Kilwa:

> The city comes down to the shore, and is entirely surrounded by a wall and towers, within which there are maybe 12,000 inhabitants. The country all round is very luxurious with many trees and gardens of all sorts of vegetables, citrons, lemons, and the best sweet oranges that were ever seen. . . . The streets of the city are very narrow, as the houses are very high, of three and four stories, and one can run along the tops of them upon the terraces . . . and in the port there were many ships.[10]

The obvious wealth of the region motivated the Portuguese to again return, bringing with them a worldview that included crusading and trade monopolizing through violence.

In 1502, da Gama returned to the Swahili Coast with fourteen armed ships and demanded a large ransom from the Sultan of Kilwa. He later went on to Calicut where he bombarded the city and sank a Muslim pilgrim ship returning from Mecca killing all 300 civilians aboard. But it was in 1505 when the Portuguese fleet commander Francisco de Almeida, a veteran of the 1492 *Reconquista* of Granada, ordered the most brutal attacks on the Swahili city-states.

First, the Portuguese sacked the southern city-state of Kilwa and established a fort in the area. After that the Portuguese attacked the city-state of Mombasa in today's Kenya where they burned and ransacked the city, crushing the Swahili resistance. Over 1,500 people were killed including women and children, and large amounts of the city's stock in silk and cotton fabrics, as well as expensive carpets, were plundered by the Portuguese invaders.

This pattern of violence repeated itself in other sections of the Indian Ocean World. The Portuguese conquered the strategic city of Hormuz in 1508, which put them in the position of controlling the Persian Gulf. In 1510, Portuguese forces took Goa on the western coast of India, a key access point to trade on the Indian subcontinent. In 1511, the Portuguese captured Malacca, which is today Melaka in Malaysia, giving them control over the critical Strait of Melaka, the central shipping lane that linked the Indian subcontinent to Southeast Asia and China, which lay between the Malay Peninsula and the island of Sumatra in modern Indonesia. The Portuguese attacked and plundered various other Indian Ocean port cities and raided Asian, Arab, and Swahili ships in an effort to establish their *Estado da India*—a term sometimes employed by the Portuguese to describe their maritime Indian Ocean empire.

Despite the speed and breadth of these conquests, however, the authority of the Portuguese in the region remained limited. The *Estado da India* that Portuguese colonial officials envisioned was a tentative, vague, and often imagined rule. Generally, because of their small population in the area, Portuguese forces had to rely on the military and strategic assistance of local populations. This was the case, for example, with the capture of Malacca, when members of the Chinese diaspora community there provided vital support to the European invaders, and during the capture of Goa, when Alfonso de Albuquerque allied his forces with those of a local warlord against the ruler of Bjiapur to wrest control of the region. The long-term survival of several of the small Portuguese colonies frequently depended on the acceptance of their presence by local rulers. Again a case in point of this was Goa, which became the center of power in the Portuguese *Estado da India.* It survived as a colony because it was tolerated by the elites of the Mughal Empire. They saw the Portuguese as another trade diaspora in the region, saw the benefit of increased competition, and recognized the value of the trade goods the settlement brought to the region. Moreover, while the Portuguese certainly had clear advantages in maritime military engagements against Asian and African fleets, they were not able to impose an outright supremacy. For instance, in 1516, the Portuguese failed to take over the strategic port of Aden during one of the many naval engagements that the Iberian state fought with the rapidly declining Mamluk state of Egypt. The successful capture of Aden would have provided the small European maritime power a stranglehold over the Red Sea. Yet, the Portuguese failed to do so throughout the sixteenth century. After Mamluk Egypt was conquered by the Ottoman Empire in 1517, the rising power of the eastern Mediterranean and southwest Asia, also effectively blocked Portuguese attempts to take control of the Red Sea.

The overall impact of the Portuguese maritime empire on the economy of the sixteenth-century Indian Ocean World was also limited. European technology and infrastructure in the early modern period had their shortcomings and the Portuguese were only one player among many in the region. As indicated earlier, the voyage from Europe to various Indian Ocean destinations was quite a risky endeavor. From 1500 to 1634, for example, an estimated 28 percent of all Portuguese ships that sailed this route are believed to have been lost at sea. Hence, the volume of ships that participated in Indian Ocean trade during this period was relatively small. Between 1500 and 1634, there was only about an average of seven ships per year that left from Portugal to destinations in the *Estado da India.* Even accounting for the above mentioned high attrition rate of ships, only an average of four out of seven boats returned to Portugal—a total of 470 ships—a discrepancy that seems to indicate that over time a decent-sized Portuguese fleet emerged in the Indian Ocean itself. Even when we account for the outbound losses of ships at sea, about 30 percent of the Portuguese vessels that reached the Indian Ocean remained there permanently. This sizeable fleet certainly participated actively in regional trade by transporting local products, but the Portuguese presence was not large enough to dominate Indian Ocean trade in the sixteenth and seventeenth centuries. Moreover, at times, Portuguese merchants used Asian ships to transport their goods, just as Asian traders occasionally shipped their goods on Portuguese ships, which were often manned by mixed European, Asian, and African crews.[11]

Portugal lagged behind many of the major Asian economies of the Indian Ocean World, which had different commercial priorities than the small Iberian state. The great empires of the Muslim world: the Ottoman Turkish Empire, extending at its height throughout much of North Africa, Iraq, and the Arabian Peninsula; the Safavid Empire of Persia; and the Mughal Empire that controlled much of the Indian subcontinent, were all large agrarian land-based empires. These empires were predominantly tied to the overland trading networks of Asia, and maritime trade, therefore, played a less central role in their strategic interests. The Portuguese state was not able to muster a land army to challenge these formidable empires, and thus, seeking a more accommodating approach with local states often proved a more successful strategy for accessing the extremely profitable trade in spices, precious stones, and various other goods, which, by the second half of the sixteenth century, were often paid for in silver and gold from the Atlantic World.

The Portuguese were also the first among the European states to reach Chinese waters in the early sixteenth century, which was more than half a century before Spain established their colonial outpost in Manila. Using the strategy that had served their interests on the Swahili Coast and other areas of their expansion, the Portuguese were initially aggressive in their attempt to strong-arm the Chinese into favorable trade policies. This policy was unsuccessful against the formidable Ming Chinese imperial state, which retaliated by rejecting and detaining a Portuguese embassy in (1517–21), expelling Portuguese from Chinese soil, and by defeating the Iberians in several sea battles in 1521–22.[12]

The Portuguese encounter with China began a long and complex history of Sino-Western relations in East Asia. Although China at the time has been described in conventional Western historiography as resistant to change and having an isolationist attitude toward the West, the historian John Wills provides an alternative explanation for Sino-European relations before 1800. He characterizes Chinese imperial policies as "defensive." He describes "Ming-Qing China as an arena of immense and restless economic and cultural energies, in which political order was highly valued but perceived as fragile and constantly at risk, and the dangers of foreign linkages to these restless energies were especially feared."[13] Both Ming and later Qing officials worried that interactions with foreigners could threaten the security of their empire. Chinese officials were also aware of attacks on Chinese diaspora populations abroad and as a result, harbored additional wariness towards Europeans. Hence, China vigorously opposed the often violent encroachments by Europeans on its territory or into its sphere of influence. In addition, imperial officials were concerned about limiting European access to their markets. International trade meant high profits for the coffers of the Chinese state, and imperial officials had no desire to give up this lucrative revenue stream. Thus, while "China did not always welcome the new arrivals with open arms," explains the historian Joann Waley-Cohen this "approach arose more out of pragmatism than out of reactionary conservatism or primitive parochialism of which Europeans dismissively accused China."[14]

Both within the Ming and Qing Dynasties, however, the imperial state was only one of many political and economic players in China. Local officials and merchants, especially those on the coast, often pursued their own interests in conjunction with, or despite, imperial objectives. The Chinese provinces in the coastal southeast, for example, throughout the Ming and Qing Empires, as late as the eighteenth century, were active players in the global maritime trade: exporting silks, porcelains, and other products while importing cotton, spices, sandalwood, and, of course, silver. Furthermore, the early modern Sino-European trade was only a marginal part of China's economic activity. The early modern Chinese economy had a vast internal trade within the borders of the empire and was a major player in the highly lucrative trans-East Asian overland commercial exchange.

After their initial violent entrance in the region failed, Portuguese merchants were confined to playing an informal role in illicit and private trade. Commercial interaction was often conducted through Asian middlemen or by Portuguese traveling on Asian ships, often through the Southeast Asian port of Melaka. Realizing the error in their initial strategy, the Portuguese attempted to improve their strained relations with Chinese imperial officials; they changed their aggressive stance and assisted Chinese authorities in various campaigns against pirates. This strategy eventually paid off. In the 1550s, Chinese officials allowed the Portuguese to settle in Macau, a settlement on China's southern coast. Westerners were not allowed to venture into the Chinese interior. In return for the trading base, the Portuguese had to pay rent in silver, which was an arrangement that would continue until the mid-nineteenth century, and Macau only officially returned to China in 1999.[15]

In the mid-1500s the Portuguese also became the first European power to initiate trade with Japan, and the Iberian nation soon functioned as an intermediary in the exchange between the two acrimonious economic powers of the region: China and Japan. By the early sixteenth century, maritime trade between the two Asian states was restrained by Japan's domestic preoccupation with a series of civil wars and the Ming Chinese perception that Japanese merchants were increasingly involved in piracy and smuggling. For the last decades of the sixteenth century and during the first decades of the seventeenth century, the Portuguese stepped in as middlemen in the Sino-Japanese trade. They brought Japanese silver and copper to China and Chinese trade goods such as porcelain and silk to Japan. Participating in this inter-Asian trade enabled the Portuguese to purchase goods that they in turn sold on the European market for a significant profit.

Despite their role as middlemen between the two regional powers, the Portuguese position in Japan remained fragile and was soon challenged. A major reason for this was that the Portuguese merchants were accompanied by Christian missionaries. As they did in the Americas, Africa, India, and other locations throughout their Global Atlantic Portuguese Empire, Jesuit priests taught Christian principles and converted the local people to their Catholic faith. In Japan, an estimated 100,000 locals, though this number might likely have been exaggerated by the missionaries, accepted Christianity without much official Japanese interest. However, by the first decades of the seventeenth century, this changed. Several of the shogun, the de facto rulers of the island nation, came to see the Western Christian presence and their mainly peasant converts as a threat to Japanese sovereignty. The shogun began to restrict, and eventually forbade the religion as well as the presence of foreigners on the island. After a rebellion led by persecuted Christians was crushed in the mid-1630s, those who refused to renounce Christianity were killed or went into hiding. Following this rebellion, Japan began an extended period of isolation known as Sakoku, which would last over 200 years. The Portuguese were entirely replaced by the Dutch as the island's major foreign trading partner and the Dutch presence in Japan was extremely restricted to a small artificially built island in Nagasaki Bay called Deshima. Though Japan was not entirely detached from the rest of the world during this period, interactions with foreigners were strictly controlled by the elites.[16]

The Dutch Global Atlantic: Spices, Violence, Genocide, and the Limits of European Power

Japan was not the only place where the Dutch actively challenged the Portuguese trade dominance. It was, in fact, part of their global strategy to confront the centers of Iberian commerce not only in maritime Asia, but throughout the Atlantic World, including Europe, the Americas, and Africa. The Netherlands became the third European state, after Portugal and Spain, to establish a foothold in Asia and to access the profitable eastern trade.

The Dutch entered the Indian Ocean World, at least in part, as a result of European politics. For much of the sixteenth century, considerable parts of the modern nation-state of the Netherlands, as well as the Dutch-speaking regions of modern Belgium known as Flanders, were ruled by Habsburg Spain. In the second half of the 1560s, the Dutch-speaking populations went into a revolt against their rulers complaining about absenteeism and cronyism in the appointment of high-level officials. Revolts in Flanders were quickly subdued by Habsburg forces, but a Dutch rebellion persisted in the Netherlands into the mid-seventeenth century. For much of this period, the Dutch United Provinces functioned as an independent state. The Dutch not only challenged Spain, but after the Spanish annexation of its Iberian neighbor in 1580, Portugal too. Although Spain and Portugal maintained separate identities from 1580 to 1640, a period of time referred to as the Iberian Union, they cooperated closely on certain policies; one of which was banning the Dutch from the port of Lisbon, then the most important access point for Asian goods in Europe. This motivated the Dutch not only to search for alternative routes to Asia, but also to gain profits while weakening the empires of Spain and Portugal. The Dutch saw the plundering of Iberian overseas colonies as legitimate and lucrative. In the new Global Atlantic, war between two relatively small regions of Europe was played out in battles across the world.[17]

The Dutch Empire was run by a joint-stock company called the VOC (the *Verenigde Oost-Indische Compagnie*—the United East India Company or, as it is conventionally known, the Dutch East India Company). The joint-stock company was created in late sixteenth and early seventeenth century Europe to allow multiple investors to share the risks as well as the profits of overseas commerce. Joint stock companies became a tool through which merchants could pool their resources together to finance trade. In northwestern Europe, it became the major way to invest in overseas trade, and it was these companies (the world's first private corporations) that took a leading role in European expansion and empire-building in the 1600s and 1700s.

In addition to the Dutch VOC, Britain, Denmark, and Sweden also formed their own companies to focus on different regions of the burgeoning Global Atlantic and Indian Ocean trading systems. There were West India companies that focused on Atlantic trade, and Levant companies that concentrated on Mediterranean exchanges, as well as a variety of others. Most of the European East India companies, like the VOC, were initially interested in the profitable South East Asian spice trade but, over time, several East India companies, such as that of Britain, also gradually moved into the Indian subcontinent, where they competed with the Portuguese for the trade in pepper and eventually South Asian textiles. Joint-stock companies financed and provided a significant portion of the Global Atlantic trade of the seventeenth and eighteenth centuries. By bringing particular products from around the world to Europe and its colonies, they helped shape early modern consumer culture in the Atlantic World.[18]

Joint-stock companies aided in the process of privatizing empire-building. The fleets that propelled the Dutch overseas trade and expansion in the late sixteenth century were outfitted by companies controlled by extremely wealthy merchants. The Dutch ships that returned with foreign goods made huge profits; attracting both more investors and competitors. The Dutch elite began to see the fierce rivalry among its merchants as a threat to their strategic, military, and economic interests. For instance, the indigenous rulers in Southeast Asia learned to play the Dutch companies against each other and the Portuguese during trade agreements; raising levies and fees and making it more costly for them to trade spices in the region. This squeeze coincided with a greater availability of spices beginning in the late sixteenth and into the seventeenth centuries in Europe, which also led to a decline in the prices that merchants charged. Taken together, these factors led the officials in the Dutch Republic to push for the consolidation of various companies active in the easterly trade. It was from this amalgamation that in 1602 the VOC was created.

The Dutch authorities granted the new company remarkable power. It was to hold a monopoly on all eastern trade, had a license to create colonies, to build fortifications, to engage in naval and land battles, and to seize enemy ships. Significantly, it was also allowed to print money. Like several other European companies that emerged to further colonial overseas expansion in the seventeenth and eighteenth centuries, often as a result of the effectiveness of the Dutch company, the VOC was administratively, militarily, politically, judicially, and economically a sovereign entity in the areas it controlled.[19]

The VOC soon used these new powers to consolidate their hold on the eastern spice trade by aggressively obtaining colonial footholds in Southeast Asia. To do so, the historian John Wills writes, they "brought to Asian waters a level of centralized political and commercial decision making and bureaucratization of violence far beyond that of the Portuguese."[20]

The company initially established a base in Bantam on the island of Java but they found that the established local sultan could not be forced to comply with their demands. In 1618, Jan Pieterszoon Coen, the VOC's governor-general who oversaw much of the company's operations in the Indian Ocean World, decided to move further up the coast to Jayawirkata (today Jakarta in Indonesia). When part of the local population resisted the VOC's plans, Coen razed the city to the ground. On its ruins he built the new Dutch settlement of Batavia, which featured many architectural elements of the Netherlands complete with canals, windmills, and houses with steep gables.

Even in Batavia, however, the Dutch had to adapt to local realities. So far from their native country, the Dutch were dependent on other communities for the city's survival. Along with various other European migrants, the city was home to local Javanese, Chinese, Indian, and various other Asian merchants, artisans, concubines, and prostitutes. The VOC also claimed a monopoly on slaving rights in East Africa and from there they imported a significant number of slaves, mainly from Madagascar, to work in the settlement. Over time, intermarriage in the colony led to the rise of a sizable "mestizo" or mixed population.

Like the Spanish in Manila, the Dutch in Batavia had a complicated relationship with the various communities they depended on. The VOC's relationship with the Chinese provides an example. As in the Philippines, the Chinese merchants traded without the protection of the powerful imperial government; the late Ming and later the Qing Dynasties had themselves a contentious relationship with the overseas Chinese merchants. So despite the power of the Chinese state, the ethnic Chinese in Batavia were often treated as second-class citizens by the Dutch. Because of their access to coveted Chinese goods, Coen took steps to attract independent Chinese settlers and merchants to Batavia, but these actions were not necessarily beneficial to the traders themselves. For instance, the VOC commanded a blockade of the ports of Macao and Manila as part of the Dutch's global war on the Iberian states, but, also because Coen believed that this strategy would divert private Chinese merchants to seek trade with the VOC stronghold. While attempting to entice merchants to their borders, the VOC was engaged in several conflicts with China, during which the company's soldiers were ordered to kidnap Chinese residents along the coast for use in manual labor. In part through these tactics, Batavia did harbor a significant and thriving Chinese diaspora but it was often in spite of the distrust, discrimination, segregation, and acts of violence they often faced at the hands of the Dutch.[21]

The dearth of eligible Dutch wives created another opportunity for intercultural interactions. Because the VOC's settlements were widely dispersed, dangerous to reach, and relatively isolated, few Dutch women ventured to travel to the Indian Ocean World. Among the small number of Western women that had made the voyage during the early years of Dutch colonization, most had been recruited in brothels and orphanages in the Netherlands. Thus, Dutch men looked to alternative sources for mates in the colonial empire. In maritime Southeast Asia, for instance, Dutch colonists often entered into unions with local women. The wives usually came from long-established family lineages where women had been successful merchants for many generations before the arrival of Europeans. Merchant women in Southeast Asian societies had exerted control over their property, had a considerable say in their choice of husbands, and, due to frequent and long travel that accompanied their families' commercial activities, had been raised in a micro-culture that was more tolerant about extra-marital relations. Many of these female merchants were quite wealthy with substantial property, and some of their mothers or grandmothers had already intermarried with Portuguese men.

Both Dutch men and Southeast Asian or mestizo women pursued these unions. For local women, having a Dutch spouse could mean special access to trade. European husbands could provide some protection to their business in a diverse and complex intercultural commercial world, which often could turn violent. In addition, having a husband that was a counselor or high colonial official could help protect and shield a local merchant's trade activities from the Dutch East India Company's rules, regulations, and monopolies. To VOC officials, on the other hand, having a local merchant wife could have substantial economic advantages. Servants of the Dutch East India Company generally were poorly paid and with the assistance of a go-between local wife who had plenty of contacts, connections, and linguistic abilities, an official could improve his personal wealth by participating in illicit trade that came, of course, at the expense of their employer's interests.

Documentary evidence also suggests that some colonists garnered or attempted to obtain their Asian or mestizo wives' fortunes. There are several incidents where Dutch men utilized the colonial legal system, which only poorly protected the rights of indigenous or mixed-race women, to take their partners' wealth. This was an act frequently committed before these men returned back to the Netherlands, often to re-settle there, rich, with a new Dutch wife more fitting to European norms. Furthermore, on occasion, Dutch colonists wrote home about their efforts to "tame" their Asian or mestizo wives who were often accustomed to more independence than their European counterparts. Despite attempts from within the power structures of the VOC and the Dutch Reformed Church to put an end to these marriages, relationships of this kind persisted into the nineteenth century when industrial inventions such as the steamboat and the telegraph more closely connected Dutch colonial holdings with the Netherlands and Dutch women became a more prevalent element of colonial society.[22]

Regardless of these examples of accommodation, the VOC's policy featuring a systematic use of violence for commercial ends that was used on Java was applied to other locations across the Dutch seaborne empire. In Southeast Asia, the most egregious example of devastating violence took place in the Banda archipelago in today's Indonesia as means of achieving a monopoly on nutmeg. The VOC had attempted to monopolize various factions of the spice trade but because of indigenous resistance, the smuggling of contraband, the wide availability of the products they tried to monopolize, and European and Asian competition, they were initially unsuccessful. Nutmeg, however, was exclusively grown on the tiny Banda archipelago where the VOC since 1610 had squeezed the local population in pursuit of their profits. In 1621, however, to gain total control of the islands, Coen ordered a VOC force of about 2,000, consisting of Dutch regulars, slave soldiers, and Japanese mercenaries, to brutalize the local population. The VOC forces killed a large portion of the population and sold the rest into slavery. It is estimated that only about 1,000 Bandanese, of a pre-genocide population of about 15,000, survived the massacre. In the aftermath of the slaughter, the Dutch imposed a plantation system on the islands that was influenced by the forced labor system used in the Americas. The Dutch maintained a monopoly on nutmeg for nearly 200 years, until the Napoleonic Wars when the British briefly controlled the islands and appropriated some of the nutmeg trees to replant in their own colonies. Although the European efforts at empire building in the Indian Ocean World were often more peripheral to the power structure of the region than those in the Americas, they often featured the same patterns of genocidal violence and the use of forced labor that, at least in part, defined the history of European colonization in the Western Hemisphere.

Despite its aggressive posturing and the use of violence, it took the VOC several decades to consolidate its hold on its widely dispersed maritime empire, and a significant portion of its successes came as a result of Portuguese losses. The Dutch took the Indian Ocean island of Mauritius from the Portuguese and permanently settled the island in 1638, where they harvested ebony trees and experimented with sugar production. In 1641, the Dutch took the strategic city of Malacca and a base on Ceylon in modern-day Sri Lanka in the 1650s from where they were able to expand to establish trade forts on the South Asian mainland. In the early 1660s they took the city of Cochin from the Portuguese, and, after some fighting, the company was able to establish control over the Malabar region of the Indian subcontinent; an area they would control until they lost it to the British in 1795. To secure their Indian Ocean shipping routes the Dutch established what had long been their refreshment station on the tip of Southern Africa into an official colony in 1652. It was not always easy for the VOC to dislocate the Portuguese because of close relationships they had formed with various local populations, which was the reason why the Portuguese were able to maintain control of certain key holdings such as Goa and Macau.[23]

The VOC brought their commercial and colonial ambitions into Chinese waters as well, only to learn about the limits of their power. As we saw above, they had a complicated relationship with the region. As part of their failed campaign to wrest Macau from the Portuguese in 1622, the Dutch attempted several unsuccessful assaults onto the Chinese mainland in an effort to force the Chinese to accept a VOC trading foothold in the region. They also raided numerous Chinese ships en route to Manila. From 1622 to 1624, the Dutch attempted to establish a foothold on the Penghu archipelago, located between modern-day Taiwan and the Chinese mainland, only to be forced by the Chinese to leave. Finally, the VOC had to settle for an arrangement the Chinese offered them in 1604; a trading post on Taiwan.

In the 1630s and 1640s, several developments occurred that would strengthen the VOC's position on Taiwan. For one, the company's trading relationship with the wealthy and powerful merchant, mariner, and pirate Admiral Zheng Zhilong of Fujian prospered into a lucrative commerce. Second, the Dutch were now well positioned to expand their trade with the Japanese. This trade provided them access to silver, which the Dutch traded from the Japanese in exchange for various Chinese goods and for the deer skins that they hunted on Taiwan. Third, the VOC pursued several violent campaigns against the island's aboriginal groups, which opened up agricultural land for rice and sugar production, farms that would be largely cultivated by Chinese peasants who also began to settle on Taiwan during this period.

Still, by the mid-seventeenth century, the Dutch control over Taiwan began to loosen as mainland Chinese influences were increasingly being felt. Spurred in part by a war between the Ming and Manchu invaders, who would later form the Qing Dynasty, over who would rule China, the Chinese population on the island increased from 4,000 to 14,000 in the 1640s. Like the Spanish in Manila, the VOC in Taiwan imposed several taxes and tolls on the Chinese, and tax collectors generally treated the community disrespectfully. In 1652, a poorly organized Chinese uprising broke out. Without much effort at discriminating between insurgent or peaceful bystander, the VOC responded with a violent campaign, killing over 3,000 Chinese. In part, as a result of this massacre, which angered many Chinese on the mainland and in the diaspora, Zheng Zhilong's son, Zheng Chenggong, who had tightly controlled the maritime trade with Taiwan, began to starve the Dutch for profits. Moreover, Taiwan's sugar exports to Europe were also increasingly undermined by cheaper Brazilian competition, hurting another source of income in the colony. In a final blow to the Dutch presence, between 1661 and 1662, a massive Chinese army from Fujian, led by Zheng Chenggong, forced the Dutch to capitulate and Taiwan became ruled by the Chinese.[24]

As the status of its trading bases expanded and contracted over time, the VOC continued its pursuit of profits. Alongside nutmeg, other spices, silk, and several other Indian Ocean World products, the VOC also began to trade in coffee. The coffee bean, originating from Ethiopia, had been enjoyed in the Muslim World for several centuries and became known in early modern Europe as well. In the early seventeenth century, coffee began to gradually gain in popularity throughout Europe and other parts of the Atlantic World. The VOC was able to profit from this development by purchasing its coffee for Europe directly from Mocah, in modern-day Yemen on the Arabian Peninsula. Thus, they sidestepped the Muslim commercial interests in southwest Asia and northern Africa, which had until then dominated that trade with Europe. The Dutch eventually broke Yemen's monopoly on the plant's cultivation when they started to grow their own coffee, beginning in the late 1650s on Ceylon, now modern Sri

Lanka. In later years they expanded this production to the island of Java and to their colony of Suriname in South America. Over time other Europeans followed the lead of the VOC and grew coffee in plantations throughout their colonial holdings around the world.[25]

We have seen how the VOC looked to the Indian Ocean trade system for its substantial profits, but their efforts in Asia were also supported by Dutch actions in the Atlantic World; underscoring, to a degree, the Global Atlantic nature of the Dutch seaborne empire in the seventeenth century. The European nation of the Netherlands did not, within its borders, have many goods desired by Asian markets, which would allow them to participate in sustainable Indian Ocean trade. They looked, at least in part, to the Atlantic World for the wealth to finance their commercial activity in the Indian Ocean, as well as for goods that could be traded there.

To carve out for themselves some of the riches of the Americas, the Dutch, like the English and French, began in the late sixteenth century to challenge the position of the Spanish Empire through piracy. By the 1620s, however, the Dutch strategy in the Atlantic became more systemically organized. Inspired and influenced by the success of the VOC, the political power structure of the Dutch Republic, the States-General, granted a charter to the *Geoctroyeerde Westindische Compagnie*, which translates into English as the Chartered West India Company and is often known by the acronym GWIC. Because of the European war with the Habsburg Empire, but also because it was extremely profitable, the new joint-stock company focused its efforts especially on challenging the forts and colonies run by Spain and Portugal. The Dutch challenged the Spanish and Portuguese directly by establishing colonies on several Caribbean islands and on the Latin American mainland, and sought to gain footholds in western Africa. Dutch efforts were spurred by a desire to access slaves, sugar, cacao, and some of the vast quantities of silver being extracted from Spanish colonies. The GWIC sponsored corsairs like Pieterszoon Heyn and his crew, who pirated a massive sum of Peruvian and Mexican silver from the Spanish treasury.

Beyond outright piracy, the Dutch found two major channels through which they could access silver. They developed an illicit slave trade with the Iberian colonies of the Western Hemisphere, which they procured from their holdings in western Africa. In the age of the economic theory of mercantilism, which held that wealth was gained by hording more gold and silver than your rival nations, the countries of Europe generally forbade their colonies and colonists from trading with outside entities. This policy was often ignored, and Iberians at times paid the Dutch for the slaves in silver and this became a major source of bullion for the GWIC in the Americas. The GWIC's silver returned to the Netherlands where much of it would be used by the VOC to purchase Asian goods, some of them from the VOC's holdings, but many also from China. "In the half century from 1610 through 1660," writes the historian Timothy Brooks, "the headquarters of the VOC authorized the export of just slightly under fifty million guilders—almost five hundred tons of silver." The other source of Dutch silver, mentioned above, also highlights the continued global importance of the Chinese economy in this period. The massive influx of silver from the Americas was matched in the volume of silver that the VOC ferried to China from Japan through the system of trade they had established with the island nation in the 1640s.[26]

Apart from silver, the Dutch West India Company was interested in gaining access to the lucrative fur trade. These pelts, especially those of the beaver because of their ability to hold their shape and their water-resistant properties, were highly valued in Europe, especially for hat making. Fur and animal skins could also fetch a good price in various global markets. The Dutch established colonial footholds in what are today the states of New York, Connecticut, as well as in the North American mid-Atlantic region from where they could access profitable trade. While violence was part of the Dutch strategy to push their way both into the Atlantic and the Indian Ocean World, in North America, Dutch colonization relied on a strategy of accommodation with the local communities. For instance, the Dutch closely traded with the Mahican nation, the Haudenosaunee (Iroquois) Confederacy, and several other Native American groups to obtain fur; an exchange that proved both profitable and destructive for Native Americans. In 1664, the GWIC was expelled from the region by the British, which corresponded to a general weakening of the Dutch position in the Atlantic World in the 1660s and 1670s when they began to lose holdings throughout the region.[27]

The British and French Global Atlantic

The decline of the Dutch Empire corresponded to some degree with the rise of British and French power in the Atlantic. These two European states gradually became major participants in overseas expansion. They initially faced difficulties in establishing their own colonies and, anxious to benefit from the wealth of the Spanish colonies, they resorted to piracy. Gradually, during the seventeenth and the first half of the eighteenth centuries, they began to consolidate not only an Atlantic empire, but a global one. Despite their humble beginnings, by the second half of the eighteenth century, both states had emerged as the most powerful contenders among the European states.

Keeping with the pattern of their European predecessors, early French and British efforts at trans-Atlantic explorations and empire-building were at least partially motivated by the lure of finding a faster route to access trade in Asia. Many of the North American explorers had the goal of discovering a Northwest Passage that would provide a northern route to Asia. The Genovese born John Cabot, Jacques Cartier, Humphrey Gilbert, and Henry Hudson, were all caught up in this search and even as late as the seventeenth century, Samuel de Champlain, the governor of the French colony in what is today Quebec (Canada), was hoping to find a waterway through North America that would enable France to access the valuable China trade. While neither the French nor the British were ever able to find this elusive passage, their involvement in the region enabled them to build a valuable fur and animal skin trade.[28] Just as the Dutch had found before them, the markets of Europe and Asia valued the pelts and animal skins of the extensive North American woodlands.

It was not until the seventeenth century that the British and French began to pursue colonies in the Americas in a viable fashion and to pay for the endeavor they attempted a variety of revenue-generating activities. In the circum-Caribbean region, they established several colonies that grew sugar as a cash crop. Both nations also gained imperial footholds in North America: the French in what is today Canada, and the British in the Chesapeake Bay (Virginia) and in Massachusetts. In the Chesapeake, the British initially hoped to find gold and silver. Instead the British learned to cultivate a crop indigenous to the Americas—tobacco—though the variety they grew was introduced to the colony by John Rolfe (perhaps most famous for his later marriage to Pocahontas). This tobacco plant came from the Caribbean region and it was a milder type than the plant grown by the local Powhatan Indians. With the success of the crop in the Chesapeake Colony, the British were able to challenge Spain's early dominant position in the tobacco trade. Once the Europeans developed a taste for it, tobacco quickly became a lucrative cash crop on the European market, where it was, given what we know about the plant today, ironically, seen as having medicinal qualities. But tobacco did not only spread to Europe; it became a Global Atlantic consumer good that would be smoked the world over. Although it was often introduced to an area as an elite product, it eventually became a mass commodity enjoyed across the socio-economic spectrum. It thus shared a similar consumption pattern as many of the Global Atlantic commodities that came out of the Americas in this era.

As they had with the Dutch, joint-stock companies also played a role in British and French overseas expansion. The British East India Company (initially the English East India Company until 1707) was charted in 1600 and was initially one of several other companies created around that time in England, but it eventually grew to overtake even the power of the Dutch VOC. As we will see later in the chapter, the British East India Company became, by the 1830s, perhaps the most powerful entity in Asia. In its early days, however, its influence was modest. Although it enjoyed less government oversight than the VOC, the British crown provided it with significantly fewer financial resources at its creation. The French too chartered a West India Company and East India Company in 1664, which would also grow to develop colonies across the Global Atlantic.

As we have seen with the other pre-industrial European empires, the British and French influence in the early modern Indian Ocean World was limited. To be able to purchase pepper, cotton and silk textiles, saltpeter for gunpowder, and diamonds and other gemstones, from China, the Mughal Empire, and other Asian states, the British and French had to pay for them in large amounts of American silver. In South Asia, even in the eighteenth century, when the Mughal Empire was in sharp decline before being eventually replaced by a number of smaller regional states, the European presence remained marginal and their trading forts and operations generally required the permission of local rulers who often saw the various Europeans as simply another trading diaspora that could provide desired goods to their region. Greater competition among merchants, many rulers understood, meant lower prices. Europeans on the Indian subcontinent, just as in other parts of the Indian Ocean World, had to create partnerships with Asian merchants and intermediaries. As with the Dutch in Southeast Asia, in the early days of empire, the French and British traders in South Asia also intermarried with local women and learned Asian languages.[29]

The British East India Company's success was also, to some degree, dependent on the financial backing of wealthy Indians. In Calcutta,

Bombay, and Madras, much of the Anglo-Indian commerce and commercial development was, at least, partially financed by local Indian traders and financiers, many of whom had gained their fortunes in the Indian Ocean trade and saw working with the British company as a means to increasing their affluence. Some, such as Dwarkanath Tagore, came from the uppermost Brahman families, others, such as Motilai Seal and Ram Gopal Ghosh, were the architects of their own fortunes, but they formed alliances with British associates, served on boards, hired Europeans to manage their estates, and wrote large checks for reasons of business and philanthropy. Indians would continue to play a significant role in financing British efforts in South Asia until the mid-nineteenth century.[30]

The Global Atlantic and Asia's Economic Power

As we have seen, the Asian economies, particularly that of China, but also of the Mughal Empire of South Asia, dominated the commerce of the early Global Atlantic. European governments and joint-stock companies competed vigorously with each other and with local Asian traders to carve out a portion of the lucrative trade. The Europeans, including those living in the new American colonies, wanted Asian spices, silk, and coffee, and, in the seventeenth and eighteenth centuries, they demanded cotton textiles from India and tea and porcelain from China. Not having a plethora of domestic goods to trade within the Asian markets, Europeans relied largely, though, as we have seen with the slave and fur trades and will see with the emerald trade, not exclusively, on silver from the Americas to purchase their coveted Asian goods.

This dependence on silver was problematic for the European states, especially those without direct access to silver mines, driving them occasionally, as we have seen, to piracy or, as with the Portuguese and Dutch in Japan and elsewhere, to act as middlemen for silver-rich regions in order to be paid in that precious metal for the transport of their goods. Relying on the expenditure of silver also defied the logic of the mercantilist economic policies that were *en vogue* in Europe at the time, and which argued that the constant loss of bullion would deprive the nation-state of its wealth. As a result, European nation-states constantly tried to locate and develop trade goods that could slow the flow of silver heading to Asia.

Beyond the challenge of how to access silver and the debate about whether it should be spent on items that were seen by some cultural critics as unnecessary—frivolous even—for a productive society, there was criticism from domestic manufacturers, both in Europe and the colonies, that Asian goods cut into their market share. The manufacturers and landed elites, many of whom were members of government, eventually organized to develop the early European protectionist policies that would restrict the import of many foreign goods into Europe, excepting those from their own colonies or monopolies. These developments gradually pushed to reverse the trade imbalance starting in the eighteenth century.

"The Indian Craze": The Global Atlantic and the Trade in South Asian Cotton Textiles

In the early modern period, the demand for Indian Ocean World textiles in the Global Atlantic was one factor that helped push the flow of silver eastward. Asian silk and cotton fabrics were not only popular in Europe, but also in Atlantic Africa, and the Western Hemisphere. The most popular of the Asian textiles in Europe, however, became the "calicoes"—a name taken from the city of Calicut, where Vasco da Gama first landed. These vivid, bright textiles were produced across the subcontinent. Thus, their secondary English name, "Indian stuffs," or the French and Spanish terms, *indienne* and *Indiana*, respectively, provided a slightly more accurate nomenclature. Starting in the seventeenth century, calicoes became available and sought after by European consumers, who were accustomed to the locally produced wool and linens, because they were soft, durable, cheaper than silk, and perhaps most importantly, held their colors even after long use and frequent washing.

The amount of South Asian cotton textiles imported to Europe provides an interesting glimpse into the growing popularity of this trade. In the early 1600s, European merchants tended to purchase only a few yards of calico cloth from the Indian Ocean World. By the mid-seventeenth century, however, this number had risen to an estimated 35–40 million yards per year. In 1684, the British East India Company alone transported 45 million yards of cotton to Atlantic markets, which averages to more than six yards of cloth per person living in Britain at that time. Such rising demand led to a massive increase in cotton fabric production in South Asia. Despite the growing role of the Global Atlantic in South Asia's calico market, European companies and merchants played only a limited role and the region continued to cater to older, more established, markets in Asia and in East Africa.[31] As the numbers of the calico trade above suggest, what initially started out as a high-status luxury item in the early seventeenth century, would, by the early 1700s, become a commonly purchased product in Europe. Some British contemporaries described this phenomenon as the "Indian craze." South Asian cotton fabrics were not only a commodity consumed by the elite, but became widely embraced by a more general public throughout the Global Atlantic to produce clothing, wall coverings, tableware, pillowcases, tissues, sheets, scarfs, curtains, and bedspreads.[32] Indian Ocean textiles, as mentioned in Chapter 2, also played a prominent role in the Atlantic slave trade as an exchange commodity. Furthermore, Native Americans from all over the Western Hemisphere incorporated Asian-made silks and cotton fabrics as part of their dress in the late seventeenth and the early eighteenth centuries.[33]

The new mass consumption of Indian textiles brought with it a series of criticisms from various writers, commentators, intellectuals, and manufacturers. In Britain, some worried that, because noble women now wore the same cloth as their maids and country women, it disrupted social norms and threatened to destabilize the entire class structure. Several Europeans were also concerned that the importation of South Asian textiles, bought in silver, reinforced a trade deficit and, according to mercantilist policies, would impoverish the national European economies. The third great complaint saw the foreign-produced fabrics as a threat to local industries. The wool, linen, and growing cotton textile manufacturing sector, clearly interested in keeping the cheaper, higher quality competition out of their respective countries, lobbied their governments for protectionist measures. Animosity rose to the extent that, in Britain, weavers and wool makers would, on occasion, attack people wearing calico fabrics. Thus, it was in this period that various European states, such as Britain and France, passed laws that undermined the demand and curtailed the import of foreign fabrics. As a result, by the second half of the eighteenth century, much of the trans-Atlantic trade in cotton fabrics was comprised of European made products.[34]

The Global Atlantic Trade and Qing China: Tea, Porcelain, Sugar, and Silver

Like the textiles of South Asia, Chinese goods also became a major feature in the Global Atlantic economy. In the second half of the seventeenth and throughout the eighteenth centuries, Europe continued to look to the Chinese as an important source for silk, porcelain, lacquer goods, and tea.

By the 1500s, when Europeans developed a taste for tea, Chinese farmers had been cultivating and processing tea for many centuries. Tea production had long satisfied the demands of a massive domestic market and had been exported to neighboring regions too. The beverage is the result of an infusion of the leaves of the evergreen tea bush or *Camellia sinensis* plant, which, in China to this day, is grown in the tropical and sub-tropical southern provinces, such as Fujian. The leaves of the tea bush are processed in various ways to create a wide variety of teas, such as green and oolong, traditionally preferred in Asia, and the more oxidated black tea, which became popular in Europe and its colonies.[35]

The British were not the first Europeans to develop a taste for tea, the Portuguese and Dutch, perhaps unsurprisingly given their pioneering roles in the Indian Ocean region, beat them to that distinction. Nevertheless, when in the eighteenth century the British came to see tea as a nourishing and healthy drink, they began to consume it in greater quantities than their fellow Europeans. Continental Europe, despite drinking some tea, continued to prefer hot chocolate and coffee.

By the eighteenth century, tea was China's main export commodity to Europe. The import of tea in Britain alone rose from 20,000 pounds in 1700, to 5 million pounds in 1760, to 20 million pounds by 1800. From Britain, it would be exported throughout the British Atlantic World. These substantial numbers reflect only tea that was legally imported. The scholar Sidney Mintz reminds us that with the increasing popularity of tea drinking "the smuggling of tea grew into a major business and, for the tax agents of the crown, a major headache."[36]

Unlike the Chinese, the British drank their tea with local milk, sweetened with sugar from the Americas, preferably in Chinese porcelain, valued as one of the few vessels that would not contaminate the flavor of the drink. Increasingly, this concoction was enjoyed, not just by the privileged classes, but by the average consumer, including laborers in the emerging factory systems. For them the drink became a significant source of daily calories. As a result, tea, sugar, and Chinese porcelain became, along with coffee, cocoa, and South Asian textiles, some of the first global non-elite consumer items in the Atlantic World.[37]

The importation of tea meant the export of silver since the British were unable to break the Chinese monopoly until the nineteenth century. With few exceptions, the Europeans were confined by Chinese law to Guangzhou (Canton) on the southern coast and very few were able to venture into the interior and study how the tea was grown and processed. Eventually the British experiments with growing tea plants in India were successful, which allowed them to undermine the Chinese market. By that time, however, the British had already discovered opium as an alternative method for reversing the trade imbalance.

As large as the British tea trade was it accounted for only a portion of the vast Chinese economy. It certainly was not insignificant. In the late eighteenth century, as Mark Elliott a historian of the Qing Dynasty writes: "One-seventh of all the tea in China was being exported to England."[38] But tea was only one of the products for which China was known. The empire had a highly specialized economy where certain regions focused on the production of one or two commodities such as rice, cotton, tea, porcelain, or tobacco. These items would then be distributed over long distances, some for export, but most for domestic consumption. Attesting to the size and integration of the Chinese economy, one Jesuit resident observed that "the inland trade of China is so great that the commerce of all Europe is not to be compared therewith; the provinces being like too many kingdoms, which communicate to each other their respective productions. This tends to unite several inhabitants among themselves, and make plenty reign in all cities."[39]

One of the regionally produced commodities was porcelain, which had been popular in Europe for a long time, but became increasingly so with tea drinking. China had several centers of porcelain production, the largest and most famous of which was Jingdezhen in Jiangxi province. The kilns there, famous for their blue and white ware, had a long history of exporting porcelain around the world. In the eighteenth century they are believed to have produced more than one million pieces of porcelain per year alone.

Although the Chinese porcelain producers catered predominantly to its much larger domestic market, and exports of Chinese porcelain rarely constituted more than 5 percent of the net worth of its exports to Europe, the relationship between the Chinese producer and European consumer was a complex one that demonstrates the increasingly interconnected spheres of the two regions. By the early eighteenth century, Chinese porcelain makers began to specifically accommodate the tastes of European consumers. John Wills writes that "export merchants at Canton cooperated with the manufacturers in developing wares in shapes and sizes that made them useful as well as ornamental in European homes: cups with handles, pots for coffee or chocolate as well as tea, soup bowls . . . and plates and platters of various sizes."[40] The models and drawings for these designs were provided by European merchants and were specialty ordered for the European market. The porcelain featured images of what China looked like in the minds of Europeans, and the porcelain drawings were generally not a Chinese portrayal of their own society. By 1730, the designs and paintings for the European market were actually produced by workshops in Guangzhou, and were far away from the porcelain producing centers in Jiangxi province. By the 1740s, European consumers increasingly desired matching porcelain sets. Western tastes and expectations would demand new products frequently, at times changing on a yearly basis. This required tremendous flexibility on the part of Chinese porcelain makers. To make matters even more complicated, the porcelains were produced in spread out networks of specialized kilns, in which one manufacturer would produce cups, while still others would specialize in plates, saucers, or pots. Thus, Chinese porcelain manufacturers had to coordinate a massive production volume working within a tremendous infrastructure, prepared for fast-changing designs and decorations.

Perhaps unsurprisingly, given its complexity, the trade in porcelain between the Chinese and the Europeans was marred with difficulties. The low profits and fast-paced changes expected by European consumers made this a very fickle business. The trade in porcelain often made Sino-European business relations unreliable and unstable. There were also complaints about Chinese officials' demands for payments from local porcelain makers and traders. Some European records suggest that the quality of porcelain might have somewhat deteriorated over time, perhaps due to the low profit margins and the general headache that the porcelain trade constituted to Chinese producers and merchants.

During the last three decades of the eighteenth century, Europeans made progress in developing a domestic industry that could compete with Chinese porcelain. High-quality porcelains from Meissen, Copenhagen, or Sevres, and stoneware producers such as Wedgewood in England began to chip away at the Chinese market share. European porcelain and tableware products could finally compete with Chinese quality. As with the textile industry, European states instituted protectionist measures against Chinese imports as a means to bolster their manufacturers' production. While

Chinese tea remained an important commodity in the Global Atlantic economy until the nineteenth century, Chinese-made porcelain was a product of fading relevance by the late eighteenth century.[41]

The Emerald Trade in the Global Atlantic

The worldwide commerce in emeralds from the early 1500s to the late 1700s, which Kris Lane examines in his book *The Colour of Paradise*, is another example of the Global Atlantic commodities' trade. Emeralds always remained a luxury product and could not, because of their scarcity, reverse the trade imbalance that Europe had with the Indian Ocean World. Still, the emerald trade gives us a further glimpse into the exchange patterns of the Global Atlantic. It provides us an example of the routes that some of the highly valued goods from the Atlantic World, such as precious stones and furs, took traveling to Afro-Eurasia.

Although they can be found in many areas of the world, in the early modern period, emeralds originated largely from South America, in what is today the modern state of Colombia. As they had for centuries, the crowned heads of Europe and other members of the elite coveted gems for high-status jewelry, religiously motivated artwork, and other ornaments, but given the special relevance that the color green has in Islam, the emeralds had an even wider appeal as a luxury commodity in the Muslim empires of Afro-Eurasia. In the Ottoman, Safavid, and Mughal empires, rulers and members of the elite contracted pieces that were either intended as displays of power and wealth or as religious icons. Emeralds were incorporated into artwork, furnishings, and weaponry. These included such important pieces as the Mughal Emperor Shah Jahan's famous Peacock Throne, which not only included the legendary Koh-i-noor diamond, but also numerous emeralds. The Topkapi Dagger is another famous example, which features three beautiful emeralds and has become one of the centerpieces in the collection of the treasury of the Ottoman Empire (its popularity boosted in part by its central role in a Hollywood heist film—*Topkapi*, 1964).

While the emerald trade was a highly lucrative business, only a portion of that wealth reached the mine owners who were mainly of European descent, and nothing of it trickled down to the local Native American population who were forced to work the mines. Labor conditions were wretched. Workers were undernourished and endured violent treatment by overseers. Landslides, a common occurrence in the industry, killed many workers and diseases such as mosquito-borne malaria, killed even more. Moreover, unsanitary living conditions in the mining settlements could lead to cholera and dysentery. Given the high mortality rate of workers, emerald mine operators began to draw in labor from outside the region to extract the stones; Native American forced labor from the Andean Highlands and enslaved west and central Africans. These workers continued to suffer from the miserable conditions and high mortality rates.

The example of the emerald trade gives us an opportunity to see how local intermediaries played an important role in distributing the precious stones from the Americas to the Asian markets. One of the central trading communities involved in the dispersion of emeralds were Sephardic Jews of the Spanish and Portuguese empires. Despite having lived on the peninsula for centuries, Sephardic Jews had been forced to convert to Christianity, or face exile and confiscation of their property as a result of the Edicts of Expulsion (1492). These "New Christians," as historians often refer to them, continued long-established trading patterns with members of the Jewish diaspora in other parts of Eurasia or with Asian traders who then distributed their merchandise further inland. Furthermore, and as a result of the Inquisition that persecuted numerous "New Christians" throughout the Spanish and Portuguese empires, many would flee to places such as the Netherlands, England, France, and the Ottoman Empire taking their trade with them.

The emerald trade underscores the complex world of the Global Atlantic. It demonstrates how a green South American stone, extracted by forced Native American and African slave labor, distributed through long-established trading networks, could became a luxury item consumed by elites around the world.[42]

The Cultural Encounter between China and the West

The commercial interactions between the Atlantic World and Asia led to various intellectual and cultural encounters and had an impact on the cultures of the West and Asia. This section focuses in particular on the cultural exchanges between Europe and China.

One of the main sources for cultural translation in this encounter was the members of the Society of Jesus—the Jesuits. This Catholic order was founded in 1540 by Ignatius of Loyola, a former Basque soldier. Members of the new order were often known for their scholarly and missionary zeal and they agreed to go anywhere and live in difficult conditions in the service of their faith. As we have seen, when the nations of Europe began to expand into the Global Atlantic, their missionaries came along to convert people to Christianity. Their methods of conversion and their success rate varied widely throughout the world, since all those who were exposed to the teaching of missionaries brought with them their own cultural frameworks. In addition, encounters between missionaries and local populations were also shaped by the unique and diverse political and economic realities on the ground.

In China, the Jesuits, for a variety of reasons, did not succeed in converting more than a fraction of the population. Their presence there, however, had a large impact on Europe. The missionaries' writings on their experiences and observations helped to spark a scholarly movement sometimes referred to as "sinophilism." Furthermore, the Jesuit Matteo Ricci translated the writings of Confucius into Latin, which allowed them to be read by Europeans. These developments had a dramatic influence on several Enlightenment intellectuals in Europe. The philosopher and mathematician Gottfried Wilhelm Leibnitz, for example, became infatuated with Chinese society, Confucian thought, and came to see the Qing emperor Kangxi as an exemplar of a virtuous ruler. The famous French writer Voltaire also became a great admirer of China. While the works of intellectuals like Leibniz and Voltaire certainly attempted to examine Chinese culture and society, they also provide an insight into what these writers saw as an idealized blueprint of a more perfect Western society. They used an imagined and romanticized version of China as a mirror for Europe.

The encounter with China also had an impact on European art and material culture in the seventeenth and eighteenth centuries. We have already seen how "Chinoiserie," or Chinese-inspired design and imagery, influenced European porcelain makers who desperately attempted to produce not only tableware of comparable quality to that originating from China, but also put interpretations of Chinese patterns on their dishes. Chinoiserie-inspired designs influenced Western art, architecture, landscaping, interior decorating, and furniture making; influences that can be observed in the Prussian King Frederick the Great's summer palace of Sanssouci, as well as in many other European palaces and residences of the Baroque and Rococo styles.

Europe also had an influence on China in the seventeenth and eighteenth centuries, especially among elite society. As members of the Emperor's court, the Jesuits were in contact with those officials interested in Western arts, knowledge, science, and technology, where they acted as intermediaries and tutors for the Chinese elite. For instance, both the Ming and especially the later Qing Dynasty used the technical assistance and know-how of Jesuits to improve their artillery as they updated their cannon technology and designs. The Qing also hired numerous Jesuits as scientists, cartographers, astronomers, architects, designers, and mathematicians. The missionaries would work as practitioners and teachers in these fields, influencing a new generation of Chinese with their knowledge and experience. Furthermore, the eighteenth-century Qianlong Emperor also had a love for European clocks and watches, and amassed a large private collection as part of his treasury. This was an interest that was shared by other members of the Chinese elite, making European clocks and watches a popular trade and collector item.

The Jesuit missionary and painter, Giuseppe Castiglione, was a favorite artist of Qianlong, and introduced elements of Western Art to court. Much of the art that was produced at the eighteenth-century Qing court was a fusion of Sino-Western styles. Furthermore, the Emperor Qianlong also ordered the construction of various European-inspired buildings and gardens, which the Chinese believed looked Western. Just as European art and architecture was influenced by China, Europe in turn inspired the Chinese artistic imagination.[43]

The Growing Global Atlantic Gap: China's and Europe's Declining Relationship

By the nineteenth century, China and Europe underwent comparatively different developments, a phenomenon that the historian Kenneth Pomeranz describes as "the great divergence."[44] While the Western World experienced an economic transformation that scholars today often describe as the Industrial Revolution, the first three decades of the nineteenth century saw a dramatic turnaround of the Qing Empire's economic fortunes. These developments were accompanied by a decline in the positive perceptions and an increase of negative views of China by Westerners, which became shaped by an ever-growing racism in Western culture.[45]

The microcosm of Western and Chinese relations was symbolic of global developments. Due to industrialization in Europe and the United States, the nineteenth century was a period in world history that saw a dramatic increase in a "gap" in power and wealth that emerged between the West and the rest of the globe. The Chinese, like many other people around the world, were increasingly tied up in a global economic system that had an unfavorable impact on their society, and which led people in many parts of the non-Western World to increasingly lose out on their political and economic sovereignty, as they experienced the encroachments that accompanied Western imperialism and domination.[46]

Starting in the 1760s, China gradually turned to more restrictive measures in their interactions with Europeans. Some historians suggest that this was an extension of the traditional isolationist position pursued by Chinese policy makers. More convincing, however, is John Wills' argument that China took on a "defensive" position. The Chinese witnessed the power of European militaries when, for example, the French and English warships clashed in Chinese waters during the War of Austrian Succession (1740–48). Several more battles between European states took place off the coast of China. Between 1760 and 1815, Great Britain and France fought a series of wars in various parts of the Atlantic World as well as Asia, turning these conflicts into a truly Global Atlantic World War. Further challenging Chinese naval sovereignty during this period, European states used allegations about local piracy as a justification for several military interventions in Chinese waters. Between the 1760s and the First Opium War in the 1830s, the Chinese responded by putting growing restrictions on European foreigners staying in China, by attempting to regulate the permission process for European businesses, and by increasing the Chinese military presence in European trade factories.

Economic and political developments were increasingly, however, beyond the control of Chinese officials, and were shaped, in part, by world historical developments in the Atlantic. After Britain lost its colonies in North America in the 1780s, a result of the American Revolution, British officials increased their presence on the Indian subcontinent, pursuing there a more consorted effort at consolidating their economic and political position, a process that unfolded in the late eighteenth and the early decades of the nineteenth centuries.

As a result of their growing presence in South Asia, the British gradually dominated the China trade among the Europeans. Recall that many

British intellectuals and officials had long been concerned about their silver trade deficit with China. While this was not a policy of the British government, or the British East India Company, British merchants would gradually find ways to spend less silver in their commercial interactions with the Chinese. There were two parts to this strategy, which over a few decades successfully reduced the flow of British silver into China. During this period British merchants finally succeeded in finding goods that would appeal to Chinese consumers. An initial easing to British spending came as a result of the introduction of South Asian cotton fabrics on Chinese markets in the last decades of the eighteenth century. This product proved to be popular with China's consumers, just as it had been in the Atlantic a century earlier. Opium, a highly addictive substance, grown by the British in India, and brought to China by British traders, proved an even more effective commodity. As a result of the opium trade, the drug became widely consumed, and wreaked social decay in Chinese society. Qing officials attempted to put an end to the opium trade, hoping it would bring down consumption in the empire. While the opium trade might not have been official British policy, the efforts by Qing officials in Guangzhou to reduce and eventually eliminate the trade of the drug, and the crisis that resulted from this effort, led the British government to initiate the First Opium War (1839–42). This was the first among several conflicts against foreign powers that China lost, which were followed by a series of treaties that left China in an increasingly disadvantaged position.[47]

Notes

1 For a spatial, temporal, and structural introduction of the extent of the Indian Ocean World and its history see K.N. Chaudhuri, *Asia before Europe: Economy and Civilisation of the Indian Ocean from the Rise of Islam to 1750* (New York: Cambridge University Press, 1990).

2 For an introduction to the history of the Indian Ocean World see, for example, K.N. Chaudhuri, *Trade and Civilization in the Indian Ocean* (New York: Cambridge University Press, 1985); and Rainer Buschmann, *Oceans in World History* (Boston: McGraw Hill, 2007), chapter 1.

3 For an introduction on this topic see Edward Dreyer, *Zheng He: China and the Oceans in the Early Ming Dynasty, 1405–1433* (New York: Pearson & Longman, 2007); Louise Levathes, *When China Ruled the Seas: The Treasure Fleet of the Dragon Throne, 1405–1433* (New York: Oxford University Press, 1996).

4 Arthur Waldron, *The Great Wall of China: From History to Myth* (New York: Cambridge University Press, 1990).
5 For a general discussion of the extremely active role that Asian traders played in the Indian Ocean World during the period of European contact and for their interactions with European companies specifically see Philip Curtin, *Cross-Cultural Trade in World History* (New York: Cambridge University Press, 1984), chapter 8.
6 Olive Patricia Dickason, *The Myth of the Savage and the Beginnings of French Colonialism in the Americas* (Edmonton, Alberta: The University of Alberta Press, 1997), 13–25.
7 See Neil MacGregor, *A History of the World in 100 Objects: From the Handaxe to the Credit Card* (New York: Viking, 2011), 482–488.
8 For Lisbon see for example Michael Krondl, *The Taste of Conquest: The Rise of the Three Great Cities of Spice* (New York: Ballantine Book, 2008), 120–124; and Timothy Walker, "Lisbon as a Strategic Haven in the Atlantic World" in Wim Klooster and Alfred Padula, eds, *The Atlantic World: Essays on Slavery, Migration, and Imagination* (Upper Saddle River, NJ: Pearson Prentice-Hall, 2004).
9 Paul Lunde, "The Coming of the Portuguese," *Saudi Aramco World*, July/August 2005, 54–61.
10 For the Gaspar Correa quote and for this issue in general see "The Story of Africa: The Swahili," *BBC World Service.* http://www.bbc.co.uk/worldservice/africa/features/storyofafrica/5chapter3.shtml (accessed May 15, 2014).
11 My discussion of the Portuguese in the Indian Ocean in this section is influenced by Curtin, 137–148; Lunde, 54–61; Sanjay Subrahmanyam, *The Portuguese Empire in Asia, 1500–1700: A Political and Economic History* (London: Longman, 1993); and A.R. Disney, *A History of Portugal and the Portuguese Empire, vol. 2: The Portuguese Empire* (New York: Cambridge University Press, 2009), chapter 19 and 20.
12 On Portuguese and Chinese interaction from 1514–24 see John E. Wills, Jr., "Maritime Europe and the Ming," in John E. Wills, Jr., ed., *China and Maritime Europe, 1500–1800: Trade, Settlement, Diplomacy, and Missions* (New York: Cambridge University Press, 2011), 25–32.
13 John E. Wills, Jr., "Introduction" in *China and Maritime Europe,* 4.
14 Joanna Waley-Cohen *The Sextants of Beijing: Global Currents in Chinese History* (New York: W.W. Norton, 1999), 92–93. See also Mark C. Elliott, *Emperor Qianlong: Son of Heaven, Man of the World* (New York: Longman, 2009), chapter 8.
15 On Portuguese Chinese relations see Wills, "Maritime Europe and the Ming," in *China and Maritime Europe*, 25–35, 39–40.
16 Buschmann, 84–85. See also Yasuko Suzuki, *Japan–Netherlands Trade 1600–1800: The Dutch East India Company and Beyond*(Melbourne, Australia: Trans-Pacific Press, 2012).

17 On this topic see Jonathan I. Israel, *The Dutch Republic and the Hispanic World, 1606–1661* (New York: Oxford University Press, 1982); and his *The Dutch Republic: Its Rise, Greatness, and Fall, 1477–1806* (New York: Oxford University Press, 1995).

18 For a readable introduction on this subject see Stephen R. Brown, *Merchant Kings: When Companies Ruled the World* (New York: Thomas Dunne Books, 2010).

19 Glenn J. Ames, *The Globe Encompassed: The Age of European Discovery, 1500–1700* (Upper Saddle River, NJ: Pearson/Prentice Hall, 2008), 99–103.

20 On Portuguese–Chinese relations see Wills, "Maritime Europe and the Ming," in *China and Maritime Europe*, 25–35, 39–40.

21 Krondl, 231–232; Buschmann, 86.

22 See Kenneth Pomeranz and Steven Topik, "How the Other Half Traded," in *The World that Trade Created: Society, Culture, and the World Economy 1400 to the Present*, 3rd edn (Armonk, NY: M.E. Sharpe, 2013), 36–39. See also Leonard Blusse, *Strange Company: Chinese Settlers, Mestizo Women and the Dutch in VOC Batavia* (Dordrecht: Foris Publications, 1986); as well as his very illuminating micro history, *Bitter Bonds: A Colonial Divorce Drama of the 17th Century*, transl. Dianne Webb (Princeton, N.J.: Markus Wiener Publishing, 2002).

23 On Dutch efforts at maritime empire building in the Indian Ocean World see Krondl, 230–236; and Buschmann, 82–83.

24 For Dutch Chinese relations see Wills, "Maritime Europe and the Ming," in *China and Maritime Europe*, 67–75; Wills, *Pepper, Guns, and Parleys: The Dutch East India Company and China, 1662–1681* (Cambridge, MA: Harvard University Press, 1974); Tonio Andrade, *How Taiwan Became Chinese: Dutch, Spanish, and Han Colonization in the Seventeenth Century* (New York: Columbia University Press, 2008).

25 On this subject see for example Nina Luttinger and Gregory Dicum, *The Coffee Book: Anatomy of an Industry from Crop to the Last Drop*, revised and updated edition (New York: New Press, 2006), chapter 1.

26 For this quote and on silver more generally see Timothy Brook, *Vermeer's Hat: The Seventeenth Century and the Dawn of the Global World* (New York: Bloomsbury Press, 2008), 160–161. For the Dutch incursions in the Atlantic World see Ames, 117–119. For a discussion of Dutch incursions alongside the French and English see Thomas Benjamin, *The Atlantic World: Europeans, Africans, Indians and Their Shared History, 1400–1900* (New York: Cambridge University Press, 2009), chapter 6. On piracy as a weapon especially against the Spanish Empire see Kris Lane, *Pillaging the Empire: Piracy in the Americas, 1500–1750* (Armonk, N.Y.: M.E. Sharpe, 1998), for the Dutch and their use of pirates in particular see chapter 3.

27 On Mahican–Dutch relations see William A. Starna, *From Homeland to New Land: A History of the Mahican Indians, 1600–1830* (Boston: Northeast Region

Ethnography Program, National Park Service, U.S. Department of the Interior, 2011), chapter 6. On Haudenosaunee–Dutch relations see Daniel K. Richter, *The Ordeal of the Longhouse: The Peoples of the Iroquois League in the Era of European Colonization* (Chapel Hill: University of North Carolina Press, 1992), chapter 4.

28 See for example Ames, 135; Brook, 45–6.

29 For an introduction to the British in the Indian Ocean World see Huw Bowen, Robert Blyth, and John McAleer, *Monsoon Traders: The Maritime World of the East India Company* (London: Scala Publisher, 2011); T.O. Lloyd, *The British Empire, 1558–1995*, 2nd edn (New York: Oxford University Press, 1996), 73–77. On the limits of empire and British power in India see, for example, Linda Colley, *Captives: The Story of Britain's Pursuit of Empire and How its Soldiers and Civilians were Held Captive by the Dream of Global Supremacy, 1600–1850* (New York: Pantheon Books, 2002), chapters 8, 9, 10. For the French see Glenn J. Ames, *Colbert, Mercantilism, and the French Quest for Asian Trade* (De Kalb: Northern Illinois University Press, 1996).

30 Pomeranz and Topik, "Empire on a Shoestring: British Adventures and Indian Financiers in Calcutta, 1750–1850," in *The World that Trade Created*, 46–48.

31 Marta V. Vicente, *Clothing the Spanish Empire: Families and the Calico Trade in the Early Modern World* (New York: Palgrave Macmillan, 2006), 9–10. For an introduction to the textile industries of the Indian Ocean World see Chadhuri, *Asia before Europe*, 306–323.

32 Vincente, 9–10.

33 For North America see, for example, Alice Nash and Christoph Strobel, *Daily Life of Native Americans from Post-Columbian through Nineteenth Century America* (Westport, CT: Greenwood Press, 2006), 21, 93.

34 Vincente, 10–11.

35 For an introduction to this subject see Mary Lou Heiss and Robert J. Heiss, *A Story of Tea: A Cultural History and Drinking Guide* (Berkeley, CA: Ten Speed Press, 2007).

36 Sidney W. Mintz, *Sweetness and Power: The Place of Sugar in Modern History* (New York: Penguin, 1985), for quote and numbers see 112–113, for a more general discussion see 108–121.

37 Wills, "Introduction," in *China and Maritime Europe*, 14; Elliott, chapter 8; Waley-Cohen, 92–93.

38 Elliott, 134.

39 Elliott, 148.

40 On this issue and for the quote see John L. Cranmer-Byng and John E. Wills, Jr., "Trade and Diplomacy with Maritime Europe, 1644–c. 1800," in *China and Maritime Europe*, 211.

41 My discussion of eighteenth century porcelain production is based on Cranmer-Byng and Wills, "Trade and Diplomacy with Maritime Europe, 1644–c. 1800," in *China and Maritime Europe,* 211–213.

42 My discussion of the emerald trade is based on Kris Lane, *The Colour of Paradise: The Emerald in the Age of Gunpowder Empires* (New Haven: Yale University Press, 2010).

43 On intercultural exchanges between China and the West see, for example, D.E. Mungello, *The Great Encounter of China and the West, 1500–1800*, 3rd edn (Lanham, MD: Rowman & Littlefield, 2009); Elliott, 116–134; Waley-Cohen, 105–121.

44 Kenneth Pomeranz, *The Great Divergence: China, Europe, and the Making of the Modern World Economy* (Princeton, N.J: Princeton University Press, 2000).

45 Mungello, 130–134; Waley-Cohen, 124–128.

46 My thinking here is influenced by Fernand Braudel, *Civilization and Capitalism, vol. 2, The Wheels of Commerce* transl. Sian Reynolds (Berkeley: University of California Press, 1992), see especially 134; and Robert Marks, *The Origins of the Modern World: A Global and Ecological Narrative from the Fifteenth to the Twenty-First Century*, 2nd edn (Lanham, MD: Rowman & Littlefield, 2007), chapter 5.

47 For the changing relationship between China and the West see Cranmer-Byng and Wills, "Trade and Diplomacy with Maritime Europe, 1644-c. 1800," in *China and Maritime Europe*, 222–235. Waley-Cohen, 124–159. Mungello, 130–134, 139–143. Elliott, 134–139.

CONCLUSION

The Decline of the Global Atlantic and a New Order of Things

The discovery of America and that of a passage to the East Indies by the Cape of Good Hope are the two greatest and most important events recorded in the history of mankind. Their consequences already have been very great; but, in the short period between two and three centuries which has elapsed since these discoveries were made, it is impossible that the whole extent of their consequences can have been seen. What benefits, or what misfortunes to mankind may hereafter result from those great events, no human wisdom can foresee. By uniting in some measure, the most distant parts of the world, by enabling them to relieve one another's wants, to increase one another's enjoyments, and to encourage one another's industry, their general tendency would seem to be beneficial. To the natives however. . . .

—Adam Smith, *Wealth of Nations* (1776)

The discovery of America, the rounding of the Cape, opened up fresh ground for the rising bourgeoisie. The East-Indian and Chinese markets, the colonization of America, trade with the colonies, the increase in the means of exchange and in commodities generally, gave to commerce, to navigation, to industry, an impulse never before known, and thereby, to the revolutionary element in tottering feudal society, a rapid development. . . . Modern industry has established the world market for which the discovery of America paved the way.

—Karl Marx and Friedrich Engels, *Communist Manifesto* (1848)

Before 1492, parts of Europe, Africa, and the Americas were connected to regional exchange networks, and between 1500 and 1750, a new Atlantic Ocean system emerged that built on and altered these traditional networks and developed into a globally integrated trade system. Thus, the Atlantic World and its peoples—Europe and Europeans, Africa and Africans, the Americas and Native Americans—participated in, and were influenced by, interregional exchanges that connected them to the larger world. In addition, the Atlantic World had biological, cultural, and economic influences on parts of the globe that lay far beyond this ocean system.

In the late eighteenth and the nineteenth centuries, however, the patterns and processes that shaped the Global Atlantic changed significantly. The industrial revolution that occurred in Europe and in the former European colonies of North America, led to a significant shift in power dynamics and a rising gap between the Western world of Europe and North America and other areas of the globe. Industrialization and the power imbalance it created also broke down the patterns of exchange that had occurred throughout the early modern Atlantic and its connections to the wider world. These developments initiated a change in the global landscape that allowed the West to play an increasingly powerful global economic, political, and cultural role.[1]

Despite the dramatic restructuring of the eighteenth and nineteenth centuries, certain regional and Global Atlantic patterns continued to persist. The wave of political revolutions of the eighteenth and nineteenth centuries, including the American, the French, and the Haitian Revolutions, as well as the numerous revolutions of Spanish South America, had their roots in older Atlantic World patterns. However, their reverberations were transformative around the globe in a variety of revolutions.[2]

Another trans-Atlantic political and cultural movement was that of Pan-Africanism, which promoted the connections of peoples of African descent in the Americas, Africa, and Europe in the nineteenth and twentieth centuries. Pan-African writers, politicians, intellectuals, and activists advocated for unity among the people of African background who had been, as a result of the slave trade, dispersed all over the Atlantic World. Pan-Africanists rallied against racism, racial violence, Western imperialism, and for the national liberation of African colonies and areas where Africans were in the majority that remained under colonial rule in the Western Hemisphere.[3]

In addition, in the late nineteenth and early twentieth centuries, as the historian Daniel Rodgers argues, there existed an "Atlantic era of social politics" a period of "institutional connections" between the United States "and the industrializing nations of Europe." Reform programs, social policies, urban planning, as well as the labor and women's movements on both sides of the North Atlantic drew intellectual inspiration, influences, and policy lessons from each other, which would eventually have global influences.[4]

The Industrial Revolution dramatically altered the patterns and processes of European overseas expansion and colonization. By the 1750s, European control in Africa and Asia was marginal, confined to small enclaves usually on the coast. Even in the Americas, where the impact of disease had been devastating to indigenous populations, the territorial control of European empires was largely confined to the eastern and western seaboards; leaving huge portions of the South and North American landmass to remain under Native American control. However, by 1900, all this changed as Western powers claimed control of large portions of the globe.

Over the course of a century and a half between 1750 and 1900, industrial technology dramatically altered the nature of European colonization. By the nineteenth century, the East and West India companies were in decline and the European nation-states began taking direct control over their colonies. For example, the Dutch nationalized the VOC's colonies in Indonesia in 1800 and the British took direct control of India from the British East India Company after the so-called Sepoy Rebellion of 1857. The new colonial powers benefited tremendously from a variety of industrial advancements, the most significant of which were: the steamship, the railroad, the telegraph, the rapid-fire machine guns, and the malaria-fighting quinine. All of these were mass produced, usually in Europe, and exported to colonies around the globe.

Telegraph, railroads, and steamships enabled Europeans to have unprecedented access to Africa and Asia. The telegraph allowed for quick communication between the far corners of the world. Steamships sped up ocean and river travel and railroads provided faster overland access to the interior. The new technologies also allowed for the transportation of much larger amounts of cargo. The railroads were built by thousands of Africans and Asians, frequently conscripted, working under difficult and dangerous conditions. This new infrastructure allowed Europeans and their merchandise to access the Asian and African interiors, and, more importantly, they were able to extract raw materials from those regions to feed the factories of Europe. These new technologies brought in the supplies to build mines and plantations, and brought out their bounty for use in a global, European-controlled, market. European-manufactured goods might then be brought back to the region as finished products where they sometimes took the place of local goods thereby damaging domestic production. For instance, this process was at work by the nineteenth century when British textiles came to be increasingly visible in the Indian market and gradually helped undermine local textile production.

Advances in transportation also enabled new forms of agriculture based not on subsistence or local needs, but on cash crops raised to feed consumers across the globe. For example, starting in the late nineteenth century, European colonial powers introduced cash crops from the Western Hemisphere, such as peanuts and cocoa, to parts of western Africa. As a result, the local populations began to practice less subsistence agriculture, as a growing number of Africans survived on rice exported from Europe's Asian colonies where rice was grown as a cash crop. This system added some efficiency to the market as well as a significant risk to the local population. If there was any disruption in this more integrated food system on either continent, mass famines and starvation could, and did, occur.

Railroads and steamships also helped to more easily deploy military forces to fight conflicts, and colonial forces, both Western and local recruits, were aided in their task of maintaining control by using new weapon technology. Rapid-fire machine guns such as the Gatling gun and the Maxim Rapid Fire gun, which were developed and mass produced in the West, were arguably the most significant among these weapons. With these new advancements, colonial forces were able to insure their control over much larger areas with more diverse populations.

Along with innovation in transportation and weapons, it was the invention of artificially produced quinine that allowed the advancement of this more invasive variety of colonization. This new medical development allowed Europeans to better deal with a slew of tropical diseases such as malaria. The story of quinine also underscores the continuous influences of the Global Atlantic patterns in world history. The active ingredient of quinine is extracted from Peruvian bark (called quina-quina in Quecha). Native Americans in South America had used this medicine for centuries to treat malaria, a mosquito-borne disease rampant in the tropical regions of Afro-Eurasia, which arrived with European ships in the Western Hemisphere where it wreaked havoc among the indigenous populations. Europeans in the Americas, learning about this treatment from the Native peoples, used the extremely bitter tasting and costly bark in their efforts to protect themselves against malaria. Wealthy Europeans in the colonies often mixed extracts of the bark with sugary water to improve the taste, thereby creating an early form of tonic water, still a popular mix with alcoholic beverages to this day. Thus, Native Americans had used and shared this medicine with the rest of the world, long before two French scientists in 1820 extracted the active ingredient of quinine. It could now be artificially and mass produced, a development that enabled Europeans to colonize tropical regions throughout the world more effectively as they now had more widely available protection against malaria.[5]

These new technologies were much more disruptive to the colonized regions than those of the early modern period. Kevin O'Rourke and Jeffrey Williamson argue that the decline in ocean transport costs due to the wide use of steamships had a massive impact by the second half of the nineteenth century and led to "globally integrated commodity and factor markets." They call this the first wave of "globalization." They argue that "[b]y 1914 there was hardly a village or town anywhere on the globe whose prices were not influenced by distant foreign markets, whose infrastructure was not influenced by foreign capital, whose engineering, manufacturing, and even business skills were not imported from abroad or whose labor markets were not influenced by the absence of those who had emigrated or by the presence of the stranger who had immigrated." They maintain that the first global wave came to an abrupt end with the start of WWI. Between 1914 and 1945, they write, "the world economy had lost all of its globalization achievements." A globalized economy would then re-emerge in the post-1945 world.[6] Although several scholars would debate this thesis and place the roots of globalization at an earlier point, O'Rourke and Williamson underscore a crucial point. By the second half of the nineteenth century, there was a period of more intensified economic interconnectedness and global interaction than had been present in the centuries before.

Much of the integration that occurred during this period in Africa and Asia was done to benefit the economies and politics of the West. The Industrial Revolution helped shape an extremely efficient and exploitative system of imperialism as Europe and North America sought to control global trade, extract raw materials, and access new markets. The form of

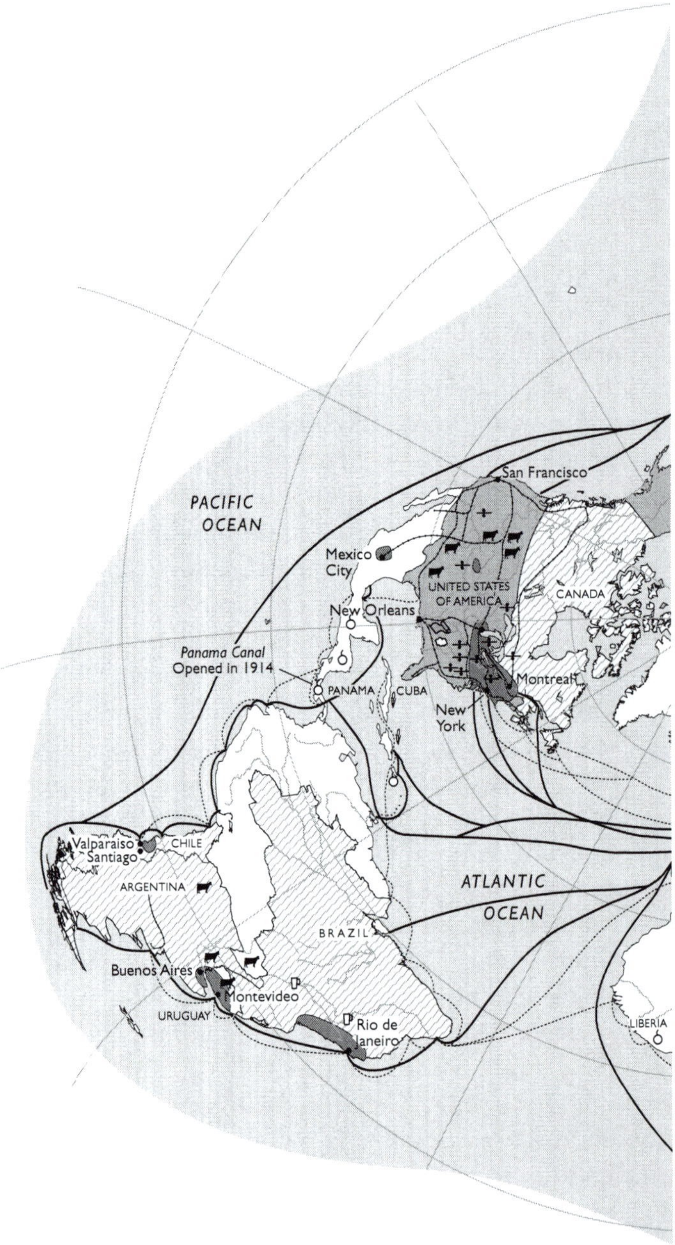

This map shows the global economic exchange networks of the late nineteenth and the early twentieth centuries. Increased technological changes led to a further increase in worldwide trade, but also began to reinforce the global gap between the West and the rest of the globe.

Source: Pomeranz, Kenneth, and Steven Topik. *The World That Trade Created: Society, Culture, and the World Economy, 1400 to the Present*, 3rd edn. Armonk, NY: M.E. Sharpe, 2013.

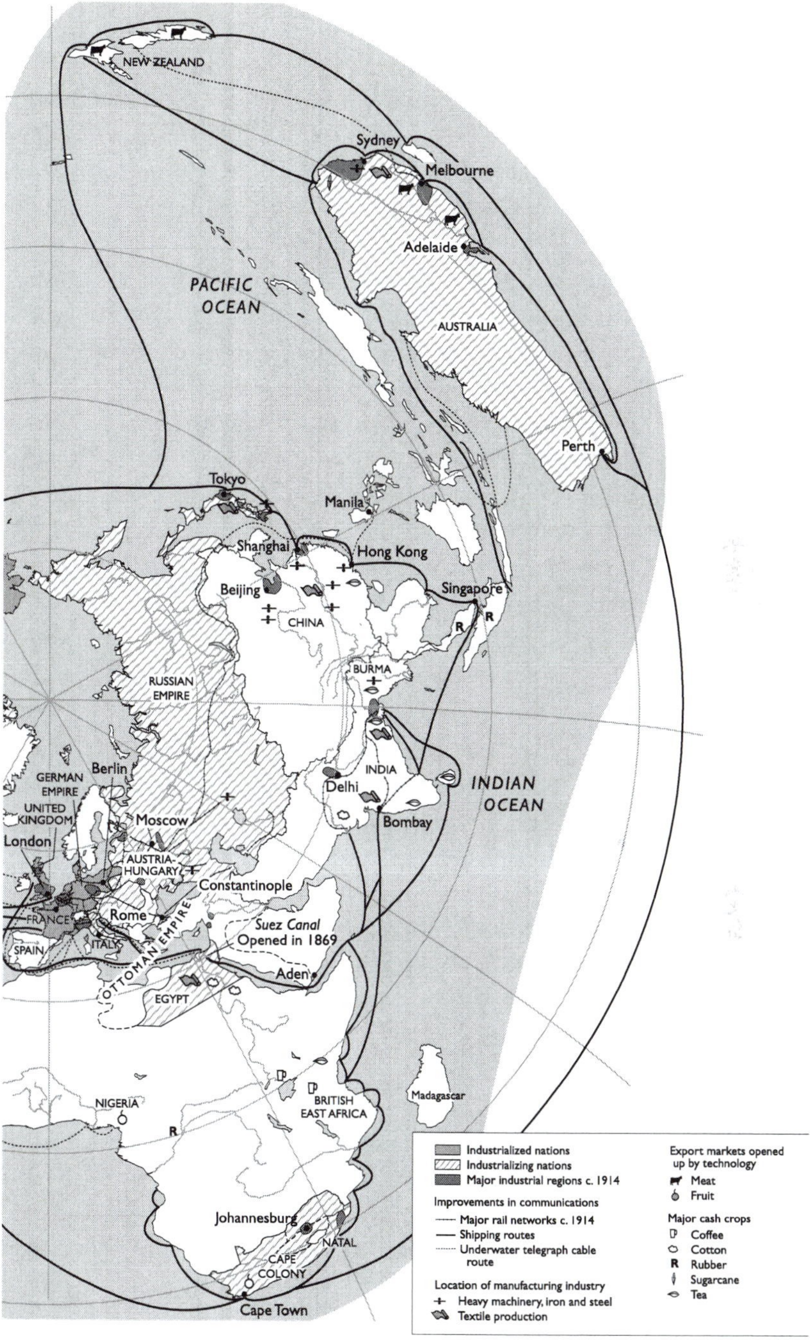
NEW ZEALAND
Sydney
Melbourne
Adelaide
PACIFIC OCEAN
AUSTRALIA
Perth
Tokyo
Manila
Shanghai
Hong Kong
Singapore
R
R
Beijing
CHINA
BURMA
RUSSIAN EMPIRE
INDIA
Delhi
INDIAN OCEAN
Bombay
Berlin
GERMAN EMPIRE
UNITED KINGDOM
London
Moscow
AUSTRIA-HUNGARY
Constantinople
FRANCE
Rome
SPAIN
ITALY
OTTOMAN EMPIRE
Suez Canal
Opened in 1869
Aden
EGYPT
NIGERIA
R
BRITISH EAST AFRICA
Madagascar
Johannesburg
NATAL
CAPE COLONY
Cape Town
Industrialized nations
Industrializing nations
Major industrial regions c. 1914
Improvements in communications
Major rail networks c. 1914
Shipping routes
Underwater telegraph cable route
Location of manufacturing industry
Heavy machinery, iron and steel
Textile production
Export markets opened up by technology
Meat
Fruit
Major cash crops
Coffee
Cotton
R Rubber
Sugarcane
Tea

colonization in Africa and Asia that developed as a result of these desires and practices was justified, in the minds of many Westerners, by sentiments of cultural superiority and racism.

Similar global transformations to the nature of intercultural and commercial exchange also occurred in Latin America. Even though the revolutions against Spanish rule in the early decades of the nineteenth century had produced a number of politically independent states, Western powers continued to obtain significant financial and commercial control in the region. Several scholars have described the capitalist system that developed there as "economic" or "free trade imperialism." In the nineteenth century Britain had the economic upper hand in the region until the United States gradually challenged that position starting in the latter half of that century. The economic historian Frederick Weaver describes this situation in his book *Latin America in the World Economy*. "In the era of Free Trade Imperialism," he writes, "international economic relationships for the first time were significantly conditioned by the dominant international power's need to reproduce its economic and social order through foreign markets by selling domestically produced product and buying foreign raw materials." This economic system provided a "definite departure" from the early modern period, "in which European merchants and rulers cooperated to maximize commercial profits and fiscal revenues from a foreign trade that had little directly to do with domestic production." Latin America, similar to parts of Africa and Asia, became an export economy for sugar, coffee, minerals, hardwood, vanilla, spices, cotton, tobacco, guano, grains, nitrates, and various other goods. As in Africa and Asia, these developments were spurred by economic growth and increases in consumption in the Western World, alongside a decline in transportation costs. But Latin America, like the European and US colonies in Africa and Asia, also provided the West with a market for its manufacturing goods.[7]

The practice of using violence and exploitation in the pursuit of profits that we have seen in the Global Atlantic of the early modern era continued during the period of imperialism in the late nineteenth and early twentieth centuries. For instance, in the Peruvian Putumayo region, a de facto slave labor system was imposed on the Native American population to force them to extract the natural rubber that was in extremely high demand in the factories of Europe and the United States to make tires and various other products. Beheadings, shootings, mutilations, abuse, severe labor conditions, abductions, and whippings were part of this extractive economy. On a much larger scale, a similar horror occurred in the tropical forests of the Belgian Congo in the late nineteenth century. Here too the population was forced to collect rubber sap in the most inhumane and terrifying conditions. Violence, mutilations, and genocidal warfare accompanied European colonization and rubber production under the Belgian King Leopold II's misrule of the Congo—a period often called the "rubber terror"—where an estimated 8 to 10 million Africans were killed.[8]

Interaction with Latin America, just as with African and Asian colonies, also had an impact on investments and finance capitalism in the Western World. Again Frederick Weaver provides a succinct description: "When British capitalists built a railroad in Argentina or expanded nitrate production in Chile, these investments meant the export of British rails, engines, rolling stock, and mining equipment, along with the need for steamships. This increased market demand reduced excess capacity and raised profits in British Finance Capitalism's leading industrial branches." Thus, in the late nineteenth century there emerged an intrinsically interconnected and complex economic system that benefited especially Western as well as some local business and political elites in the non-Western World.[9]

Thus, the "modern world" that began to emerge in the late eighteenth and nineteenth centuries saw a gradual change of the diverse and complex processes and patterns that had once shaped the Global Atlantic. Before industrialization created a significant shift in the power dynamics between Europe, North America, and the rest of the world, Europeans often had to temper their interactions with and show deference to Africans, Native Americans, and Asians. This old reality was, however, increasingly replaced with a system where power dynamics shifted more decisively in favor of Western nations in Europe and North America and in which the trends and dynamics that had shaped earlier interaction were soon forgotten.

Notes

1 See especially Robert Marks, *The Origins of the Modern World: A Global and Ecological Narrative from the Fifteenth to the Twenty-First Century*, 2nd edn (Lanham, MD: Roman & Littlefield Publishers, 2007), chapter 4; and Kenneth Pomeranz, *The Great Divergence: China, Europe and the Making of the Modern World Economy* (Princeton, NJ: Princeton University Press, 2000).

2 On these issues see for example Wim Klooster, *Revolutions in the Atlantic World: A Comparative History* (New York: New York University Press, 2009); David Armitage and Sanjay Subrahmanyam, eds, *The Age of Revolutions in Global*

Context, c. 1760–1840 (New York: Palgrave Macmillan, 2010); and David Armitage, *The Declaration of Independence: A Global History* (Cambridge, MA: Harvard University Press, 2007).

3 See, for example, Imanuel Geiss, *The Pan African Movement: A History of Pan-Africanism in America, Europe, and Africa*, transl. by A.E. Keeps (Teaneck, NJ: New Holmes & Meier Publishing, 1974).

4 Daniel T. Rodgers, *Atlantic Crossings: Social Politics in a Progressive Age* (Cambridge, MA: Harvard University Press, 1998), for quotations see 4. See also Patricia Greenwood Harrison, *Connecting Links: The British and American Woman Suffrage Movements, 1900–1914* (Westport, CT: Greenwood Press, 2000).

5 Jack Weatherford, *Indian Givers: How the Indians of the Americas Transformed the World* (New York: Crown, 1988), 176–179.

6 Kevin H. O'Rourke and Jeffrey Williamson, *Globalization and History: The Evolution of a Nineteenth-Century Atlantic Economy* (Cambridge, MA: MIT Press, 1999), 2. On this issue see also Ralph A. Austen, *Trans-Saharan Africa in World History* (New York: Oxford University Press, 2010), chapter 6.

7 Frederick Stirton Weaver, *Latin America in the World Economy: Mercantile Colonialism to Global Capitalism* (Boulder, Col.: Westview Press, 2000), for quotes see 33, for a general discussion see 32–35, 39–54, 63–66.

8 On the rubber terrors see Adam Hochschild, *King Leopold's Ghost: A Story of Greed, Terror, and Heroism in Colonial Africa* (Boston: Houghton Mifflin Company, 1998), for the Putumayo region see 269–270.

9 Weaver, 63.

CHRONOLOGY

700–1550	Mississippian chiefdoms dominate what is today the southeastern United States
1000s	Vikings establish settlements in Greenland and North America
*c.*1230s	Mansa Sundiata believed to have founded the Mali Empire
*c.*1312–37	Rule of Mansa Musa. Mali Empire at its height of power. Mali Empire extends to the Atlantic coast
1324–25	Mansa Musa's Hajj
1340	Europeans reach the Canary Islands
1352	The North African Muslim traveler Ibn Battuta reaches the empire of Mali. This voyage was part of Ibn Battuta's impressive Afro-Eurasian journeys, which covered over 70,000 miles and took place over almost 30 years
1368–1644	Ming Dynasty
Late 1300s	Songhay splits from Mali and begins its ascent at the expense of the once powerful empire of Mali
1400s	Triple Alliance between the Mexica and their Nahuatl-speaking allies—conventionally referred to as the Aztec Empire
1405–33	Chinese Admiral Zheng He leads several expeditions to the Indian Ocean
1415	Portuguese take the North African city of Ceuta
1434	Portuguese sailor Joao Diaz and his crew sail around Cape Bojador—a crucial step that eventually leads the Portuguese to become the first European state to learn the wind patterns of the Atlantic Ocean
1438	Pahacutec establishes rule of Inca Empire in Peru—empire lasts from *c.*1430s–1533

1441	Portuguese navigators encounter African populations near Cape Blanc in western Africa—early efforts at slave trading
1453	Ottomans take Constantinople
1460–70s	Period of dramatic expansion of Songhay Empire
1470	Portuguese navigators explore "Gold Coast" of West Africa
1471	Portuguese set up a trading post at El Mina
1480s	European fishing expeditions off the coast of Newfoundland
1484	Kongo and Portugal establish diplomatic relations and exchange ambassadors
1488	Bartolomeu Dias sails around the African Cape of Good Hope into the Indian Ocean
1491	First Kongolese ruler converts to Christianity
1492	Expulsion of Muslims and Jews from the kingdom of Castile and Aragon. Columbus' first voyage to the Americas
1492–1900	Waves of epidemics introduced by Europeans and Africans lead to the death of millions of Native Americans all over the Western Hemisphere
1494	Treaty of Tordesillas divides the non-Christian globe between the kingdoms of Castile and Portugal
1497	Venetian navigator John Cabot, commissioned by the English Crown to discover a trade route to Asia, reaches the east coast of North America. Portuguese sailor Vasco Da Gama sails around the South African Cape, reaches the East African Swahili coast, and continues to India
1499	Amerigo Vespucci and his crew set out for an exploratory mission to South America
1500	Portuguese mission to India led by Pedro Alvares Cabral reaches land in the Western Hemisphere (later known as Brazil)
1502	Montezuma becomes the *tlatoani* of the Mexica
1505	Portuguese establish *feitorias* (trading posts) on the Swahili coast of eastern Africa
1509	The Spanish Catholic missionary, Bartolome de las Casas, proposes the use of African slave labor to lessen the abuse of Native American forced labor
1510	Portuguese conquer the Indian city of Goa (western India) and establish a permanent colony there
1511	Portuguese conquer Malacca (today Melaka in Malaysia)
1513	Blasco Nunez de Balboa and his crew reach the Pacific by crossing the Panama Isthmus. Portuguese expedition reaches Canton in China—the Portuguese traveled by Chinese junk from Malacca

1515	Portuguese take Hormuz Albrecht Dürer produces the woodcut "Rhinoceros"—a fictionalized image of a real-life creature brought to Europe by the Portuguese from India
1516	West African state of Benin outlaws slave trade
1517	Portuguese establish a *feitoria* in Ceylon (Sri Lanka). Portuguese king orders a diplomatic and trade mission to Canton (Guangzhou)—Portuguese envoys meet with Chinese hostility
1519–22	Spanish invasion of the Aztec Empire. The likely period of the introduction of horses to the Americas. Spanish expedition commanded by Portuguese navigator Ferdinand Magellan completes the first circumnavigation of the globe
1530	Portuguese establish several captaincies in Brazil and introduce sugar cane brought from Madeira
1530–33	Francisco Pizarro and his forces invade the Inca Empire
1530s–50s	Spain takes over and develops silver mines in New Spain and in the Andes
1542–1605	Rule of third Mughal Emperor Akbar
1542–1638	Macau–Nagasaki trade route
1557	The Chinese provide the Portuguese permission to settle in Macau
1565	Andres de Urdaneta explores a route from the Philippines to the Americas, which will be later used by the Manila galleons. This trip also initiates the Spanish colonization of the Philippines
1568–1648	Dutch Revolt
1577–80	Francis Drake's expedition around the world via Cape Horn
1580	Spanish annexation of Portugal
1590	Dutch merchant mariners aggressively expand their presence in West Africa, the Mediterranean, and in the Indian Ocean (especially Indonesia)
1591	Moroccan forces gain a decisive victory against Songhay's army
1598	Dutch take Mauritius and begin to use the island as a refreshment station for their ships. They establish a permanent settlement there in 1638 in an effort to keep out European competitors
1600	English (later British) East India Company established
1602	Dutch East India Company established (*Vereenigde Oost-Indische Compagnie*, VOC). VOC is dissolved in 1795
1603	Samuel de Champlain founds a French settlement in Acadia (today Canada)
1605	England claims the island of Barbados in the Caribbean as a colony
1607	Founding of Jamestown colony in Virginia
1608	Ships of the English East India Company are beginning to dock in Surat (today in the state of Gujarat in western India). The city would become the seat of the presidency of the company

1609	Dutch East India Company ships Chinese tea to Europe. Hugo Grotius writes *Mare Liberum*, a book that advocates for the freedom of the sea under international law
1611	Japanese authority allow Dutch merchants trade privileges
1613	Stock Exchange built in Amsterdam
1614	Dutch navigators explore Long Island Sound and the Delaware Bay and River. Dutch establish trading post near modern Albany, New York. These developments aid in the creation of the colony of New Netherlands (1614–67)
1617	Dutch take over Goree Island on the West African coast
1618	Nzinga becomes ruler of the state of Ndongo (today's Angola). Dutch bring coffee from Mocha (a coastal city in modern day Yemen) to the Netherlands via the Indian Ocean World trade routes
1618–48	Thirty Years War
1619	Dutch attack and destroy the city of Jayawirkata and establish a fort and settlement named Batavia (location of today's Jakarta in Indonesia)
1620	Runaway slaves in Brazil establish the "maroon" state of Palmares. Puritan Separatists (the Pilgrims) establish a colony at Plymouth on land that had been cleared by Wampanoag inhabitants and abandoned after a small pox epidemic that swept the northeast of the modern United States from 1616 to 1619
1621	Dutch West India Company established. First experimentation with potato plant in Germany
1626	Settlement of Salem, Massachusetts. French settlement on the Senegal River, West Africa
1630	Pirate settlement of Tortuga founded on the northwest coast of the present day Dominican Republic
1638	Dutch only European state allowed to trade with Japan, but only at Dejima, a small island at Nagasaki Bay
1640s–50s	First coffee houses open in various European cities such as Venice and Oxford
1641	Dutch capture Malacca from Portuguese. Massachusetts legalizes slavery—the first mainland British colony to do so in the Americas
1644–1911	Qing Dynasty
1652	Dutch settlement at Cape of Good Hope (South Africa)
1658	Dutch begin coffee cultivation in Ceylon (modern day Sri Lanka)
1659	French establish settlement of St. Louis on the Senegal River
1660	Founding of Royal African Company
1661	British obtain Bombay (today Mumbai India) from Portuguese who had controlled the islands from 1534 to 1661

1661–1722	Rule of Kangxi Emperor
1668–69	French East India Company (*La Compagnie Française des Indes Orientales*) establishes its first trading posts on the Indian subcontinent
1685	Kangxi Emperor opens Canton region of China to limited trading with foreigners
1690	Major gold deposit found in Brazil. British obtain three villages in the Bengal region of India, one of them named Kalikata. Job Charnock renamed this growing settlement Calcutta (today Kolkata)
1691	Virginia passes anti-miscegenation laws and anti-manumission laws
1690s	Portuguese colonists in the Sao Paulo region of Brazil defeat the quilombo (runaway slave community) of Palmares
1697	Gottfried Wilhelm Leibniz (1646–1716) publishes *Novissima Sinica*, one of several of his works, in which the philosopher's thinking is influenced by his interest in China. The "Middle Kingdom" also occupies the writing of several other European enlightenment thinkers such as Voltaire
1699	Pierre Lemoyne establishes the first French settlement in the present state of Louisiana
1701	The Society for the Propagation of the Gospel in Foreign Parts is established by the Anglicans to convert Native Americans and Africans. Origin of the Asante state
1710	Mass production of porcelain in Meissen (German principality of Saxony) begins. This was arguably the first successful European attempt at making hard-paste porcelain, though the quality of the product was still inferior to Chinese ceramics. Earlier European attempts to imitate Chinese porcelain had only been able to produce soft-paste porcelain, such as the Medici porcelain produced in Florence from 1575 to 1587, or at Rouen in France from 1673 to 1696
1711	The British establish first trading post in Canton
1722	Founding of Herrnhut settlement in Saxony by the Moravian Church—Moravians send missionaries throughout the world in the eighteenth and nineteenth centuries. First coffee planted in Brazil
1730	Oyo defeats Dahomey
1735–99	Rule of Qianlong Emperor
1740	Chinese are massacred at Batavia
1748	French capture Madras (today Chennai) from the British and occupy it until 1749
1754–63	"Seven Years"/"French and Indian" War (Britain only declares war officially on France in 1756, but the fighting precedes this date)
1755	Earthquake and tsunami hits Lisbon—kills over 30,000 people in the city

1756	Voltaire publishes *An Essay on the Customs and Spirit of Nations*. This work includes a significant favorable portion on China
1758	Quakers prohibit their members to either own or to participate in the trade of slaves
1759	Battle of Chinsurah: Asked by Mir Jafar, the Nawab of Bengal, and also to get a foothold in the lucrative India trade, the Dutch East Indian Company, alongside their Bengali allies, unsuccessfully attack the British
1760	Battle of Wandiwash (today Vandavasi)—French are decisively defeated by the British, which provides an end to their presence in India
1764	Battle of Buxsar brings a decisive victory for the British East India Company's army, consisting predominantly of Indian sepoys, over the armies of several Indian rulers.
	Modified version of Sugar and Molasses Act passed by British Parliament
1765	Stamp Act passed by British Parliament, which taxes its American colonies—repealed in 1766. Act feeds a debate in the North American colonies about Great Britain's right to tax its colonies. The South American potato is believed to have become the most widely consumed food in Europe
1768–71	James Cook circumnavigates the globe
1771	First spinning mill in England
1770s–1820s	Madagascar functions as prominent base for pirates
1775	James Watt designs a steam engine.
	Pierre-Simon Girard designs a water turbine
1775–83	American Revolution
1776	Adam Smith publishes "An Inquiry into the Nature and Causes of the Wealth of Nations"
1779–1880	Hundred Years War of the Xhosa in southern Africa
1780–83	Tupac Amaru rebellion in the Andes
1789	First steam-powered cotton mill opens in Manchester, UK
1789–99	French Revolution
1791–1804	Haitian Revolution
1794	Eli Whitney patents the cotton gin
1795–1803	British occupy the Dutch colony of Cape of Good Hope in southern Africa
1800–65	Apex of whaling industry
1803–15	Napoleonic Wars
1806	British re-occupy the Cape Colony—this time they stay
1807	French invasion of Portugal—Portuguese royal family flees to Brazil
1810s–20s	Revolutionary struggles all over Latin America

1819	First steamship crosses the Atlantic
1820	American Colonization Society founds Liberia intended as a settlement for free African Americans
1820s–40s	Numerous Eastern Woodland Indian nations, including the Ottowas, Miamies, Shawnees, Seminoles, Muskogee, Choctaw, and Cherokees, are removed from their homelands and moved to Oklahoma, Kansas, and Iowa
1823	Monroe Doctrine—declares that US would interfere should any European states attempt to interfere with any states in the Americas
1824	British rule begins in Burma
1826–28	Numerous Latin American countries default on their foreign debt
1833	British Empire abolishes slavery—this leads to an increase of the use of indentured servants around the British Empire
1839–42	First Opium War
1840s	Irish potato famine, crop failures in Germany, as well as a wave of failed revolutions throughout Europe spur a wave of trans-Atlantic migrations
1846–48	Mexican American War—Mexico loses more than half of its territory to the United States
1848–49	Various revolutions rage throughout Europe
1856–60	Second Opium War
1857	Transatlantic investments in US railroad company shares going bust cause a financial crisis in Europe. Indian rebellion by sepoys
1858	British Raj over India
1857–65	Trans-Atlantic cable is being laid
1861–65	United States Civil War
1867	Discovery of diamond fields in South Africa
1871	British Empire annexes the diamond fields of Kimberley in southern Africa
1876–1902	A series of droughts cause famine in several British colonies in Asia and Africa resulting in an estimated 30–50 million casualties
1884	Gold found in the southern African Transvaal—rise of Johannesburg
1884–85	Berlin Conference—European colonial powers divide up Africa and begin the colonization of the continent
1885	Congo becomes King Leopold's private colony—his rule in the Congo is believed to have killed eight to ten million people
1887	Establishment of French Indochina
1890	Worldwide influenza epidemic. French introduce cocoa to the Gold Coast
1898	Spanish American War

SELECTED BIBLIOGRAPHY

Abu-Lughod, Janet L. *Before European Hegemony: The World System A.D. 1250–1350.* New York: Oxford University Press, 1991.

Alchon, Suzanne Austin. *A Pest in the Land: New World Epidemics in a Global Perspective.* Albuquerque: University of New Mexico Press, 2003.

Ames, Glenn J. *Colbert, Mercantilism, and the French Quest for Asian Trade.* De Kalb: Northern Illinois University Press, 1996.

Ames, Glenn J. *The Globe Encompassed: The Age of European Discovery, 1500–1700.* Upper Saddle River, NJ: Pearson/Prentice Hall, 2008.

Andrade, Tonio. *How Taiwan Became Chinese: Dutch, Spanish, and Han Colonization in the Seventeenth Century.* New York: Columbia University Press, 2008.

Armitage, David. *The Declaration of Independence: A Global History.* Cambridge, MA: Harvard University Press, 2007.

Armitage, David and David Braddick, eds. *The British Atlantic World, 1500–1800.* New York: Palgrave Macmillan, 2002.

Armitage, David and Sanjay Subrahmanyam, eds, *The Age of Revolutions in Global Context, c. 1760–1840.* New York: Palgrave Macmillian, 2010.

Austen, Ralph A. *Trans-Saharan Africa in World History.* New York: Oxford University Press, 2010.

Bailyn, Bernard. *Atlantic History: Concepts of Contours.* Cambridge, MA: Harvard University Press, 2005.

Barrett, Ward. "World Bullion Flows, 1450–1800," in J.D. Tracy, ed., *The Rise of Merchant Empires: Long-Distance Trade in the Early Modern World, 1350–1750* New York: Cambridge University Press, 1990.

Bender, Thomas. *A Nation among Nations: America's Place in World History*. New York: Hill and Wang, 2006.

Benjamin, Thomas. *The Atlantic World: Europeans, Africans, Indians and Their Shared History, 1400–1900*. New York: Cambridge University Press, 2009.

Benjamin, Thomas, Timothy Hall, and David Rutherford, eds. *The Atlantic World in the Age of Empire*. Belmont, CA: Wadsworth, 2001.

Bentley, Jerry H. *Old World Encounters: Cross-Cultural Contacts and Exchanges in Pre-Modern Times*. New York: Oxford University Press, 1993.

Bentley, Jerry H. "Sea and Ocean Basins as Frameworks of Historical Analysis." *The Geographical Review* 89 (April 1999): 215–224.

Blusse, Leonard. *Bitter Bonds: A Colonial Divorce Drama of the 17th Century*, translated by Dianne Webb. Princeton, N.J.: Markus Wiener Publishing, 2002.

Blusse, Leonard. *Strange Company: Chinese Settlers, Mestizo Women and the Dutch in VOC Batavia*. Dordrecht: Foris Publications, 1986.

Bowen, Huw, Robert Blyth, and John McAleer, *Monsoon Traders: The Maritime World of the East India Company*. London: Scala Publisher, 2011.

Boxer, Charles R. *The Dutch Seaborne Empire, 1600–1800*, reprinted edn. New York: Penguin, 1990.

———. *The Portuguese Seaborne Empire, 1415–1825*. New York: Alfred A. Knopf, 1969.

Braudel, Fernand. *Civilization and Capitalism 15th–18th Century, vol. 3: The Perspective of the World*. Translated by Sian Reynolds. Paperback edn. Berkeley: University of California Press, 1992.

Bronsted, Johannes. *The Vikings*. Baltimore: Penguin Books, 1965.

Brook, Timothy. *Vermeer's Hat: The Seventeenth Century and the Dawn of the Global World*. New York: Bloomsbury Press, 2008.

Brooks, George. *Landlords and Strangers: Ecology, Society, and Trade in Western Africa, 1000–1630*. Boulder, CO: Westview Press, 1993.

Brotton, Jerry. *The Renaissance Bazaar: From the Silk Road to Michelangelo*. New York: Oxford University Press, 2002.

———. *A History of the World in 12 Maps*. New York: Viking, 2013.

Brown, Stephen R. *Merchant Kings: When Companies Ruled the World*. New York: Thomas Dunne Books, 2010.

Buschman, Rainer F. *Oceans in World History*. Boston: McGraw-Hill, 2007.

Butel, Paul. *The Atlantic*. New York: Routledge, 1999.

Calloway, Colin. *New Worlds for All: Indians, Europeans, and the Remaking of Early America*. Baltimore, MD: Johns Hopkins University Press, 1997.

Canizares-Esquerra, Jorge and Eric R. Seeman, eds, *The Atlantic in Global History, 1500–2000*. Upper Saddle River, NJ: Pearson & Prentice Hall, 2007.

Canny, Nicholas and Philip Morgan, eds, *The Oxford Handbook of the Atlantic World: 1450–1850*. New York: Oxford University Press, 2011.

Canny, Nicholas and Anthony Pagden, eds. *Colonial Identity in the Atlantic World, 1500–1800*. Princeton, N.J.: Princeton University Press, 1987.

Carrasco, David and Scott Sessions, *Daily Life of the Aztec Peoples of the Sun and Earth*, 2nd edn. Westport, CT: Greenwood Press, 2008.

Chaudhuri, K.N. *Trade and Civilization in the Indian Ocean*. New York: Cambridge University Press, 1985.

———. *Asia before Europe: Economy and Civilisation of the Indian Ocean from the Rise of Islam to 1750*. New York: Cambridge University Press, 1990.

Clendinnen, Inga. *Aztecs: An Interpretation*. New York: Cambridge University Press, 1991.

Coclanis, Peter A. "Drang Nach Osten: Bernard Bailyn, the World Island, and the Idea of Atlantic History," *Journal of World History*, vol. 13 (2002), 169–182.

———. "Beyond Atlantic History" in *Atlantic History*, 342, 337–356.

———. "Atlantic World or Atlantic/World?" *William and Mary Quarterly*, 63 (October 2006): 725–742.

———. *The Columbian Exchange: Biological and Cultural Consequences of 1492*. Westport, CT: Greenwood Press, 1972.

Colley, Linda. *Captives: The Story of Britain's Pursuit of Empire and How its Soldiers and Civilians were Held Captive by the Dream of Global Supremacy, 1600–1850*. New York: Pantheon Books, 2002.

Columbus, Christopher. *The Four Voyages of Columbus*, ed., Cecil Jane. New York: Dover, 1988.

Cranmer-Byng, John L. and John E. Wills, Jr., "Trade and Diplomacy with Maritime Europe, 1644–c. 1800," in *China and Maritime Europe*.

Crosby, Alfred W. *Ecological Imperialism: The Biological Expansion of Europe, 900–1900*. New York: Cambridge University Press 1986.

Curtin, Philp. *Cross-Cultural Trade in World History*. New York: Cambridge University Press, 1984.

Davidson, Basil. *The Lost Cities of Africa*. Boston: Little & Brown, 1959.

Dickason, Olive Patricia. *The Myth of the Savage and the Beginnings of French Colonialism in the Americas*. Edmonton, Alberta: The University of Alberta Press, 1997.

Disney, A.R. *A History of Portugal and the Portuguese Empire: From Beginnings to 1807*, 2 vols. New York: Cambridge University Press, 2009.

Dreyer, Edward L. *Zheng He: China and the Oceans in the Early Ming Dynasty, 1405–1433*. New York: Pearson & Longman, 2007.

Dunn, Ross E. *The Adventures of Ibn Battuta: A Muslim Traveler of the 14th Century*. Berkeley: University of California Press, 1986.

Egerton, Douglas R., Alison Games, Jane Landers, Kris Lane, and Donald Wright. *The Atlantic World: A History, 1400–1888*. Whelling, Ill.: Harland Davidson, 2007.

Elliott, Mark C. *Emperor Qianlong: Son of Heaven, Man of the World*. New York: Longman, 2009.

Falola, Toyin, and Kevin D. Roberts, eds, *The Atlantic World, 1450–2000*. Bloomington: Indiana University Press, 2008.

Fernandez-Armesto, Felipe. *Before Columbus: Exploration and Colonization from the Mediterranean to the Atlantic, 1229–1492.* Philadelphia: University of Pennsylvania Press, 1987.

Forbes, Jack D. *Africans and Native Americans: The Language of Race and the Evolution of Red-Black Peoples*, 2nd edn. Urbana and Chicago: University of Illinois Press, 1993.

Franklin, Simon and Jonathan Shepard. *The Emergence of the Rus, 750–1200.* New York: Longman, 1996.

Freedman, Paul. *Out of the East: Spices and the Medieval Imagination.* New Haven, Conn.: Yale University Press, 2008.

Geiss, Immanuel. *The Pan African Movement: A History of Pan-Africanism in America, Europe, and Africa*, translated by A.E. Keeps. Teaneck, NJ: New Holmes & Meier Publishing, 1974.

Gilbert, Erik and Jonathan T. Reynolds. *Africa in World History: From Prehistory to the Present*, 2nd edn. Upper Saddle River, NJ: Pearson, 2008.

Gilbert, Erik and Jonathan Reynolds. *Trading Tastes: Commodity and Cultural Exchange to 1750.* Upper Saddle River, NJ: Pearson, 2006.

Girshick Ben-Amos, Paula. *The Art of Benin*, revised edn. Washington, D.C.: Smithsonian, 1995.

Greene, Jack P. and Philip D. Morgan. eds., *Atlantic History: A Critical Appraisal.* New York: Oxford University Press, 2009.

Harrison, Patricia Greenwood. *Connecting Links: The British and American Woman Suffrage Movements, 1900–1914.* Westport, CT: Greenwood Press, 2000.

Heiss, Mary Lou and Robert J. Heiss. *A Story of Tea: A Cultural History and Drinking Guide.* Berkeley, CA: Ten Speed Press, 2007.

Hobson, John M. *The Eastern Origins of Western Civilisation.* Cambridge: Cambridge University Press, 2004.

Hochschild, Adam. *King Leopold's Ghost: A Story of Greed, Terror, and Heroism in Colonial Africa.* Boston: Houghton Mifflin Company, 1998.

Hodgson, Marshall G.S. *Rethinking World History: Essays on Europe, Islam, and World History.* Edited with an introduction and conclusion by Edmund Burke III New York: Cambridge University Press, 1993.

Ibn Battuta. *The Travels of Ibn Battuta in the Near East, Asia and Africa, 1325–1354*, translator and ed. Samuel Lee. Mineola, NY: Dover Publications, 2004.

Ingstad, Helge and Anne Stine Ingstad. *The Viking Discovery of America: The Excavation of a Norse Settlement in L'Anse aux Meadows, Newfoundland.* New York: Checkmark Books, 2001.

Israel, Jonathan I. *The Dutch Republic: Its Rise, Greatness, and Fall, 1477–1806.* New York: Oxford University Press, 1995.

Israel, Jonathan I. *The Dutch Republic and the Hispanic World, 1606–1661.* New York: Oxford University Press, 1982.

Kamen, Henry. *Empire: How Spain Became a World Power, 1492–1763.* New York: Harper Collins Publisher, 2003.

Karras, Alan L. and J.R. McNeill, eds. *Atlantic American Societies: From Columbus through Abolition, 1492–1888.* New York: Routledge, 1992.

Katzew, Ilona. *Casta Painting: Images of Race in Eighteenth Century Mexico.* New Haven: Yale University Press, 2004.

Kicza, John. *Resilient Cultures: America's Native Peoples Confront European Colonization, 1500–1800.* Upper Saddle River, NJ: Prentice Hall, 2003.

Klooster, Wim. *Revolutions in the Atlantic World: A Comparative History.* New York: New York University Press, 2009.

Klooster, Wim, and Alfred Padula, eds. *The Atlantic World: Essays on Slavery, Migration, and Imagination.* Upper Saddle River, NJ: Pearson Prentice-Hall, 2004.

Krondl, Michael. *The Taste of Conquest: The Rise and Fall of the Three Great Cities of Spice.* New York: Ballantine Book, 2008.

Kupperman, Karen Ordahl. *The Atlantic in World History.* New York: Oxford University Press, 2012.

Lane, Kris E. *Pillaging the Empire: Piracy in the Americas, 1500–1750.* Armonk, NY: M.E. Sharpe, 1998.

Lane, Kris E. *The Colour of Paradise: The Emerald in the Age of Gunpowder Empires.* New Haven, CT: Yale University Press, 2010.

Las Casas, Bartolome de. *A Short Account of the Destruction of the Indies.* New York: Penguin, 1992.

Levathes, Louise. *When China Ruled the Seas: The Treasure Fleet of the Dragon Throne, 1405–1433.* New York: Oxford University Press, 1996.

Lewis, Martin W. and Karen Wigen. *The Myth of Continents: A Critique of Metageography.* Berkeley: University of California Press, 1997.

Lloyd, T.O. *The British Empire, 1558–1995*, 2nd edn. New York: Oxford, 1996.

Lunde, Paul. "The Coming of the Portuguese," *Saudi Aramco World*, July/August 2005, 54–61.

Luttinger, Nina, and Gregory Dicum. *The Coffee Book: Anatomy of an Industry from Crop to the Last Drop*, revised and updated edition. New York: The New Press, 2006.

MacGregor, Neil. *A History of the World in 100 Objects: From the Handaxe to the Credit Card.* New York: Viking, 2011.

Magnusson, Magnus, and Hermann Palsson, *The Vinland Sagas: The Norse Discovery of America.* Baltimore: Penguin Books, 1965.

Mancall, Peter C., ed. *Travel Narratives from the Age of Discovery: An Anthology.* New York: Oxford University Press, 2006.

Mann, Charles C. *1493: Uncovering the New World Columbus Created.* New York: Alfred A. Knopf, 2013.

Marks, Robert B. *The Origins of the Modern World: A Global and Ecological Narrative from the Fifteenth to the Twenty-First Century*, 2nd edn. Lanham, MD: Rowman and Littlefield Publishers, 2007.

Meinig, D.W. *The Shaping of America: A Geographical Perspective on 500 Years of History. Vol 1: Atlantic America, 1492–1800.* New Haven, Conn.: Yale University Press, 1986.

Milner, George R. *The Moundbuilders: Ancient Peoples of North America*. London: Thames & Hudson, 2004.

Mintz, Sidney W. *Sweetness and Power: The Place of Sugar in Modern History*. New York: Penguin Books, 1985.

Morgan, Philip D., and Moly A. Warsh, eds. *Early North America in Global Perspective*. New York: Routledge, 2014.

Mungello, D.E. *The Great Encounter of China and the West, 1500–1800*, 3rd edn. Lanham, MD: Rowman & Littlefield, 2009.

Nash, Alice, and Christoph Strobel. *Daily Life of Native Americans from Post-Columbian Through Nineteenth Century America*. Westport, CT: Greenwood Press, 2006.

Nellis, Eric. *Shaping the New World: African Slavery in the Americas, 1500–1888*. Toronto: University of Toronto Press, 2013.

Niane. D.T., ed. *Sundiata an Epic of Mali*. Translated by G.D. Pickett. London: Longman, 1965.

O'Rourke, Kevin H., and Jeffery G. Williamson. *Globalization and History: The Evolution of a Nineteenth Century Atlantic Economy*. Cambridge, MA: Massachusetts Institute of Technology Press, 1999.

Pomeranz, Kenneth and Steven Topik. *The World that Trade Created: Society, Culture, and the World Economy, 1400 to the Present*, 3rd edn. Armonk, NY: M.E. Sharpe, 2013.

Pomeranz, Kenneth. *The Great Divergence: China, Europe and the Making of the Modern World Economy*. Princeton, NJ: Princeton University Press, 2000.

Reinhardt, Steven G., and Dennis Reinhartz, eds, *Transatlantic History*. College Station: Texas A&M University, 2006.

Richter, Daniel K. *The Ordeal of the Longhouse: The Peoples of the Iroquois League in the Era of European Colonization*. Chapel Hill: University of North Carolina Press, 1992.

Rodgers, Daniel T. *Atlantic Crossing: Social Politics in a Progressive Age*. Cambridge, MA: Harvard University Press, 1998.

Saliba, George. *Islamic Science and the Making of the European Renaissance*. Cambridge, MA: MIT Press, 2011.

Salisbury, Neal. "The Indians' Old World: Native Americans and the Coming of Europeans." *William and Mary Quarterly* 53 (July 1996): 435–458.

Schurz, William Lytle. *The Manila Galleon*. New York: E.P. Dutton and Company, 1939.

Seed, Patricia. *Ceremonies of Possession in Europe's Conquest of the New World, 1492–1640*. New York: Cambridge University Press, 1995.

Shaffer, Lynda Norene. *Native Americans before 1492: The Moundbuilding Centers of the Eastern Woodlands*. Armonk, NY: M.E. Sharpe, 1992.

Shillington, Kevin. *History of Africa*, 3rd edn. New York: St. Martin's Press, 1989.

Smith, Bonnie G., Marc van de Mieroop, Richard von Glahn, and Kris Lane. *Crossroad and Cultures: A History of the World's Peoples*. Boston: Bedford/St. Martins, 2012.

Starna, William A. *From Homeland to New Land: A History of the Mahican Indians, 1600–1830*. Boston: Northeast Region Ethnography Program, National Park Service, US Department of the Interior, 2011.

Strobel, Christoph. *The Testing Grounds of Modern Empire: The Making of Colonial Racial Order in the American Ohio Country and the South African Eastern Cape, 1770s–1850s*. New York: Peter Lang Publishing, 2008.

Subrahmanyam, Sanjay. *The Portuguese Empire in Asia, 1500–1700: A Political and Economic History*. London: Longman, 1993.

Suzuki, Yasuko. *Japan–Netherlands Trade 1600–1800: The Dutch East India Company and Beyond*. Melbourne, Australia: Trans-Pacific Press, 2012.

TePaske, John J. "New World Silver, Castile and the Philippines, 1590–1800," in J.F. Richards, ed., *Precious Metals in the Later Medieval and Early Modern Worlds*. Durham, NC: Carolina Academic Press, 1983.

Thornton, John K. *Africa and Africans in the Making of the Atlantic World, 1400–1800*, 2nd edn. New York: Cambridge University Press, 1998.

———. *A Cultural History of the Atlantic World, 1250–1820*. New York: Cambridge University Press, 2012.

Tracy, James D. Editor. *The Rise of Merchant Empires: Long Distance Trade in the Early Modern World, 1350–1750*. New York: Cambridge University Press, 1990.

———. Editor. *The Political Economy of Merchant Empires: State Power and World Trade, 1350–1750*. New York: Cambridge University Press, 1991.

Vicente, Marta V. *Clothing The Spanish Empire: Families and the Calico Trade in the Early Modern World*. New York: Palgrave Macmillan, 2006.

Waldron, Arthur. *The Great Wall of China: From History to Myth*. New York: Cambridge University Press, 1990.

Waley-Cohen, Joanna. *The Sextants of Beijing: Global Currents in Chinese History*. New York: Norton, 1999.

Walker, Timothy. "Lisbon as a Strategic Haven in the Atlantic World" in Wim Klooster and Alfred Padula, eds, *The Atlantic World: Essays on Slavery, Migration, and Imagination*. Upper Saddle River, NJ: Pearson Prentice-Hall, 2004.

Weatherford, Jack. *Indian Givers: How the Indians of the Americas Transformed the World*. New York: Crown, 1988.

Weaver, Frederick Stirton. *Latin America in the World Economy: Mercantile Colonialism to Global Capitalism*. Boulder, Col.: Westview Press, 2000.

Weber, David J. *The Spanish Frontier in North America*. New Haven, CT: Yale University Press 1992.

Williams, Robert. *The American Indian in Western Legal Thought: The Discourses of Conquest*. New York: Oxford University Press, 1990.

Wills, John E. Jr. ed. *China and Maritime Europe, 1500–1800: Trade, Settlement, Diplomacy, and Missions*. New York: Cambridge University Press, 2010.

Wills, John E. *Pepper, Guns, and Parleys: The Dutch East India Company and China, 1662–1681*. Cambridge, MA: Harvard University Press, 1974.

Wolf, Eric R. *Europe and the People without History*, new edn. Berkeley: University of California Press, 1997.

Wood, Peter. *Black Majority: Negroes in Colonial South Carolina from 1670 through the Stono Rebellion*. New York: Knopf, 1974.

Wright, Donald R. *The World and a Very Small Place in Africa: A History of Globalization in Niumi, The Gambia*, 3rd edn. Armonk, NY: M.E. Sharpe, 2010.

INDEX